IMPORTANT NOTICE

The Forest Service is in the process of renumbering all of the forest roads in western Washington.

The present numbering system was derived thirty years ago before road planners had any indication of the maze of roads that would eventually be developed. The new numbering system should make road directions easier to follow.

Mt. Baker-Snoqualmie and Gifford Pinchot National Forests made their changes in 1981; these changes are reflected in this edition of **102 Hikes**. Wenatchee and Okanogan National Forests will not change over until 1984, or later. Olympic National Forest has made the change but may do so again. Expect considerable confusion until all the changes are completed and forest maps revised.

Gnome Tarn and Prusik Peak in the Enchantment Lakes area of the Alpine Lakes Wilderness

102 hikes

IN THE ALPINE LAKES, SOUTH CASCADES AND OLYMPICS

Text: Ira Spring and Harvey Manning
Photos: Bob and Ira Spring

THE MOUNTAINEERS • SEATTLE

Third edition

The Mountaineers: Organized 1906 ". . . to explore, study, preserve and enjoy the natural beauty of the Northwest."

Copyright © 1971, 1974, 1978, 1983 by The Mountaineers

Published by The Mountaineers, 715 Pike Street
Seattle, Washington 98101

Published simultaneously in Canada by
Douglas & McIntyre Ltd., 1615 Venables Street
Vancouver, British Columbia V5L 2H1

Manufactured in the United States of America
First edition, June 1971; revised September 1974
Second edition, June 1978; second printing, August 1979;
third printing, May 1980; fourth printing (revised), June 1981
Third edition, March 1983; second printing, March 1984

*Series design by Marge Mueller; layout by Barbara Haner; maps by
  Helen Sherman, Gary Rands and Judith Siegel*
Cover: Camping near Moose Lake, Olympic National Park (Hike 90).

Library of Congress Cataloging in Publication Data

Spring, Ira.
  102 hikes in the Alpine Lakes, South Cascades, and Olympics.

  Includes index.
  1. Hiking—Washington (State)—Guide-books. 2. Trails—Washington
(State)—Guide-books. 3. Washington (State)—Description and
travel—1981- —Guide-books. I. Manning, Harvey. II. Spring, Bob, 1918-
III. Mountaineers (Society) IV. Title. V. Title: One hundred two hikes in the Alpine
Lakes, South Cascades, and Olympics.
GV199.42.W2S67 1983   917.97   82-7857
ISBN 0-89886-067-9

TABLE OF CONTENTS

SAVING OUR TRAILS
The Preservation Agenda for the 1980s

Most hikers are surprised that only 48 trails described in this book are safe from bulldozers. That is, only 48 trails are in designated wilderness areas or national parks. The other 54 trails have no legal protection.

In the back of this book, in the section "Still More Hikes," is a list of another 149 trails. Of these only 63 have protection; 86 do not. In the **101 Hikes** book only 40 trails have protection and 61 do not. In the "Still More Hikes" section, 34 trails have protection and 79 do not.

In a variety of ways over the years The Mountaineers have worked "to preserve the natural beauty of Northwest America." One means, adopted in the early 1960s, is the publication of hiking guides, the aim being to put more boots on certain trails, into certain wildlands. The organization doesn't suffer from any delusion that large numbers of boots improve trails, enhance wildness. However, it is ruefully certain that only by making new friends for threatened areas will they be preserved.

Those who benefit from the guidance of this book have the obvious obligation to become defenders of trails and wilderness. Nowadays, when the large numbers of wilderness lovers are in themselves a threat of sorts, more attention is required to rules of "walking light," as discussed later herein. Yet the ultimate threat to natural beauty is not hikers, no matter how destructive their great, vicious boots may be, but doomsday, as represented by motorcycles, bulldozers, and forces for change in the name of "progress."

Some things have been won since The Mountaineers began guidebook publishing — a North Cascades National Park, to cite the grandest victory of the 1960s. In 1976 came that decade's triumph, the Alpine Lakes Wilderness — too small, of course, the preserves always are, but a splendid foundation for future expansion.

Folks who arrived late need have no fear there's nothing left for them to do. The situation cries out for heroes and heroines. Following is a capsule summary of the current preservation agenda for the many provinces of the Cascades and Olympics to which the 102 hikes offer an introduction. Those who find this book a useful guide to hours and days of wandering forests and meadows owe it to themselves, and to their children and grandchildren, to make the agenda their own.

De Facto Wilderness

A quarter-century ago the mountain areas of Washington were mostly pretty much as they always had been — wild. Then, after World War II, the loggers and road-builders began pushing deeper into the backcountry, farther up valleys, higher on ridges. The action caused an equal and opposite reaction in the form of a great reinforcement of the preservation movement. By the 1970s all observers realized that exploiters and preservers were both so busy there soon would be no overlooked lands. Everything was either going to be "locked up" or logged.

The U.S. Forest Service, manager of most of the "de facto" (just sitting there) wilderness, is in the middle, and as is usual with compromises, making both sides unhappy. The odds are that in the future, as in the recent past, there'll be a dogfight over each wild valley and hill. Therefore, every hiker should participate, striving to preserve as much wilderness as should and can be preserved in the Olympics and Cascades.

Alpine Lakes

With several exceptions, Hikes 1-44 all are in either the Alpine Lakes Wilderness or the surrounding Alpine Lakes Management Area. The first of these units now needs protection mainly from over-loving boots. For the second, the Forest Service is implementing a plan that balances commodity exploitation with recreation and, in the latter category, road recreation, motorcycle trail recreation, and hiker-horse trail recreation.

It is not a plan fixed in concrete for all time, it is subject to change when and where a case is made. For example, preservationists feel certain localities were unwisely omitted from the Wilderness and that certain roads—such as that up the Middle Fork Snoqualmie—ought to be truncated to enwilden the Wilderness. Further, they object to certain areas being converted into motorcycle romper rooms. (See "Hiker/Motorcycle Scoreboard," below.) These matters will continue to be brought to the attention of the Forest Service.

However, on one subject there is whole-hearted unanimity. The Alpine Lakes Act of 1976 established "instant" Wilderness and Intended Wilderness, the latter consisting of private lands in the checkerboard ownership dating from that criminally scandalous Northern Pacific Land Grant, to be automatically added to the Wilderness when acquired by the Forest Service by purchase or land exchange. The Forest Service is vigorously pursuing acquisition and needs the vigorous support of every Wilderness user.

Cougar Lakes

Hikes 46-58 are in the proposed two-section Cougar Lakes (or possibly, William O. Douglas) Wilderness; a bill to establish this area was introduced in Congress in 1970 and hearings held in 1977-78; as of 1982 the legislative process was moving along as rapidly as could be expected in view of the situation in Washington, D.C. The north section is bounded on the south by the Chinook Pass Highway, on the west by the Crystal Mountain Ski Area, and on the north by the lowering of the crest into wooded terrain. The larger south section includes the entire Cascade Crest between Chinook Pass and the White Pass Highway, bounded on the west much of the way by Mount Rainier National Park, and extends eastward over valleys of virgin forests and ridges of flowers punctuated by such rugged peaks as Mt. Aix.

The Cougar Lakes Wilderness is needed as wild living room to complement increasingly-crowded Mount Rainier National Park and to prevent high-use road-oriented recreation (and logging) the fragile beauty cannot tolerate.

Mount Rainier National Park

Ultimately the National Park boundaries must be pushed outward on the south, west, and north to take in the entirety of Mt. Rainier and all its flanking ridges and the intervening valleys; though many of these have been savagely clearcut, the Park is for the centuries and in time wounds will heal. Certain as yet unspoiled lands, notably in the Tatoosh Range, should be placed in the Park immediately.

On the north, where the Forest Service is thrusting logging roads almost to the boundary, logging should be halted, or at the very least, the roads "put to bed" when the cutting is complete in order to preserve the remoteness of Park meadows. Hunting should be controlled in all areas adjacent to the Park to maintain a complete summer-and-winter range for the animal population.

Pacific Crest Trail

The route of the Pacific Crest National Scenic Trail southward from Snoqualmie Pass should be designated as a no-logging strip, and protected from any further road intrusions.

The historic Naches Wagon Trail (Hike 46) deserves particularly urgent attention. The little that remains of the old emigrant route should be saved by placing it entirely off-limits to jeepers and trailbikers and loggers.

South Cascades

The area sampled by Hikes 59-76 is large, varied, and badly abused. The Goat Rocks and Mt. Adams Wildernesses consist mainly of snow and rocks and meadows; boundaries should be adjusted outward to include more of the approach ridges and valleys.

The Mt. St. Helens area before 1980 was one of the worst examples of mismanagement in the Northwest. Faced by an impossible checkerboard of private and public ownership, the U.S. Forest Service had capitulated to the exploiters. On three sides the graceful volcano rose above a sea of stumps, only the Spirit Lake side spared. Because the Forest Service seemed totally unwilling to radically alter its management philosophy, conservationists began seeking a Mt. St. Helens National Monument.

On May 18, 1980, the ground rules of the controversy were abruptly changed. The devastation done by pre-eruption logging is, over a broad area, no longer noticeable. But incredibly, no sooner had bodies of victims been recovered than Weyerhaeuser loggers were bulldozing into the blast zone to salvage blown-down timber. "It's our property," the company said, citing the $6 an acre it paid for Northern Pacific Land Grant forests in 1900. The loggers who see wilderness only as a tree mine similarly view the scene of the most dramatic geological event in the nation since it became a nation. Preservationists still seek protection for islands of old-growth forest that survived the blast. Additionally, they now seek a truly meaningful Mt. St. Helens National Volcanic Area that is managed as a living exhibit of nature at work, a place generations of world citizens can watch the decade-by-decade transformation of raw ash and dead trees into lush forest—a process that has been repeated over and over again on volcanoes of the Cascades but in our time has been witnessed on this scale only once. (So far.)

The broad expanse of forested valleys and ridges between Adams and St. Helens has been criss-crossed with a spider web of roads in the years since World War II, obliterating hundreds of miles of trails. But small pockets of splendor remain relatively pristine and to preserve these a number of small Wildernesses are proposed.

Olympics

Hikes 78-102 are on the Olympic Peninsula, for the most part in Olympic National Park, most of which soon will be permanently classified as wilderness. The Park Service must be strenuously urged to acquire private lands within the Park, particularly in the Quinault Valley, and under no circumstances to eliminate from the Park portions of the Valley now included.

Eventually the Park must be enlarged along the eastern side, where, for example, the summits of such peaks as Cruiser, The Brothers, and Constance lie exactly on the boundary, their east slopes and drainage valleys excluded. Looking west from Seattle to the Olympic horizon, the only portions of the Park that can be seen are the summits of several peaks. All the rest of the visible range is in Olympic National Forest, subject to logging, as can be vividly realized in winter, when snows demark the clearcuts, which grow larger year by year. To prevent further damage, Wildernesses must be established bordering the National Park on the northeast, southeast, and southwest.

The Mountaineers: An Invitation

The Mountaineers, with groups based in Seattle, Everett, Tacoma, and Olympia, warmly invite the membership of all lovers of outdoor life who sympathize with the purposes of the organization and wish to share its activities.

The Mountaineers sponsor a year-around program of climbing, hiking, camping, ski-touring, snowshoeing, canoeing and kayaking, and bicycling. Many hundreds of outings are scheduled each year, ranging from afternoon walks to trips lasting 2 weeks or more. On a typical weekend as many as 50 excursions may be offered, from ocean beaches to the summit of Mt. Rainier. In addition, members engage in countless privately-organized trips of all kinds; the opportunity is boundless to make new friends with similar interests.

Enjoying wildlands is one side of the coin; the other is working to preserve the natural beauty of Northwest America. Here, The Mountaineers continue their role of leadership as they have for 76 years, and seek new members to share the effort.

For membership application, and further information on club activities, write The Mountaineers, 719 Pike Street, Seattle, Washington 98101.

HARVEY MANNING

HIKER/MOTORCYCLE SCOREBOARD

A dozen-odd years ago hiking trails were seldom if ever molested by motorcycles. It wasn't until Yankee ingenuity and Japanese mass production combined that the trouble began; since then the situation has gotten completely out of hand.

When Congress enacted the "Multiple Use Concept," it certainly never intended the Forest Service to adhere to the literal interpretation and mix together every use everywhere no matter how incompatible. However, some forest supervisors do just that, saying, "Let the hikers and motorcyclists learn to live together." But they can't. A major reason hikers go hiking is to get away from machines, and until the middle 1960s, once on the trail they were free of noise and pollution. But where, now, can they escape? In dedicated Wilderness areas—that are so full of people escaping machines one needs a permit to enter. In the European Alps all trails are closed to motorcycles. Even service roads used by farmers and foresters are closed to recreational use of motors. In Japan where most of the machines come from, things are not as bad as here. Only in America . . .

Unlike the trees, wildlife, water, and minerals of national forests, whose benefits are measurable in dollars, the benefits of hiking trails are hard to determine. Who can put a cash value on the mental stimulation of meeting a challenge? The spiritual and physical therapy of getting away from the contraptions of civilization? As any doctor will testify, hiking is one of the best exercises known for lungs, heart, and muscles. And many a case of hypertension, many a case of crumbling nerves, has been successfully treated by a walk in the wildlands. While the Forest Service hasn't yet put a dollar value on good health, some health insurance companies are beginning to.

The Forest Service has been conditioned to think in terms of the value of logs; rangers are trained to manage timber, not to provide mental and physical therapy, much less esthetic pleasure. As a consequence, unless an area is specifically set aside by Congress as a Wilderness, some forest supervisors adhere to a literal interpretation of "multiple-use," meaning every use everywhere, no matter how incompatible. Even the best supervisors, placed in the position of compromising between user-group pressures, make terrible blunders of judgment. Congress is going to have to set strict controls. Until it does, though, we hikers have to keep after the supervisors, letting them know where we stand (and where we walk).

Recreational use of off-road vehicles had become so serious a problem by 1976 that the President ordered all federal land-managers to inventory off-road vehicle use, listing where environmental damage had been done, where user conflict existed, and where off-road vehicle use should be permitted. It was a golden opportunity to give hiking trails back to the hiker. It failed. After months of study, public reviews costing millions of dollars nationwide, virtually nothing happened. Except the roar went on.

Though the framework of policy is set at a higher level, trail-by-trail decisions are made by individual district rangers in consultation with their staffs—often after considerable internal controversy. The rangers are just like other people, which is to say, of different sorts. When the Japanese started mass-producing trail machines in the 1960s, a few rangers were far-sighted enough to forbid machines on trails in their districts. Some simply didn't care and a few thought (and still think) that machines are great. Though the rangers responsible for the boo-boos have moved on, the districts that were let wide-open to wheels then are the ones with the most problems now. Hikers now must fight to attain the status that once existed.

In general, district rangers now are much more aware of the environmental and psychological damage done by motorcycles, are much more sympathetic to hikers. Even where the ranger himself is a fan of racket, on his staff are sure to be a certain number of people arguing the case for peace and quiet. These, our friends, need our support. Specifically, they need our letters. If a ranger is able to show a lot of letters complaining about the incompatible use or specific examples of environmental damage done by machines, chances are he will rule favorably. Unfortunately, most letters presently are written by motorcyclists wanting more trails open, arguing their right as free-born Americans to screw up the earth any way they want—and increasingly arguing "historic rights" dating from the Forest Service's failure of the 1960s.

Big strides have been made since 5 years ago, when the situation seemed hopeless. For example, the Twisp Ranger District, then wide open, had all its trails leading to the Chelan Crest closed. Now, the bad news: the ranger was overwhelmed with complaints from motorcyclists, didn't receive a single thank-you letter from hikers, and ended up reopening four of the trails. We blew it. The trails around Spirit Lake were crowded with motorcycles. It took hundreds of complaints to overcome the ranger's bias, but the motors finally were abolished in 1978. Unfortunately, 2 years later Mt. St. Helens abolished the trails.

At the moment, some rangers are gradually cleaning up their trails—as public support makes it possible for them to act. Others personally love motorcycles, ride them on their own days off, but even they will bend under pressure. Sad to say, some are using state "ORV money"—a portion of the gasoline tax devoted to non-highway purposes, and contributed to by you and me every time we drive our family car on Forest Service roads, making it, under the law, an "off-road vehicle"—to build ORV "trails." A fact to remember is that district rangers are regularly transferred. Never consider any district a lost cause. The motorcycle mania is still with us but year by year is recognized by thoughtful forest managers as a thing of the past, like smallpox.

We by no means are opposed to motorcycles, in their place. Where is their place? **On roads**. With thousands of miles of logging roads built in the years since World War II—in most cases replacing trails, thus reducing the extent of quiet country—there is plenty of room to exercise the wheels and the gluteal muscles. We have so little quiet land left we cannot afford to give up a single mile.

Repeatedly Forest Service personnel tell me they need letters. They literally are **begging** for complaints! Therefore, when you find machines on a good hiking trail, or when you see the Forest Service spending your ORV money to "upgrade" a trail for wheels, complain. Write the district ranger, write the forest supervisor, write your Congressman. The letter will be read and a copy will find its way to the right person who will use it for support the next time that particular trail comes up for review.

—And remember the Twisp! Keep in mind that letters **complimenting** the Forest Service for a wise decision are also welcome!

Ira Spring

INTRODUCTION

The country sampled by the 102 hikes has many characteristics in common throughout, but also significant differences from place to place caused by variations in climate and geology and elevation and people-pressure. Three "provinces" may be distinguished.

First, the Alpine Lakes Cascades (Hikes 1-44), extending some 50 or so miles west to east from maritime greenery of Puget Sound lowlands to golden hills above the semi-arid Columbia River valley, and roughly 25-35 miles south to north from the Snoqualmie Pass Highway to the Stevens Pass Highway—beyond which lies the domain of a companion book, **101 Hikes in the North Cascades**.

On the windward slopes of the Cascades the precipitation is heavy enough to nourish near-rain forests. The leeward slopes, in the rainshadow, often are sunny when the crest is lost in mists and drizzles, and the forests are generally more open. However, the range is much narrower here than it is to the north and the contrasts in climate from one edge to the other less marked. The hiking season is everywhere about the same because though snows pile deeper on the west, elevations average higher on the east. Past glaciation has left in all parts a legacy of sharp-sculptured peaks, plus cirque basins and scoured valleys now filled by lakes high and low—some 600 in all.

The second province, the Washington South Cascades (Hikes 45-76), is really an assemblage of quite diverse sub-provinces: the 25 miles south from Snoqualmie Pass, in which the Cascade Crest follows relatively low and heavily-wooded ridges; the next 25-odd miles from north of Chinook Pass to White Pass, with the Crest rising to meadows and small crags of the proposed Cougar Lakes Wilderness; the 30 miles south from White Pass, where the Crest climbs more, from flowers to glaciers of the Goat Rocks and finally to the nearly 2½-mile-high summit of Mt. Adams; and a last 30 miles in which the Crest drops to the Columbia River. But the Cascade Crest is not the whole story: though the alpine realm of the Crest proper is rather narrow, westward 35 miles from Adams over forested ridges is the formerly graceful and now "interesting" volcano of Mt. St. Helens; and of course, adjoining the Cougar Lakes area is the grandest volcano of them all, and the trail country described in a companion book, **50 Hikes in Mount Rainier National Park**.

The South Cascades offer isolated eruptions of spectacular violence—the volcanoes, the ice-plucked Goat Rocks and a few other peaks—but also the friendliest parklands of the entire range, and because of the distance from major cities, and the overshadowing fame of mountains farther north, some of the lonesomest.

The third province, the Olympic Peninsula (Hikes 78-102), extends some 55-85 miles from the Pacific Ocean east to Hood Canal and roughly 70 miles from the Strait of Juan de Fuca south to foothills, encompassing wilderness ocean beaches, west-side rain forests, a wilderness interior of glaciers and rock needles and flower gardens, and rainshadow ridges standing high above lowlands of Hood Canal and Puget Sound.

Within these three provinces many varieties of trail experience are available. There are short and easy hikes that can be done by small children and old folks with no training or equipment for mountain travel. And also there are long hikes, and difficult hikes, and long-and-difficult hikes, which should be attempted only by experienced wilderness roamers.

There are hikes that can be done by any person capable of putting one foot in front of another for a morning or afternoon. And there are adventures that can take a party back through time to the frontier, into wildlands where the walker is utterly on his own, with no help from anyone if things go wrong.

Administration

The three provinces are administered by the National Park Service, by the U.S. Forest Service in the Mt. Baker-Snoqualmie, Wenatchee, Gifford Pinchot, and Olympic National Forests, and in small but important part by the Washington State Department of Natural Resources. Because regulations on use vary, hikers should be aware of which administrative units they are traveling.

Mount Rainier and Olympic National Parks have been set aside, to use the words of the National Park Act of 1916, "to conserve the scenery and the natural and historic objects and wildlife . . ." Each visitor must therefore enjoy the Parks "in such manner and by such means as will leave them unimpaired for the enjoyment of future generations." A good motto for Park users is: "Take only a picture, leave only a footprint."

Much of both Parks soon will be dedicated as wilderness, so that not only the National Park Act of 1916 but the Wilderness Act of 1964 will apply, giving a still higher degree of protection. Motorized travel on Park trails is forbidden and horse travel closely regulated. Hunting is banned—but not fishing. Pets are not allowed on trails, since their presence disturbs wildlife.

Backcountry permits are required for all overnight hikers in National Parks, and may be obtained at ranger stations on the entry roads.

Under U.S. Forest Service jurisdiction are the Goat Rocks, Mt. Adams, and Alpine Lakes Wildernesses (and hopefully, in the near future, the proposed Cougar Lakes Wilderness), where "the earth and its community of life are untrammeled by man, where man himself is a visitor who does not remain." Motorized travel is forbidden absolutely and horse travel is beginning to be regulated or even eliminated at some points; foot travel and camping are currently less restricted, though the backcountry population explosion will require increasing controls to protect the fragile ecosystems. Wilderness permits, available at ranger stations and National Forest headquarters, are required for all travelers in the Goat Rocks and Mt. Adams Wildernesses but as of 1982, not in the Alpine Lakes Wilderness, where a management plan is still being pondered.

Other portions of the National Forests, such as the Alpine Lakes Management Area, have certain limitations on commodity exploitation and recreation. Multiple-use areas are devoted mainly to logging, but even here the Forest Service increasingly is trying to preserve trail systems.

Large areas of the Alpine Lakes and South Cascades are in a checkerboard ownership dating from the Northern Pacific Land Grant. The presence of private land intermixed with public land so far has interfered with trail use only here and there, but poses a future threat. The Forest Service is seeking to "block up" the public land by exchanges.

Maps

Each hike description in this book lists the appropriate topographic maps (if such are available) published by the U.S. Geological Survey. These can be purchased at mountain equipment shops or map stores or by writing the U.S. Geological Survey, Federal Center, Denver, Colorado 80225. The USGS maps are the hiker's best friend.

The National Forests publish recreation maps which are quite accurate and up-to-date. Excellent topographic maps are available for the Goat Rocks and Mt. Adams Wildernesses. These maps may be obtained for a small fee at ranger stations or by writing the Forest Supervisors at:

Mt. Baker-Snoqualmie National Forest
1022 1st Avenue
Seattle, WA 98104

Gifford Pinchot National Forest
500 W. 12th Street
Vancouver, WA 98660

Wenatchee National Forest
P.O. Box 811
Wenatchee, WA 98801

Olympic National Forest
Federal Building
Olympia, WA 98501

Clothing and Equipment

Many trails described in this book can be walked easily and safely, at least along the lower portions, by any person capable of getting out of a car and onto his feet, and without any special equipment whatever.

To such people we can only say, "welcome to walking—but beware!" Northwest mountain weather, especially on the ocean side of the ranges, is notoriously undependable. Cloudless morning skies can be followed by afternoon deluges of rain or fierce squalls of snow. Even without a storm a person can get mighty chilly on high ridges when—as often happens—a cold wind blows under a bright sun and pure blue sky.

No one should set out on a Cascade or Olympic trail, unless for a brief stroll, lacking warm long pants, wool shirt or sweater, and a windproof and rain-repellent parka, coat, or poncho. (All these in the rucksack, if not on the body during the hot hours.) And on the feet—sturdy shoes or boots with a 5-9-inch top to keep out mud and dirt plus two pair of wool socks and an extra pair in the rucksack.

As for that rucksack, it should also contain the Ten Essentials, found to be so by generations of members of The Mountaineers, often from sad experience:

1. Extra clothing—more than needed in good weather.

2. Extra food—enough so something is left over at the end of the trip.

3. Sunglasses—necessary for most alpine travel and indispensable on snow.

4. Knife—for first aid and emergency firebuilding (making kindling).

5. Firestarter—a candle or chemical fuel for starting a fire with wet wood.

6. First aid kit.

7. Matches—in a waterproof container.

8. Flashlight—with extra bulb and batteries.

9. Map—be sure it's the right one for the trip.

10. Compass—be sure to know the declination, east or west.

Camping and Fires

Indiscriminate camping blights alpine meadows. A single small party may trample grass, flowers, and heather so badly they don't recover from the shock for several years. If the same spot is used several or more times a summer, year after year, the greenery vanishes, replaced by bare dirt. The respectful traveler always aims to camp in the woods, or in rocky morainal areas. These alternatives lacking, it is better to use a meadow site already bare—in technical terminology, "hardened"—rather than extend the destruction into virginal places nearby.

Particularly to be avoided are camps on soft meadows (hard rock or bare-dirt sites may be quite all right) on the banks of streams and lakes. Delightful and scenic as such sites are, their use may endanger the water purity, as well as the health of delicate plants. Moreover, a camp on a viewpoint makes the beauty unavailable to other hikers who simply want to come and look, or eat lunch, and then go camp in the woods.

Carry a collapsible water container to minimize the trips to the water supply that beat down path.

As the age of laissez faire camping yields to the era of thoughtful management, different policies are being adopted in different places. For example, in such high-use places as Snow Lake a large portion of the shore has been designated "Day Use Only," forbidding camps. In others there is a blanket rule against camps within 100 feet of the water. However, in certain areas the rangers have inventoried existing camps, found 95 percent are within 100 feet of the water, and decided it is better to keep existing sites, where the vegetation long since has been gone, than to establish new "barrens" elsewhere. The rule in such places is "use established sites"; wilderness rangers on their rounds dis-establish those sites judged unacceptable.

Few shelter cabins remain—most shown on maps aren't there anymore—so always carry a tent or tarp. **Never** ditch the sleeping area unless and until essential to avoid being flooded out—and afterward be sure to fill the ditches, carefully replacing any sod that may have been dug up.

Always carry a sleeping pad of some sort to keep your bag dry and your bones comfortable. **Do not** revert to the ancient bough bed of the frontier past.

The wood fire also is nearly obsolete in the high country. At best, dry firewood is hard to find at popular camps. What's left, the picturesque silver snags and logs, is part of the scenery, too valuable to be wasted cooking a pot of soup. It should be (but isn't quite, what with the survival of little hatchets and little folks who love to wield them) needless to say that green, living wood must never be cut; it doesn't burn anyway.

Both for reasons of convenience and conservation, The Mountaineers strongly urge the highland hiker to carry a lightweight stove for cooking and to depend on clothing and shelter (and sunset strolls) for evening warmth. The pleasures of a roaring blaze on a cold mountain night are indisputable, but for the sake of these pleasures a single party on a single night may use up ingredients of the scenery that were long decades in growing, dying, and silvering.

At remote backcountry camps, and in forests, fires perhaps may still be built with a clear conscience. Again, one should minimize impact by using only established fire pits and using only dead and down wood. When finished, be certain the fire is absolutely out—drown the coals and stir them with a stick and then drown the ashes until the smoking and steaming have stopped completely and a finger stuck in the slurry feels no heat. Embers can smoulder underground in dry duff for days, spreading gradually and burning out a wide pit—or kindling trees and starting a forest fire.

If you decide to build a fire, **do not make a new fire ring**—use an existing one. In popular areas patroled by rangers, its existence means this is an approved, "established" or "designated" campsite. If a fire ring has been heaped over with rocks, it means the site has been dis-established.

Litter and Garbage and Sanitation

Ours is a wasteful, throwaway civilization—and something is going to have to be done about that soon. Meanwhile, it is bad wildland manners to leave litter for others to worry about. The rule among considerate hikers is: **If you can carry it in full, you can carry it out empty**.

On a day hike, take back to the road (and garbage can) every last orange peel and gum wrapper.

On an overnight or longer hike, burn all paper (if a fire is built) but carry back all unburnables, including cans, metal foil, plastic, glass, and papers that won't burn.

Don't bury garbage. If fresh, animals will dig it up and scatter the remnants. Burning before burying is no answer either. Tin cans take as long as 40 years to disintegrate completely; aluminum and glass last for centuries. Further, digging pits to bury junk disturbs the ground cover, and iron eventually leaches from buried cans and "rusts" springs and creeks.

Don't leave leftover food for the next travelers; they will have their own supplies and won't be tempted by "gifts" spoiled by time or chewed by animals.

Especially don't cache plastic tarps. Weathering quickly ruins the fabric, little creatures nibble, and the result is a useless, miserable mess.

Keep the water pure. Don't wash dishes in streams or lakes, loosing food particles and detergent. Haul buckets of water off to the woods or rocks, and wash and rinse there. Eliminate body wastes in places well removed from watercourses; first dig a shallow hole in the "biological disposer layer," then touch a match to the toilet paper (or better, use leaves), and finally cover the evidence. So managed, the wastes are consumed in a matter of days. Where privies are provided, use them.

Party Size

One management technique used to minimize impact in popular areas is to limit the number of people in any one group. For example, the Glacier Peak Wilderness permits a maximum of 12 people, 15 horses. The Alpine Lakes Wilderness allows 12 people and/or horses. —But in the Enchantments, where horses can't go at all, the top is 6 people.

The figures may change as years go on; hikers with large families (or outing groups from clubs or wherever) should check the rules when planning a trip.

Pets

The handwriting is on the wall for dog owners. Pets always have been forbidden on national park trails and now the Enchantments have been closed; other heavy-use areas are bound to follow soon. How fast the ban spreads will depend on the owners' sensitivity, training, acceptance of responsibility, and courtesy—and on the expressed wishes of non-owners.

Where pets are permitted, even a well-behaved dog can ruin someone else's trip. Some dogs noisily defend an ill-defined territory for their master, "guard" him on the trail, snitch enemy bacon, and are quite likely to defecate on the flat bit of ground the next hiker will want to sleep on.

For a long time to come there will be plenty of "empty" country for those who hunt upland game with dogs or who simply can't enjoy a family outing without ol' Rover. However, the family that wants to go where the crowds are must leave their best friend home.

Do not depend on friendly tolerance of wilderness neighbors. Some people are so harassed at home by loose dogs that a hound in the wilderness has the same effect on them as a motorcycle. They may holler at you and turn you in to the ranger.

Dogs belong to the same family as coyotes, and even if no wildlife is visible, a dog's presence is sensed by the small wild things into whose home it is intruding.

Hoh River trail to Glacier Meadows on side of Mt. Olympus

Theft

Twenty years ago theft from a car left at the trailhead was rare. Not now. Equipment has become so fancy and expensive, so much worth stealing, and hikers so numerous, their throngs creating large assemblages of valuables, that theft is a growing problem. Not even wilderness camps are entirely safe; a single raider hitting an unguarded camp may easily carry off several sleeping bags, a couple tents and assorted stoves, down booties, and freeze-dried strawberries — maybe $1000 worth of gear in one load! However, the professionals who do most of the stealing mainly concentrate on cars. Authorities are concerned but can't post guards at every trailhead.

Rangers have the following recommendations.

First and foremost, don't make crime profitable for the pros. If they break into a hundred cars and get nothing but moldy boots and tattered T shirts they'll give up. The best bet is to arrive in a beat-up 1960 car with doors and windows that don't close and leave in it nothing of value. If you insist on driving a nice new car, at least don't have mag wheels, tape deck, and radio, and keep it empty of gear. Don't think locks help — pros can open your car door and trunk as fast with a picklock as you can with your key. Don't imagine you can hide anything from them — they know all the hiding spots. If the hike is part of an extended car trip, arrange to store your extra equipment at a nearby motel.

Be suspicious of anyone waiting at a trailhead. One of the tricks of the trade is to sit there with a pack as if waiting for a ride, watching new arrivals unpack — and hide their valuables — and maybe even striking up a conversation to determine how long the marks will be away.

The ultimate solution, of course, is for hikers to become as poor as they were in the olden days. No criminal would consider trailheads profitable if the loot consisted solely of shabby khaki war surplus.

Water

Hikers traditionally have drunk the water in wilderness in confidence, doing their utmost to avoid contaminating it so the next person also can safely drink. But there is no assurance your predecessor has been so careful.

No open water ever, nowadays, can be considered safe for human consumption. Any reference in this book to "drinking water" is not a guarantee. It is entirely up to the individual whether he wants to take a chance.

In the late 1970s began a great epidemic of giardiasis, caused by a vicious little parasite that spends part of its life cycle swimming free in the water, part in the intestinal tract of beavers and other wildlife, dogs, and people. Actually, the "epidemic" was solely in the press; giardia were first identified in the 18th century and are present in the public water systems of many cities of the world, including Paris and Moscow. Long before the "outbreak" of "beaver fever" there was the well-known malady, the "Boy Scout trots." This is not to make light of the disease; though most humans somehow feel no ill effects (but become life-long carriers), others have serious symptoms which include devastating diarrhea, and the treatment is nearly as unpleasant. The reason giardiasis has become "epidemic" is that there are more people in the backcountry—more people drinking water contaminated by animals—more people contaminating the water.

Whenever in doubt, boil the water 10 minutes. Keep in mind that giardia can survive in water at or near freezing for weeks or months—a snow pond is not necessarily safe. No other treatment, by chemicals or filter, is 100 percent effective. Boiling is.

Protect This Land, Your Land

The Cascade and Olympic country is large and rugged and wild—but it is also, and particularly in the scenic climaxes favored by hikers, a fragile country. If man is to blend into the ecosystem, rather than dominate and destroy, he must walk lightly, respectfully, always striving to make his passage through the wilderness invisible.

The public servants entrusted with administration of the region have a complex and difficult job and they desperately need the cooperation of every wildland traveler. Here, the authors would like to express appreciation to these dedicated men for their advice on what trips to include in this book and for their detailed review of the text and maps. Thanks are due the Superintendent of Olympic National Park, the Supervisors of the Mt. Baker-Snoqualmie, Wenatchee, Gifford Pinchot, and Olympic National Forests, the director of the Washington State Department of Natural Resources, and their district rangers and other staff members.

On behalf of the U.S. Forest Service and National Park Service and the Washington State Department of Natural Resources and The Mountaineers, we invite Americans—and all citizens of Earth—to come and see and live in their Washington Cascades and Olympics, and while enjoying some of the world's finest wildlands, to vow henceforth to share in the task of preserving the trails and ridges, lakes and rivers, forests and flower gardens for future generations, our children and grandchildren, who will need the wilderness experience at least as much as we do, and probably more.

1 Deception Creek

Round trip 6 miles (to campsite)
Hiking time 4 hours
High point 3200 feet
Elevation gain 1400 feet
Best June to early July
One day or backpack
USGS Scenic and Mt. Daniel

Hike this lovely forest trail in late May or June when the high country is still buried deep under the winter snow cap. There are no spectacular views, but the forest floor is covered with moss, dotted with Canadian dogwood and queen's cup. Here and there are patches of delicate maidenhair ferns and wicked-looking devil's club. While the trees are not the largest, they are protected by the Alpine Lakes Wilderness.

This is not an easy valley walk as the trail climbs high above cliffs with stretches of mud and a few boulders to trip over. There are no spectacular viewpoints, so if Alpine Lakes is the destination, there are easier, more scenic trails to follow. There will still be patches of snow in June, so check the condition of the trail with the Forest Service before starting out.

Drive east on US 2, the Stevens Pass highway, 8 miles beyond the town of Skykomish (0.2 miles beyond the Deception Falls parking area), and turn right on forest road No. 6088 signed "Deception Creek Trail." Follow this road 0.4 of a mile, passing under a railroad trestle to the road's end and trailhead, elevation 2000 feet.

The trail, No. 1059, follows Deception Creek a short ½ mile, then crosses the creek at the wilderness boundary. From there the way leaves the river, climbing 1000 feet over forested cliffs. At 2 miles the way crosses a scary foot log suspended high over Sawyer Creek. When the creek is flooding, this is the only way across. At 2½ miles reach the 3200-foot high point and then descend 400 feet to a delightful campsite beside Deception Creek, elevation 2800 feet, and a good turnaround spot.

The trail continues, crossing Deception Creek two more times in the next 2 miles. There are numerous ups and downs and several less-crowded campsites. At 5 miles there is a junction with a shortcut trail from the Tonga Ridge road. At 7½ miles there is a junction with the Deception Lakes trail and at 10½ miles the trail ends at Deception Pass and a junction of the Pacific Crest Trail.

Deception Creek trail

2 Dorothy, Bear, Deer, and Snoqualmie Lakes

Round trip to Lake Dorothy from Miller
River 10½ miles
Hiking time 6 hours
High point 3058 feet
Elevation gain 1700 feet
Best June through October
One day or backpack
USGS Skykomish, Grotto, Snoqualmie
Lake

Round trip to Snoqualmie Lake from Taylor
River 14½ miles
Hiking time 8 hours
High point 3147 feet
Elevation gain 2000 feet
Best June through October
One day or backpack
USGS Snoqualmie Lake

Lying in a string on both sides of the Snoqualmie-Skykomish divide, these four large subalpine lakes once were so remote that only the sturdiest Scouts and fishermen could visit on a weekend; the usual trip was a week. Then logging roads pushed so far up the valleys that Dorothy was a mere 1½ miles from the car and Snoqualmie 2¼ miles—and there even were plans for a Lake Dorothy Highway that would have skirted all the shores! But with the Alpine Lakes Wilderness came a new attitude toward roads, not every one of which now is considered permanently sacred. Permitting logging roads to dwindle to footroads, transitional to trails, has made the four lakes much lonesomer.

The end lakes, Dorothy and Snoqualmie, have become quite long day hikes from the Miller River and Taylor River, respectively, and the middle lakes, Bear and Deer, are pretty much purely for backpacking. The route will be described here as a cross-divide one-way walk from the north—keep in mind the reverse direction and the variations.

Drive US 2 east 17½ miles from Gold Bar and just before the highway tunnel turn right, at a sign for Money Creek Campground, on Old Cascade Highway. At a Y in 1¼ miles turn right onto gravel Miller River road and drive 5.5 miles to a gate. Park here, elevation 1400 feet.

Walk the road 3.8 miles in alternating clearcuts and forests, crossing many fine creeks which vigorously attack the road to enlarge the wildland, to the trailhead, 2200 feet.

The trail climbs through forest to Dorothy Lake at 1½ miles, 3058 feet. It follows the east side of the 2-mile-long lake, crosses the marshy inlet, begins climbing, and at 4½ miles from the road tops the 3800-foot ridge dividing the Miller and Taylor Rivers. Views are down to island-dotted Dorothy amid forest and gray-white cliffs and southeast to the dominant peak of the area, 6670-foot Big Snow Mountain.

From the pass the way is downhill to Bear Lake, 3610 feet, and, at 6 miles, Deer Lake, 3583 feet. At 6½ miles is Snoqualmie Lake, 3147 feet, second-largest of the group. The trail continues 2¼ miles down the Taylor River to the end of another abandoned logging road become pleasant footroad, elevation 1865 feet. Amble on down a scant 5 miles, pausing to admire a series of spectacular granite-slab waterfalls, to the parking area at 1225 feet.

To drive to this point, follow the Middle Fork Snoqualmie road (see Hike 16, Hester Lake) to the Taylor River bridge and turn left 1 mile to where the Quartz Creek road goes left and the old Taylor road is barricaded.

To protect the vegetation, campers are asked to use sites 100 feet from lakeshores.

Snoqualmie Lake

	OLD	NEW
Miller River road	2522	6412
Middle Fork Snoqualmie road	2445	56

SKYKOMISH RIVER

3 Tonga Ridge- Mount Sawyer

Round trip to pass 6½ miles
Hiking time 3 hours
High point 4800 feet
Elevation gain 400 feet
Best July through October
One day or backpack
USGS Scenic

The easiest ridge walk on the west side of the Cascades, with grand views, beautiful meadows, and flowers throughout the summer.

Drive US 2 east from Skykomish 1.8 miles and turn right on the Foss River road. At 1.2 miles keep right on the main road. At 2.5 miles go straight ahead at the intersection just after passing under a railroad bridge. At 3.6 miles turn left on Tonga Ridge road 7 miles. Turn right at a junction on No. 6830-310 and continue 1.5 miles to the road-end, elevation 4400 feet.

The hike begins on an old fire trail climbing to the ridge crest. In a couple hundred feet the foot trail turns off the fire trail into forest, winds through woods a while, and then follows the ridge top in meadows. At about 1½ miles the trail leaves the crest to contour around Mt. Sawyer, finally dropping a bit to Sawyer Pass, 3 miles, 4800 feet, dividing the drainages of Burn Creek and Fisher Creek. Good campsites, and also the first water of the trip, in the gentle swale of the pass, a large green meadow (commonly called N. P. Camp) that turns a brilliant red in fall.

For a wide-view sidetrip, scramble up 5501-foot Mt. Sawyer, the second large hill seen from the Tonga River approach. Leave the trail wherever the slopes look appealing and plow upward in huckleberry brush, gaining 700 feet. Try it in late August and eat your way through delicious berries. The summit panorama includes Mt. Rainier, Mt. Baker, and Glacier Peak, plus Hinman, Daniel, Sloan, and more. Immediately below are two lakes of the Jewel Lake string, easily reached from Sawyer Pass by consulting a contour map.

The most obvious tread at Sawyer Pass is on the west side, but this is a fishermen's path toward Fisher Lake and soon fades out. The main trail stays to the east side of the pass, then descends 1600 feet into valley forest, crossing several small creeks. At 5½ miles skirt a clearcut, cross another clearcut and road, and at 6 miles reach Deception Creek trail.

If pickup transportation can be arranged, interesting one-way hikes can be made

	OLD	NEW
Foss River road	2622	68
Tonga Ridge road	2605	6830
	2605A	6830-310

Tonga Ridge trail

from here, exiting via Deception Creek, or Deception Lakes and Surprise Creek (Hike 6), or Deception Pass, a sidetrip to Marmot Lake, and Hyas Lake (Hike 40).

Note: Road No. 6830 is open to public travel to the end; to get there, instead of turning right at the junction 7 miles from Foss River road No. 68, one would continue on road No. 6830 for 11 miles to the trailhead below Sawyer Pass. Obviously this shortcut would give much quicker access to goals in and beyond upper Deception Creek. However, hikers seek challenges, not shortcuts, and it is therefore fervently urged (and demanded) that the Forest Service live up to its "multiple use" theory by closing off the last 3-4 miles of road No. 6830 once the logging is finished, thus preserving as trail country an area that is very heavily used as such, and that certainly doesn't need "improved" access by automobile.

Necklace Valley, LaBohn Gap in distance

SKYKOMISH RIVER

4 Necklace Valley

Round trip to Jade Lake 16 miles
Allow 2-3 days
High point 4600 feet
Elevation gain 3000 feet
Best late July through October
USGS Skykomish, Big Snow Mountain,
    Mt. Daniel

A narrow alpine valley carved from the side of Mt. Hinman and appropriately named for its string of small gems—Jade, Emerald, and Opal Lakes. Nearby are Locket and Jewel Lakes. And others. Thanks to the long trail, this is much more lonesome country than the Foss Lakes area described in Hike 5.

Drive US 2 east from Skykomish 1.8 miles. Turn right on the Foss River road 3.6 miles to the Tonga Ridge junction, as described in Hike 3, and continue to the East Fork Foss River trail at 4.2 miles. On the left side of the road find a small parking area and the trailhead, elevation 1600 feet.

The first 5 miles gain only 600 feet and are very pleasant going through forest, following the valley bottom, passing the marshes of Alturas "Lake."

The trail this far is very worthwhile in its own right, and can be hiked on a day walk or a weekend backpack in May and June when the high country is buried in snow.

The trail crosses a log over the river which flows from the Hinman Glacier on Mt. Hinman and from the Lynch Glacier on Mt. Daniel. On the far bank the trail leaves the river and climbs into the hanging glacial trough, gaining 2400 feet in the 3 miles to the first gem of the necklace, Jade Lake, 4600 feet.

Necklace Valley is a delightful mixture of forest, heather, ice-polished granite—and of course, the lakes. Possibilities for roaming are endless. Campsites are available along the river and at most of the lakes; the best are at Emerald.

From Emerald Lake, about ¼ mile upvalley from Jade Lake, cross a low saddle west to Jewel and Locket Lakes or cross the ridge east to Lake Ilswoot.

From the east side of Opal Lake, another ¼ mile upvalley from Emerald Lake, climb a short step up a tributary creek to Cloudy Lake.

Tougher to attain are La Bohn Lakes, set in granite bowls near the summit of 5600-foot La Bohn Gap. The off-trail route from the head of Necklace Valley goes abruptly up through cliffs, and though an easy way can be found in the vicinity of the waterfall tumbling down from the east, the "obvious" chute to the south has killed at least one hiker. No route from valley to gap can be recommended for any but experienced mountain travelers.

To preserve vegetation, campers are asked to use sites 100 feet from lakeshores. Firewood is extremely scarce; carry a stove.

	OLD	NEW
Foss River road	2622	68

SKYKOMISH RIVER

5 Foss Lakes

Round trip to Copper Lake 8 miles
Hiking time 6-8 hours
High point 3961 feet
Elevation gain 2300 feet
Best July through October
One day or backpack
USGS Big Snow Mountain

Lovers of alpine lakes look at the Big Snow Mountain topog map and drool. Crowded onto this single sheet are 10 large lakes and numerous small ones, the rich legacy of ancient glaciers. The West Fork Foss River trail passes four of the lakes and fishermen's paths lead to others. Don't expect privacy—the area has long been famous and extremely popular for its numerous, unusually big, and readily accessible lakes.

Drive US 2 east from Skykomish 1.8 miles. Turn right on the Foss River road 4.2 miles to the East Fork Foss River trail, as described in Hike 4, and continue to West Fork Foss River road at 4.8 miles. Turn left 2 miles to the road-end and trailhead, elevation 1600 feet.

Hike an easy 1½ miles in cool forest to the first of the chain, Trout Lake, 2000 feet. Trees line the shore; through branches are glimpses of rugged cliffs above. This far makes a leisurely afternoon, and the trail is free of snow in May.

The steep, hot, 2-mile climb to Copper Lake, gaining 2000 feet, is something else in late summer. Water is plentiful but always out of reach—splashing in falls on the far hillside, rushing along a deep gully below the trail. The way at last opens into the cliff-walled basin of 3961-foot Copper Lake, surrounded by alpine trees and meadows and talus slopes.

Though much can be seen in a day or weekend, 3 days or more are needed for a

Copper Lake

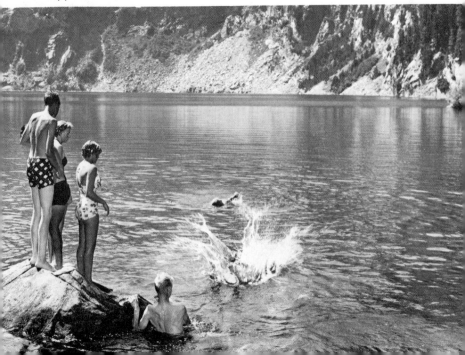

satisfying exploration. Copper Lake is the beginning of highland terrain, with miles of heather and blueberries amid groves of alpine trees, and glacier-smoothed rock knolls and granite buttresses. The crowds steadily diminish beyond Copper.

The lovely cirque of Malachite Lake, 4089 feet, is reached by a steep ¼-mile path branching from the main trail ½ mile before Copper Lake.

Beyond Copper Lake the main trail climbs gently along a stream, passing the best and maybe the only flower display of the trip, to 4204-foot Little Heart Lake, 1 mile from Copper, then crosses a 4700-foot ridge and drops to 4545-foot Big Heart Lake, 2½ miles from Copper; during the ridge crossing take a short sidetrip from the trail for an overlook of three lakes.

The formal trail continues beyond the outlet of Big Heart Lake 1 mile over the end of the ridge to the outlet of 4609-foot Lake Angeline. Chetwoot Lake, 4905 feet, coldest and rockiest of the group, may be reached by leaving the formal trail at about its high point on the ridge and traveling south over the very summit of the high and narrow ridge between Big Heart and Angeline Lakes, down into a saddle, and up once more over the next ridge. The route is a bit rugged but quite feasible, with a beaten footpath much of the way. From Chetwoot the upper end of Lake Angeline is readily accessible.

There are also Delta, Azurite, and Otter Lakes, and a dozen or more smaller ones, many visible from the trail and each a jewel in its own right. Routes known to hardy fishermen exist to all of them, and even semblances of boot-beaten track, but essentially these lakes are for the experienced cross-country hiker.

All camps at all the lakes are heavily used and usually crowded. Carry a stove if you want hot food or boiled drinking water. To preserve vegetation, use sites 100 feet from the shores. At Trout Lake only several sites are designated and no others may be used; due to sanitation problems, do not fail to boil the water. Camping is very limited at Malachite, Little Heart, and Chetwoot Lakes and virtually impossible at Angeline. Copper has a large expanse of comfortable people-beaten dirt. The most scenic camping is at Big Heart.

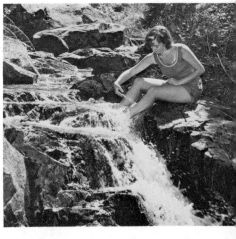

	OLD	NEW
Foss River road	2622	68
West Fork Foss River road	2622	6840

SKYKOMISH RIVER

6 Surprise Lake and Mountain

Round trip to Surprise Lake 8½ miles
Hiking time 5 hours
High point 4500 feet
Elevation gain 2300 feet
Best late June through October
One day or backpack
USGS Scenic

Round trip to Surprise Mountain 15½ miles
Hiking time 9-12 hours
High point 6330 feet
Elevation gain 4100 feet
Best late July through October
One day or backpack
USGS Scenic

Surprise Lake mirrors a ring of green trees and white granite. Glacier Lake adds the cliffs of Surprise Mountain, whose summit is the supreme grandstand for viewing the glacial brilliance of Daniel and Hinman, forest deeps of Deception Creek, and peaks from Baring to Monte Cristo to Glacier to Cashmere.

Drive US 2 east from Skykomish 10 miles. Just after the highway makes a bend left, go off right on an unsigned road that crosses the Tye River to the hamlet of Scenic, service center for the Burlington-Northern Railroad's Cascade Tunnel, whose west portal is nearby. Drive over the railroad tracks and in a hundred feet turn right on a sideroad with a hiker-trail symbol. In about ¼ mile, before the road starts a rough ascent, park, elevation 2200 feet.

Walk the road (some cars drive, but not happily) ¼ mile, following the powerline swath to the trail, which quickly leaves hot brush for cool trees. No hike in the vicinity offers a more joyful forest, so many excellent waterfalls, and exactly the proper trickles and gushes to solace mouth and head; despite green shadows these can become quite dry, particularly on switchbacks of the final mile, where the trail parallels a continuous cataract up into the hanging valley. A picnic lunch atop a granite buttress at Surprise Lake, 4508 feet, 4 miles from the trailhead, climaxes a nice day.

Having passed the old route of the Pacific Crest Trail just before Surprise Lake, on the way to Glacier Lake the valley trail passes the new route. The valley trail avoids Glacier, 4806 feet, but sidepaths give easy access. At 1½ miles from the Surprise

Mt. Daniel from Surprise Gap

outlet the trail passes the site of the old shelter cabin and in a scant ½ mile more opens out in a basin of granite blocks and green lawns and meltwater creeks and flowers a-rioting. Here at the foot of Surprise Mountain's 1000-foot walls is a junction, 5100 feet.

The new Crest Trail turns right and climbs to 5900-foot Peiper Pass, the (long) way to Deception Lakes and points south and the start of off-trail explorations to Spark Plug Mountain and Spark Plug Lake.

The old, abandoned Crest Trail climbs in a scant ½ mile of rock gardens (or snow—in early summer, be careful) to Surprise Gap, 5780 feet. This is the short way, 1¼ miles from the gap, down to 5053-foot Deception Lakes, very nice. For the views turn right at the gap and climb 1 steep mile through parkland and meadows and marmots to the summit of Surprise Mountain, 6330 feet. Naught remains of the lookout cabin except a litter of fragments—and the metal post that was the base of the firefinder. The views! Precipitously down spectacular cliffs to the lakes. Across the broad valley to the gleaming ice. West to saltwater, north to volcanoes, east to Enchantments.

Camps are numerous at and near both lakes and at the site of the old shelter cabin. Wood is scarce at most; carry a stove. To preserve vegetation, campers are asked to shun the shores. Carry water and camp near the summit of Surprise and see more stars than are dreamt of in your astronomy charts.

NASON CREEK

7 Larch Lake

Round trip via Chiwaukum Creek 20 miles
Allow 2-3 days
High point 6078 feet
Elevation gain 3700 feet
Best mid-July through October
USGS Chiwaukum Mountains

A high mountain lake, rimmed by rocks and groves of larch, in the shadow of the tall and rugged Chiwaukum Mountains on the northeast edge of the Alpine Lakes Wilderness.

Tragically, much of the surrounding region is privately owned as a consequence of the infamous Northern Pacific Land Grant of 1864, and in 1973, despite strenuous efforts by conservationists, Wenatchee National Forest and Pack River Lumber Company began building a system of new roads to allow logging of both private and public timber. Take the hike—and return mourning the destruction.

There are two approaches to Larch Lake: a well-graded trail over McCue Ridge; or a valley walk along Chiwaukum Creek, easy except for 2 very steep, hot miles. Despite the mean stretch, the creek route is recommended. The forest is lovely, there are frequent charming views of the stream, and the way crosses three nice bridges, one of them just below a waterfall. Both approaches are the same length but the ridge trail climbs 300 feet higher going in and makes a 500-foot ascent coming out.

For the McCue Ridge route, which has been messed up by Pack River's logging operations, drive US 2 east from Stevens Pass 17 miles. Just opposite a highway rest area turn south around a pasture. There are numerous logging spurs but the correct way is well-marked. At 0.5 mile find Lake Julius trail No. 1584, elevation 2500 feet.

The trail follows a ridge above Roaring Creek, crossing a private (gated) logging road four times, climbing to a junction with McCue Ridge trail No. 1574 at 5½ miles, 5600 feet. (Note: Loggers leave the gate open while they're at work, but lock it when they leave, with no mercy for unwary hikers who may have driven on through for the sake of a shortcut.) Keep left, ascending to the ridge top at 5750 feet. At this point the ridge is timbered; for views, walk a path a few hundred feet east on the crest and look over a big patch of snowbrush (ceanothus). Below is the vast Chiwaukum valley, west are the Chiwaukum Mountains, and south are Snowgrass Mountain and the Stuart Range. From the ridge the trail drops 550 feet to Chiwaukum Lake at 7½ miles;

Larch Lake and Chiwaukum Mountains

campsites near the shores and in a large, horsey area at the head of the lake in Ewing Basin. A way trail traverses the long basin and climbs steeply into meadowlands, at 10 miles reaching 6078-foot Larch Lake and many good camps.

For the Chiwaukum Creek route, drive US 2 east from Stevens Pass 25 miles and about ½ mile before reaching Tumwater Campground turn south on a rough road leading in 2 miles to the trailhead, elevation 2200 feet.

Trail No. 1571 follows close by the creek in deep forest, gradually ascending. At 4 miles turn right on trail No. 1573 and at 5 miles begin climbing steeply, with many switchbacks, on a badly-eroded tread consisting mainly of loose schist, gaining 1200 feet in a little more than a mile. At 7 miles the unpleasantness ends as 5210-foot Chiwaukum Lake is attained. Follow the shore ½ mile to a junction with the McCue Ridge trail described above and continue to Larch Lake at 10 miles.

Among the possible explorations from Larch Lake are a scramble up among the 8000-foot Chiwaukum Mountains and a walk to tiny Cup Lake, set in a little north-facing cirque that doesn't melt free of snow until September, if then.

To preserve the vegetation, campers are asked to use established sites.

33

Lake Viviane

ICICLE CREEK

8 Enchantment Lakes

Round trip to Snow Lakes 13½ miles
Allow 2 days
High point 5415 feet
Elevation gain 3800 feet
Best July through October
USGS Mt. Stuart and Liberty

Round trip to Lower Enchantment Lakes 20
 miles
Allow 3-4 days
High point 7000 feet
Elevation gain 5400 feet
Best late July through mid-October

A legendary group of lakes in rock basins over 7000 feet high amid the Cashmere Crags of the Stuart Range; one of the most famous places in the Cascade Mountains. Large lakes, small ponds, gigantic slabs of ice-polished granite, flower gardens, heather meadows, trees gnarled and twisted by the elements, waterfalls, snowfields, and glaciers. Visit in summer for flowers, in late September to see the autumn gold of larch.

This is not a trip for beginners. The way is long, steep, and grueling. A strong hiker needs at least 12 hours to reach the high lakes. The average hiker takes 2 days. The rest never make it.

It also is not a trip for hermits. The scene is mobbed from early summer, when the snow is still deep, until late fall, when it's piling up again. It's mobbed on holidays, mobbed on weekends, mobbed in midweek.

If you decide to come anyhow, be prepared to obey as stringent a moral code as any in American wilderness. The fragility of the vegetation requires it. So does the population density. Motorcycles were the first superconsumers to be prohibited. Then came horses. —And then, **dogs**—do not expect law-abiding hikers to accept your excuse that "Gee, I never go no place without good ol' Slasher." Bring a stove—wood fires are banned. Camp on bare ground at established sites. Walk on rock or snow rather than plants. Limit party size to six. If you can't live with all that, do without.

Drive US 2 east from Stevens Pass to Leavenworth. On the west outskirts of town turn south on Icicle Creek road. At 4 miles turn left into the Snow Lakes trail parking area, elevation 1600 feet.

Snow Lakes trail No. 1553 crosses the river and immediately starts up—and up. The way switchbacks upward in forest, with views in the early part to the granite cliffs of Snow Creek Wall. Small camps at approximately 2 miles, 2800 feet, offer a break in the journey for parties with heavy packs or not too much energy and wishing to make the approach in easy stages. At 5½ miles is Nada Lake, 5000 feet, and good camps. At 6¾ miles the trail passes between the two Snow Lakes at 5415 feet. For camping here, find sites to the left at the lower lake and all the way around the left side of the upper lake to where the trail finally starts up. To the north rises 8292-foot Mt. Temple and to the south 8364-foot Mt. McClellan. All beginners and most average hikers find this far enough, and these lakes magnificent enough—as indeed they are, but it just happens their beauty can't hold a candle to what lies above.

To continue to the Enchantments, cross the low dam between the two lakes. Pause to note this rather weird interference with nature: like a bathtub, water is drained through a hole in the bottom of the upper lake (which thus has a fluctuating shoreline) and is used to guarantee a pure intake for the Leavenworth Fish Hatchery; probably few people imagined, when the project was perpetrated back in the 1930s, that Snow Lakes would become as popular as they now are.

Follow the trail winding along the left shore. At the south end cross the inlet stream and proceed up Snow Creek, climbing into granite country.

The area was discovered by A.H. Sylvester, a topographer for the U.S. Geological Survey for some 13 years and then, from 1908 to 1931, supervisor of Wenatchee National Forest. In his years of exploring he placed thousands of names on maps of the West. "Enchantment" expressed his reaction—and that of all who have followed. The one name covered everything until climbers arrived in the late 1940s and began assigning vivid names to "The Crags." Then came Bill and Peg Stark, who over many years drew on various mythologies to name the lakes and other features. A lake and its sword-like rock peninsula became Lake Viviane and Excalibur Rock. Other lakes and tarns they called Rune, Talisman, Valkyrie, Leprechaun, Naiad, Lorelei, Dryad, Pixie, Gnome, Brisingamen, Brynhild, Reginleif, Sprite, and Titania. And there is Troll Sink (a pond), Valhalla Cirque, Tanglewood, and many more.

Lower Enchantment Basin, at 7000 feet, is friendliest. Upper Enchantment Basin, at 7500 feet, has a desolate splendor. Some of its lakes are clear and some are jade-colored by rock milk and some are frozen solid all summer. When Sylvester was here—not all that long ago—nearly the whole basin was occupied by the Snow Creek Glacier.

ICICLE CREEK

9 Lake Caroline

Round trip 11 miles
Hiking time 8 hours
High point 6190 feet
Elevation gain 2400 feet
Best mid-July through October
One day or backpack
USGS Chiwaukum Mountains

Another delightful spot of the Alpine Lakes Wilderness, a high tree-lined lake, meadows, and a wealth of rocky cliffs. A special treat is the great north face of 9415-foot Mt. Stuart, seen from close enough to make out crevasses in the hanging glaciers.

The trail to Lake Caroline crosses the checkerboard ownership inherited from the railroad land grants. Lake Caroline itself is on private land. The present owners are cutting their land and the trail is disrupted in several places.

Drive US 2 east from Stevens Pass to Leavenworth. On the west outskirts of town turn south on Icicle Creek road. At 8.5 miles turn left across a bridge on road No. 2412 up Eight Mile Creek, climbing steeply 3 miles to the trailhead, elevation 3800 feet. Eight Mile Lake trail No. 1552, on the uphill side of the road, is clearly signed.

The trail ascends moderately following Eight Mile Creek with about ½ mile of road walking. At 2½ miles, the trail reaches Little Eight Mile Lake, elevation 4400 feet, and a junction. The left fork goes another ½ mile up the valley to 4641-foot Eight Mile Lake and good camps. The lake is ringed by woods but awesome rock walls rise far above the trees.

The right fork climbs an endless series of switchbacks (hot and thirsty on sunny days) up from the valley, first in timber, then emerging into meadows. The labor is rewarded by steadily improving views to the jagged spires of the Stuart Range and finally the tall thrust of Mt. Stuart itself. At 5½ miles the way reaches the alpine basin of Lake Caroline, 6190 feet. The most attractive campsites are ½ mile farther and 200 feet higher at Little Lake Caroline, surrounded by meadows.

The best is yet to come. The 2-mile hike to 7200-foot Windy Pass, on good trail amid flowers and larches, is an absolute must. For broader views walk the ridge towards 8501-foot Mt. Cashmere—but don't try for the summit; the last pitches are strictly for climbers.

An alternate return route (not too practical unless one can hitch a ride back to the

36

Lake Caroline (Vicky Spring photo)

car) can be made by going 8 miles from Windy Pass down Trout Creek to the Chatter Creek Guard Station. This trail passes through a mile of clearcuts on more railroad grant land.

To preserve vegetation, campers are asked to use only established campsites.

10 Lake Stuart- Colchuck Lake

Round trip to Colchuck Lake 9 miles
Hiking time 8 hours
High point 5570 feet
Elevation gain 2000 feet
Best mid-July through October
One day or backpack
USGS Chiwaukum and Mt. Stuart

Round trip to Lake Stuart 10 miles
Hiking time 7 hours
High point 5064 feet
Elevation gain 1500 feet
Best mid-July through October
One day or backpack

Two large lakes amid alpine forests and granite cliffs of the Stuart Range. Hike to emerald waters of Colchuck Lake and contemplate towering crags above, decorated with two small glaciers. Or, to cure itchy feet, visit nearby Lake Stuart. Or, if it's peace and quiet you want, don't come here at all because this is the most heavily-used trail and lake system in the vicinity—even more so than the Enchantments!

From Icicle Creek road (Hike 9) drive 4 miles on road No. 2412 to the trailhead, elevation 3600 feet. Find Lake Stuart-Colchuck Lake trail No. 1599 at a sharp turn of the road on the creek side.

The trail parallels Mountaineer Creek on a constant upward grade for 1 mile, then switchbacks up the steepening valley to a junction at 1½ miles, 4600 feet.

The left trail (a rough path) crosses Mountaineer Creek and ascends with many switchbacks, in open forest among numerous granite knolls, along the cascading waters of the East Fork Mountaineer Creek. During the final ¼ mile the way bypasses a waterfall, leaves the creek, and comes to a tiny, almost landlocked lagoon of Colchuck Lake, 5570 feet, 3½ miles. Incredibly, this lovely blue-green lake, like others in the area, is drained for use by the Icicle Irrigation District. Camping all the way around the right side of the lake.

The right trail proceeds gently up the main fork of Mountaineer Creek to the wooded shores, clear blue water, and tall cliffs of Lake Stuart, 5064 feet, 4½ miles. Campsites near the point where the trail first reaches the lake and around the south shore. Follow

Mt. Stuart from Lake Stuart

the trail ¾ mile beyond the lake to a marshy meadow under the towering cliffs of Mt. Stuart. Beyond lies **wild** wilderness, brushy and craggy, mean and dangerous; Horseshoe Lake and Jack Ridge are strictly for the super-doughty.

To preserve the vegetation, campers are asked to use established sites.

Icicle Ridge trail, Mt. Stuart in distance

ICICLE CREEK

11 Lake Mary

Round trip to Lake Mary 16 miles
Allow 2-3 days
High point 6200 feet
Elevation gain 3300 feet
Best mid-July through October
USGS Chiwaukum Mountains

If the Enchantments are the granite classic of the Alpine Lakes Wilderness, Snowgrass Mountain is the supreme green. This is the place for dreamlike wanderings along tundra ridges and through lake basins and around corners to magic surprises. But there is a price to pay: gangs of dreamers, hordes of dreamers, wandering everywhere—many on horseback.

Drive US 2 east from Stevens Pass to Leavenworth. On the west outskirts of town turn south on Icicle road. At 8.5 miles pass Eight Mile junction and at 16.7 miles cross Icicle Creek on a concrete bridge (road No. 2512). At 18.5 miles are the road-end and trailhead, elevation 2900 feet.

Icicle Creek trail No. 1551 goes upstream in lovely forest, over several creeks with campsites, to a junction at 2½ miles, 3000 feet. Turn right on Wildhorse trail No. 1592, cross Icicle Creek, and start up. Soon cross Frosty Creek; fill canteens, there's a dry hill coming, with many a dusty switchback. But the worst is over at 6 miles, 4900 feet, when the way emerges from trees into the little basin of Packrat Camp. At 6¾ miles a short sidepath drops a bit to woodsy Lake Margaret, 5409 feet; camping is very limited. At 7½ miles the trail tops Frosty Pass, 5800 feet, and opens out into meadow-and-parkland that stretches in every direction as far as eye can see. Where to start?

An unsigned, unmaintained trail contours northwest from the pass to an excellent camp and continues sketchily onward—ultimately to Doelle Lakes. The Wildhorse trail sidehills north, giving off-trail (meadow) access to Grace Lakes.

Eventually one must proceed east from Frosty Pass on Icicle Ridge trail No. 1570, in ½ mile reaching the sidetrail dropping to Lake Mary, 6100 feet, the popular place for a basecamp, and a superb spot it is—if you can find a vacancy. If not, climb the garden-wall trail ¾ mile to Mary Pass, 6800 feet, and drop ½ mile to Upper Florence Lake, 6400 feet, with the most scenic—and most exposed—camps of all.

Why stop? Just 1¼ flowery miles from Marys Pass is Ladies Pass, 6800 feet, above Lake Brigham and Lake Flora in headwaters of Chiwaukum Creek. In another mile, beyond the shoulder of 7300-foot Cape Horn, is Lake Edna, 6735 feet, a cold and rocky tarn. Spanish Camp Basin, below the trail to Ladies Pass, is well worth an afternoon; an old trail enters the basin from Upper Florence Lake. For high panoramas leave the trail at Marys Pass and strike directly up the flowers to the 7600-foot ridge of Snowgrass Mountain and views from Cashmere and Stuart to Monte Cristo and Glacier to Index and Baring. Or leave the trail between Lake Mary and Marys Pass and climb to a hidden basin and continue upward to an even higher ridge of Snowgrass. (The several summits of the 4-mile-long mountain, the highest 8000 feet, require climbing experience and equipment, but easy hiking takes a person high enough to feel on top of the world.)

To preserve vegetation, campers are asked to use established sites.

PESHASTIN CREEK

12 Ingalls Creek

Round trip to Falls Creek Camp 12 miles
Hiking time 6 hours
High point 3200 feet
Elevation gain 1200 feet
Best late May through November
One day or backpack
USGS Liberty and Mt. Stuart

Round trip to Stuart Pass 32 miles
Allow 3-5 days
High point 6400 feet
Elevation gain 4400 feet
Best July through October

The longest wilderness valley remaining in the Cascades outside the far north, 16 miles of trail climbing from low forest to high meadows, passing constantly changing views of the spectacular Stuart Range.

Hike this trail the first week of June when the first 5 miles are lined with trillium, gold-colored paintbrush, and a few calypso orchids thrown in. If you're too early for trillium, there will be glacier lilies. If you're too late for trillium, there will be queen's cup.

Drive US 97 north from Swauk (Blewett) Pass 12.5 miles and turn left on Ingalls Creek road about 1 mile to the road-end and trailhead, elevation 1953 feet.

The trail ascends steadily but gently, alternating between groves of trees and patches of avalanche brush, mostly in sight and always in sound of roaring Ingalls Creek, with tantalizing glimpses of the rocky summits of the Stuart Range, and later, looks to fantastic spires.

In early June hikers usually will encounter snow patches from 4 miles or so, and difficult going beyond the vicinity of Falls Creek, 6 miles, 3200 feet. The lovely Falls Creek Camp is reached by a sidetrail across Ingalls Creek, which is much too deep and swift to ford while meltwater is rushing. In any season this point makes a good turnaround for day-trippers.

The way continues upward along the almost-straight fault-line valley (granite on one side, sediments and metamorphics on the other), the forest becoming subalpine and open, the views growing. Tributary creeks are crossed often enough to satisfy thirst; pleasant camps are frequent.

Ingalls Creek near Falls Creek

From Porcupine Creek, about 10 miles, 4100 feet, the path steepens a bit and sidehills above Ingalls Creek, the timber increasingly broken by meadows. Now the cliffs and buttresses of 9415-foot Mt. Stuart, second-highest nonvolcanic peak in the state, dominate the scene.

At about 13½ miles, 4800 feet, the trail nears Ingalls Creek and commences a rather earnest ascent, climbing parkland and flowers and talus to Stuart Pass, 16 miles, 6400 feet. On the far side the tread descends Jack Creek to Chatter Creek Forest Station on Icicle Creek.

All along the upper valley the open country invites easy off-trail wanderings, such as to Longs Pass (Hike 43). From a camp in the delightful basin under Stuart Pass one can spend days exploring—begin by contouring meadows from the pass to 6463-foot Ingalls Lake (Hike 44).

**NORTH FORK
SNOQUALMIE RIVER**

13 Bare Mountain

Round trip 8 miles
Hiking time 6 hours
High point 5353 feet
Elevation gain 3250 feet
Best late June through October
One day
USGS Mt. Si and Grotto

A lonesome trail up a green hillside to a former fire lookout with panoramic views north to Mt. Baker and south to Mt. Rainier and west to the Olympics. So little-walked is the path that the tread is grown up in moss and grass—and may be lost under a canopy of flowers and bracken.

Drive Interstate 90 to North Bend, take Exit 31 into town and onto the main street, the former highway. Go two blocks east of the stoplight and turn north on Ballaratt Street, which leads to North Fork County Road. At 4 miles from North Bend is a Y; take the left, uphill, signed "Lake Hancock." In 7.5 miles pass the Lake Hancock junction and proceed onward. At about 21 miles enter National Forest, the road now becoming Lennox Creek road No. 57. At the boundary the road forks; keep right, crossing Lennox Creek. At 23 miles from North Bend (what with all the chuckholes on the county segment, allow an hour for the drive) is the trailhead, signed "Bare Mountain trail No. 1037." Park here, elevation 2100 feet.

The first 2 miles follow an abandoned mining road, crossing Bear Creek on a wide bridge near a beautiful pool. (Note: It's "Bare" Mountain and "Bear" Creek. Were they named for two different reasons?) In ¼ mile the way recrosses the creek on a footbridge, enters the Alpine Lakes Wilderness, and climbs another ¼ mile to a large meadow covered with waist-high bracken. Find the trail with your feet—but watch out for hidden holes! At about 2 miles from the car is (1981) a small white post obscurely marking a junction, 3650 feet. Go left. (The right fork ascends the valley to private property. If after crossing the large meadow you enter forest you are ¼ mile beyond the junction on this, the wrong way.)

The left (correct) fork sets out from the junction so deep under ferns the boots can feel it but the eyes can't see it. Eventually, though, the path comes out in the open and after gaining 1700 feet in 46 switchbacks attains the 5353-foot summit.

	OLD	NEW
Lennox Creek road	250	57

Bare Mountain

All that remains of the lookout cabin, which was removed in 1973, is broken glass, rusting cables—and a grand view.

The three Paradise Lakes sparkle below, a tempting 1000-foot dive; due to formidable cliffs, this seems the only practical way to get there from here.

Anderson Lake, snow-covered in late June; Treen Peak, left, and Garfield Mountain, center

NORTH FORK
SNOQUALMIE RIVER

Round trip to Anderson Lake 7¼ miles
Hiking time 5 hours
High point 4600 feet
Elevation gain 1900 feet in, 400 feet out
Best July to early November
One day or backpack
USGS Mt. Si and Snoqualmie Lake

14 Lennox Creek

Waterfalls, broad slopes of heather meadows, views of peaks and valleys, and a quiet lake—all in a little-traveled portion of the Cascades. After lying in limbo for many years, this particular trail was reopened in 1970, and hikers gradually are coming to discover the beauties of the North Fork Snoqualmie country.

Drive about 21 miles from North Bend to the boundary of Mt. Baker-Snoqualmie National Forest and keep right at the fork here. (See Hike 13, Bare Mountain.) From the boundary drive 4 miles to two small bridges over island-divided channels of Lennox Creek. About ¼ mile farther is a fork; keep right on road No. 5700210, heading up Cougar Creek drainage a short, switchbacking mile to the road-end at a hogback in a clearcut, elevation 2700 feet.

The trail starts steeply up the hogback on a bulldozer track, in less than ¼ mile going from logged barrens into forest and passing a miner's cabin. Now the way contours the east side of Dog Mountain, traversing shoulders of a large avalanche chute. At about 2 miles the route enters a land of heather laced by numerous creeklets. Directly below the meadows and a bit hard to see is the spectacular waterfall of one of the tributaries of Lennox Creek.

At about 3¼ miles, 4600 feet, the trail gains a wooded saddle in the ridge. Enjoy the views down to Taylor River and across the valley to Treen Peak and a most unfamiliar aspect of Garfield Mountain.

From the saddle the trail switchbacks down 400 feet in a rough ½ mile to little Anderson Lake, surrounded by patches of heather and lots of trees. Camping is nice and quite private but wood is scarce.

	OLD	NEW
Lennox Creek road	250	57
Cougar Creek road	250B	5700210

**MIDDLE FORK
SNOQUALMIE RIVER**

15 Mount Si

Round trip 8 miles
Hiking time 8 hours
High point 4167 feet
Elevation gain 3500 feet
Best April through November
One day
USGS on the corner of Mt. Si, Snoqualmie,
North Bend, and Bandera

Climb steeply to the top of a fault scarp rising high above lowlands at the west edge of the Cascades. Look down to the Snoqualmie River meandering by the towns of North Bend and Snoqualmie and through green farms. If the smog isn't too thick, look west to Seattle and Puget Sound and the Olympic Mountains.

Si is a striking landmark at the gateway to the Cascades and is close to the city and therefore is perhaps the most heavily-traveled peak in the state. Mountaineers use the trail for conditioning, Scouts come in troops, and families with little children, and elderly folk and young lovers and lone roamers — a cross-section of humanity (in fact, about 10,000 hikers a year) may be encountered on a typical Sunday.

By May of normal years the way is entirely clear of snow. Sometimes the mountain is briefly bare even in midwinter, and the trail usually can be hiked to high viewpoints in any month.

Drive Interstate 90 to North Bend, take Exit 31 into town, and continue east on North Bend Way, the old route of Interstate 90. Exactly 1 mile from the east edge of town turn left on 432nd S.E. (Stilson Road) and cross the Middle Fork Snoqualmie River. Turn right at the first intersection. Drive 2.5 miles to a parking lot for 175 cars, a picnic area, and the trailhead, elevation 650 feet. The trail is signed for hikers only.

The first ½ mile is in alders, then second-growth firs 60-70 years old—except for a 1976 clearcut. At 1 mile is a vista point on a big rock alongside the trail. At 1¾ miles enter Snag Flat, covered by a mixture of old snags and huge fir trees, some 8 feet in diameter, that survived the fires. Water here about 200 feet off the main trail on a spur going ½ mile to a viewpoint.

The trees get smaller but views are scarce until the old trail is intersected at 3 miles, just below the ridge, a mile from the top. The way follows a rocky shoulder with broad panoramas to Haystack Basin, at the foot of the cliffs of the final peak. The Department of Natural Resources, which relocated the trailhead and built the new path after the old one was partially obliterated by logging operations, has installed pit toilets and

North Bend from edge of Haystack Basin

primitive campsites. However, there is no water after the last snow melts, usually in May, so carry enough for cooking or else hike up after dinner, enjoy the night on top—thousands of lights below and millions of stars above—and return to the car for breakfast. There are no other camps on the route.

The Haystack can be climbed by crossing the basin to the northeast side and scrambling a steep, loose-rock gully, but the ascent is a bit difficult and quite hazardous, and the summit view is only slightly better than that from the basin.

**MIDDLE FORK
SNOQUALMIE RIVER**

Round trip to Myrtle Lake 10 miles
Hiking time 7 hours
High point 3777 feet
Elevation gain 2400 feet
Best July through October
One day or backpack
USGS Snoqualmie Lake

16 Hester Lake-Myrtle Lake

Round trip to Hester Lake 9 miles
Hiking time 7 hours
High point 3886 feet
Elevation gain 2500 feet

Two high lakes, one offering some scenery and lots of solitude, the other lots of scenery—and people. However, the fishermen crowds don't climb the ridge where the views and meadow-wandering are.

Drive Interstate 90 east past North Bend and go off on Exit 34. Turn left, pass Ken's Truck Town, and follow signs for Middle Fork Snoqualmie River road, which in 15 miles crosses the Taylor River bridge. Once across the bridge, go another 6 miles to Dingford Creek trailhead, elevation 1400 feet.

The trail switchbacks steeply and hotly upward 1 mile through second-growth trees seeded after logging operations in the late 1940s, then gradually gentles out in cool virgin forest of tall, old Douglas fir and hemlock, going along constantly close to the tumble and roar of Dingford Creek. At about 2 miles, 2600 feet, is a ford of Goat Creek and an unmaintained fishermen's sidetrail climbing a rough 1 mile to Horseshoe Lake and Goat Lake. At 3¼ miles, 2900 feet, the trail forks; a nice campsite here beside the creek.

The right fork, to Hester Lake, is in poor shape and will be allowed to stay that way for people wanting to get away from people. The trail crosses Dingford Creek, ascends moderately at first in subalpine meadow-marshes and patches of trees, then goes straight uphill to Hester Lake, 3888 feet, 5½ miles from the road. The deep blue

	OLD	NEW
Middle Fork road	2445	56
Beyond Taylor River	241	5620

Oyster mushrooms along the trail to Hester Lake

lake is set in a cirque gouged in the side of 5600-foot Mt. Price; impressive cliffs rise from the shores, around which are good camps.

The left fork, to Myrtle Lake, is being improved for hikers and horses. The trail ascends easily in open forest, passing several meadows; the biggest difficulty (in season) is making any progress at all through the delicious blueberries. At 3 miles from the forks is Myrtle Lake, 3777 feet, amid clumps of alpine trees interspersed with huckleberry-covered meadows. Campsites at the lake and on higher benches; to protect the vegetation, campers are asked to use sites 100 feet from the shore.

For explorations, go around the east shore and find (if possible—it's not easy) a faint trail to Little Myrtle Lake. Continue another ¼ mile to the 4400-foot top of the ridge and views north to Lake Dorothy and south to Big Snow Mountain, 6670 feet. Alternately, climb the slopes west from Myrtle Lake and roam the ridges and fields of blueberries to Merlin, Niume, and LeFay Lakes.

Williams Lake and Little Big Chief Mountain

**MIDDLE FORK
SNOQUALMIE RIVER**

17 Dutch Miller Gap-La Bohn Gap

Round trip to Dutch Miller Gap 15 miles
Allow 2-3 days
High point 5000 feet
Elevation gain 2000 feet
Best mid-July through October
USGS Big Snow Mountain and Mt. Daniel

Round trip to La Bohn Gap approximately
   16 miles
Allow 2-3 days
High point 5600 feet
Elevation gain 2600 feet
Best late July through October

Hike a glorious valley of forests and meadows and waterfalls, rockslides and cliffs and jagged peaks, to wilderness headwaters of the Middle Fork Snoqualmie River. Then follow either the main trail to Dutch Miller Gap, named for an early prospector, or a way trail to La Bohn Gap, where he dug his holes in the ground.

Drive Middle Fork Snoqualmie River road to Dingford Creek (see Hike 16) and 6 more miles to the road-end at Hardscrabble Creek, elevation 3000 feet.

The trail enters forest and ascends gently with ups and downs, passing a riverbank camp at 1½ miles.

The transition from low country to high is abrupt: at about 4 miles the trail switch-backs up a step in the valley, going by a splendid cataract of the river, and at the top emerges into heather, grass, flowers, large talus slopes, and views of craggy peaks. The way is flat and frequently marshy and muddy to 6 miles, where the river is so wide and slow and meandering as almost to be a lake, surrounded by a broad meadow. Here, at superbly scenic Pedro Camp, 4100 feet, the trail crosses a branch of the river on a bridge; shortly beyond prowl around to find remnants of an old miner's cabin (Dutch Miller's?).

The way goes moderately upward in heather and alpine trees another ½ mile to a junction with the Williams Lake—La Bohn Gap trail, an easy ¾ mile to the heather-fringed lake.

For the main event, follow tread a long mile or so and then climb rockslides and/or snowfields to a magnificent basin of cold little tarns set in granite bowls, of flower patches and waterfalls, and of the mineral outcroppings and diggings and garbage of Dutch Miller's old mine—and his contemporary successors. Climb a bit more to the 5600-foot crest of La Bohn Gap (2 miles from the junction) and more tarns and views of Bears Breast Mountain and down to Necklace Valley (Hike 4). Experienced roamers can walk to panoramas from 6585-foot La Bohn Peak west of the gap or make a more difficult scramble to the summit of 7492-foot Mt. Hinman. Many delightful camps in the basin and in the gap.

One-half mile from the Williams Lake junction the main valley trail fords the river and ascends between the walls of Bears Breast and Little Big Chief, with grand views of Little Big Chief, Summit Chief, Middle Chief, and Overcoat, to the gardens of Dutch Miller Gap, 7½ miles, 5000 feet. Look immediately below to Lake Ivanhoe and out the valley east to Waptus Lake. Look westerly back down the long Snoqualmie valley. The trail drops ½ mile to rock-shored Ivanhoe, 4652 feet, at the foot of the cliffs of Bears Breast. Good camps by the lake. The trail continues down to Waptus Lake and the Cle Elum River (Hike 36).

	OLD	NEW
Middle Fork road	2445	56
Beyond Taylor River	241	5620

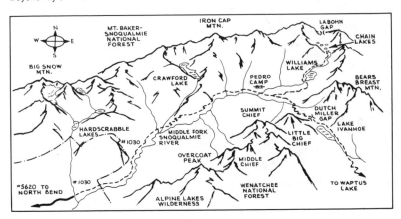

Round trip 9 miles
Hiking time 8 hours
High point 5162 feet
Elevation gain 3700 feet
Best July through October
One day
USGS Bandera

18 McClellan Butte

The sharp little peak looks formidable from Interstate 90, and because of avalanche snows in a gully it is dangerous until early July. However, a steep and rugged trail climbs to a viewpoint a few feet below the rocky summit for panoramas west over lowlands to Seattle, Puget Sound, and the Olympics, south over uncountable clearcuts to Mt. Rainier, and east to Snoqualmie Pass peaks. The lower part of the route contains numerous scars and artifacts of man's present and past activities; the recorded history of the area dates to 1853, when Captain George B. McClellan journeyed approximately this far up the valley during his search for a cross-Cascades pass suitable for Indian-fighters and immigrants. The trail is very popular even though rough in spots.

Drive Interstate 90 to Exit 42 and go off on road No. 55. Immediately beyond the Snoqualmie River bridge, turn right to the trailhead and parking lot, elevation 1500 feet.

The trail follows remnants of a wire-wrapped wooden waterline to a bridge (built by Scouts) over Alice Creek, climbs a bit, crosses a powerline swath, enters woods again, reaches a long-abandoned, overgrown railroad grade, and at ½ mile crosses the Milwaukee Railroad tracks and enters a vast clearcut. In the woods again, the trail passes mouldering mining relics and at 1 mile, 2200 feet, crosses a private (gated) logging road. Find a little spring left along the road—the last sure water after July.

The way steepens, going by a sometime spring in a cool grove of large trees, then

Yellow violets

	OLD	NEW
Tinkham road	222	55

Interstate 90 from summit ridge of McClellan Butte

switchbacks up the wooded north face of the butte. At about 2½ miles the trail rounds the east side of the butte and crosses an avalanche gully with a treacherous snow-bank that usually lasts into July. From here, with numerous switchbacks, the way sidehills below cliffs and occasional views, attaining the south ridge of the peak at 3¼ miles, 4500 feet. The trail follows the crest a short bit, with looks down into Seattle's Cedar River watershed, rounds the east side of the mountain, drops 100 feet to a small pond (possible campsites) and climbs again, passing recent mining garbage to a magnificent viewpoint on the ridge crest about 100 vertical feet from the summit.

As in the case of nearby Mt. Si, the majority of hikers are content with the ridgetop view and leave the summit for experienced mountaineers; the rocks are slippery when wet and in any conditions the exposure is sufficient to be fatal.

**SOUTH FORK
SNOQUALMIE RIVER**

19 Mason Lake-
Mt. Defiance

Round trip to Mason Lake 5 miles
Hiking time 6 hours
High point 4300 feet
Elevation gain 2200 feet
Best June through November
One day or backpack
USGS Bandera

Round trip to Mt. Defiance 10 miles
Hiking time 10 hours
High point 5400 feet
Elevation gain 3300 feet
Best July through November

Reasons this hike ought not be in this book at all: A huge and nasty boulder field. A steep, eroded, muddy path. Even to call it a "trail" requires a stretch of the imagination. Any person who makes this trip his first hike most likely never will leave the cars again. The nearby Lake Annette and Pratt Lake trails are much better suited to beginners and families with small children.

Reasons it's in this book after all: It's one of the closest-to-Seattle trails to a mountain lake. Despite the horrors it's short and on a summer's day is thronged with day hikers and dogs, young couples carrying babies on backs, and novices with enormous overnight packs. —And to give the devil its due, the alpine lakes are numerous and the views from Mt. Defiance are tremendous. (Still, the Pratt Lake trail, Hike 21, gets to the same places more sensibly.)

Drive Interstate 90 to Exit 45. Go off the freeway and under it and turn left onto forest road No. 9030. At 1 mile go straight ahead on road No. 9031, signed "Mason Lake Way." At 3.8 miles from the freeway the road is blocked. Park here, elevation 2100 feet.

Ascend the abandoned road about ½ mile to the torrent of Mason Creek; 300 feet beyond, the sign often hidden by brush, find the Mason Lake trail, which starts out switchbacking upward in fairly decent fashion—and then goes all to pieces. Beaten out by boots with rarely a helping ax or saw, the way goes nearly straight up. At about 1¼ miles the grade eases to cross the boulder field, the route marked by a confusion of cairns and plastic ribbons. A final bit of pleasant forest leads to Mason Lake, 4300

	OLD	NEW
	2218	9030
Mason Lake road	2218A	9031

Lake Kulla Kulla from Mt. Defiance, Granite Peak in distance

feet, 2½ miles. If camps are crowded here, try Little Mason Lake, reached by a swampy sidetrail that also passes a shallow pond. Within a mile are four other lakes. The Pratt Lake trail yields more.

For views, continue past Mason Lake, climbing 200 feet in ½ mile to a trail junction on the ridge crest between Mason Lake and Lake Kulla Kulla—and signs that suggest a week of explorations. Follow the ridge trail westward, ascending south slopes of Defiance. At 5200 feet, about 2 miles from the junction, traverse a large, steep meadow very near the 5400-foot summit, reached by a steep scramble up the west edge of the flower field. Look north over the Middle Fork Snoqualmie valley to Mt. Baker and Glacier Peak. Look south over the South Fork valley (with freeway) to Mt. Rainier and Mt. Adams.

The trail continues along the ridge, drops to Thompson Lake, then climbs over a spur to the enormous clearcuts of Granite Creek. If a hiker can arrange for a pickup on the Middle Fork Snoqualmie road, a one-way trip is possible.

SOUTH FORK SNOQUALMIE RIVER

20 Bandera Mountain

Round trip 7 miles
Hiking time 6 hours
High point 5240 feet
Elevation gain 2800 feet
Best mid-May through November
One day
USGS Bandera

Even though there is no real trail, just a boot-beaten track and follow-your-nose scramble, Bandera offers the easiest-to-reach summit panoramas in the Snoqualmie area, with superb views to the valley and lowlands, into the Alpine Lakes Wilderness, and up and down the length of the Cascades. Because of the southwesterly exposure, snow melts off early; the ascent can be made when trails to nearby peaks are still buried in winter white.

In the summer of 1958 a fire started by loggers swept Bandera to timberline. Long before that, in the past century, the upper slopes were burned (probably by nature's lightning, not by man's carelessness) and forest has not yet begun to come back. Thus the entire ascent is in the open, and can be hot. To compensate, scenery is continuous every step of the way.

Drive to the end of road No. 9031. (See Hike 19, Mason Lake.) Park here, elevation 2100 feet.

Walk the abandoned road, passing the Mason Lake trail, 1½ miles to the end. Fill canteens at the creek here; there is no water above.

Begin by scrambling uphill near the creek, on boot-built tread, a short bit to a bulldozer track. Go rightward up the road a few hundred feet to a point where green timber at the margin of the burn is very close above. Climb the bank (where others obviously have done so) and a few yards of sparse brush to the edge of timber and there intersect the path hacked out by the fire-fighters of 1958.

Ascend the rude, steep tread with hands and feet to the upper limit of the burn, then follow any of the paths directly upward, first over and around down logs, then in low greenery of small shrubs and beargrass. Admire picturesque bleached snags from the 19th-century blaze. Off to the left, see a lichen-gray granite talus; listen for marmots whistling there.

	OLD	NEW
	2218	9030
Mason Lake road	2218A	9031

58

Island Lake from Bandera Mountain

The ridge crest is attained at around 4700 feet; immediately below on the far side is Mason Lake. The ridge is a good turnaround point for those who've had enough; the views are nearly as broad as those from the summit. The route to here often melts free of snow in early May.

Climb east on the crest through subalpine trees, then scramble granite boulders up a step in the ridge to the first summit, 5150 feet, and down-and-up a bit farther to the highest summit, 5240 feet. Look north to lakes in forest bowls below and far away to Glacier Peak and Mt. Baker, northeasterly to Snoqualmie peaks, south down to the highway and beyond to omnipresent Rainier, and west past the portal peaks of Washington and Defiance to lowlands. Civilization is near, but also wilderness.

SOUTH FORK
SNOQUALMIE RIVER

21 Pratt Lake

Round trip to Pratt Lake 11½ miles
Hiking time 8 hours
High point 4100 feet
Elevation gain 2300 feet in, 700 out
Best July through October
One day or backpack
USGS Snoqualmie Pass and Bandera

Miles of deep forest and a lovely lake amid subalpine trees. A network of trails leads to other lakes and to meadow ridges and high views. From a basecamp hikers and fishermen can spend days exploring.

Drive Interstate 90 to Exit 47, cross over the freeway, and turn west ¼ mile to the trailhead parking area, elevation 1800 feet.

The first steep mile gains 800 feet in cool forest to a junction with the Granite Mountain trail; just beyond is a nice creek for drinking and resting. Turn left and sidehill upward on a gentler grade in young forest, through patches of twinflower, Canadian dogwood, salal, and bracken, by many nurse logs, to Lookout Point, 3 miles, 3400 feet, a much-used camp.

At 3¾ miles is a short sidepath down to Talapus and Olallie Lakes. The main trail rounds the Olallie basin in open subalpine forest to a 4100-foot saddle, 4 miles, a logical turnaround point for day hikers. Lots of huckleberries here in season, plus a view south to Mt. Rainier, and a junction with the Mt. Defiance trail (see below). The Pratt Lake trail switchbacks down a steep hillside of much mud, some of it covered with new puncheon, flattens out and contours above the lake, then drops to the outlet, 5¾ miles, 3400 feet. The once-popular campsites at the outlet have been mostly destroyed by blowdown. In any event, the lake is so heavily used the Forest Service requests campers to stay elsewhere.

Now, for explorations. (These are only a few; connoisseurs of the country have many other private favorites.)

In a short ½ mile from Pratt Lake is Lower Tuscohatchie Lake, 3400 feet, and a choice of three directions for wandering: A fishermen's path beats brush 1½ miles to 4023-foot Tuscohatchie Lake. From the outlet of Lower Tuscohatchie a trail ascends gently then steeply 3 miles, in trees with glimpses outward of alpine scenery, to 4500-foot Melakwa Lake (Hike 23). Also from the outlet of Lower Tuscohatchie, a

Pratt Lake from Pratt Mountain

less-used trail climbs northward to 4800 feet and drops past little Windy Lake to 3900-foot Kaleetan Lake, 3½ miles. The way is entirely in forest, with only occasional views over the Pratt River valley, logged in the 1930s, but the lonesome lake has a splendid backdrop in the cliffs of Kaleetan Peak.

From the Olallie-Pratt saddle (see above), the Mt. Defiance trail ascends westward through beargrass and heather and huckleberry meadows (fine views 1100 feet down to Lake Talapus) on the side of Pratt Mountain, whose 5099-foot summit is an easy scramble via huge boulder fields on the southwest side, passes Rainbow Lake (Island Lake lies ½ mile away on a sidepath and actually is a more rewarding objective for hikers than Pratt Lake), comes near Mason Lake, traverses high above Lake Kulla Kulla, and climbs in flower gardens almost to the summit of 5584-foot Defiance, about 3 miles, and broad views (See Hike 20.) The trail continues westward on the ridge a mile, drops to Thompson Lake, 3400 feet, 5½ miles, and descends to the Granite Creek road, 7 miles.

At some of the lakes campers are asked to keep 100 feet from the shores.

Mt. Rainier and the Granite Mountain trail

**SOUTH FORK
SNOQUALMIE RIVER**

22 Granite Mountain

Round trip 8 miles
Hiking time 8 hours
High point 5629 feet
Elevation gain 3800 feet
Best June through November
One day
USGS Snoqualmie Pass

The most popular summit trail in the Snoqualmie region, and for good reason. Though the ascent is long and in midsummer can be blistering hot, the upper slopes are a delightful garden of granite and flowers and the panorama includes Mt. Rainier south, Mt. Baker and Glacier Peak north, Chimney Rock and Mt. Stuart east, and infinitely more peaks, valleys, and lakes.

Drive Interstate 90 to Exit 47, cross over the freeway, and turn west ½ mile to the trailhead parking lot, elevation 1800 feet.

The first steep mile on the Pratt Lake trail gains 800 feet in cool forest to the Granite Mountain junction and a creek for drinking and resting. Be sure to fill canteens; this may be the last water.

Go right from the 2600-foot junction, traversing in trees ½ mile, then heading straight up and up in countless short switchbacks on an open south slope where fires and avalanches have inhibited the growth of forest. (On sunny days, start early to beat the heat.)

At 4000 feet the trail abruptly gentles and swings east across an avalanche gully—an area of potentially extreme danger perhaps through May. Hikers seeking the summit before Memorial Day of cold springs should be very wary of crossing this gully; a better alternative in avalanche season is to leave the trail and climb directly to the peak on the rough but safe granite felsenmeer ("rock sea") of the southwest ridge, which melts free of snow while the trail route has another month of winter whiteness left.

Beyond the gully the trail sidehills through rock gardens, passing a waterfall (early summer only) from snows above, and then switchbacks steeply to grass and flowers, reaching the summit ridge at 5200 feet. In early summer the route beyond here may be too snowy for some tastes; if so, wander easterly on the crest for splendid views over the Snoqualmie Pass peaks, down to alpine lakes, and through the pass to Lake Keechelus.

The trail ascends westward in meadows, above cosy cirque-scoop benches, and switchbacks to the fire lookout, 5629 feet, 4 miles, and full compensation for the struggle.

Experienced highland rovers depart from the trail on secret routes to solitudes of hidden lakes and alpine nooks. It is possible to camp near the summit, either for the sunset and dawn views or to allow time for exploration.

The hike has special appeal in early summer when flowers are blooming and in fall when blueberries are ripe and the slopes are flaming.

**SOUTH FORK
SNOQUALMIE RIVER**

23 Denny
Creek-
Melakwa Lake

Round trip to Melakwa outlet 9 miles
Hiking time 6 hours
High point 4600 feet
Elevation gain 2300 feet
Best mid-July through October
One day or backpack
USGS Snoqualmie Pass

The liveliest valley of the Snoqualmie Pass vicinity, a series of waterfalls fluming and splashing. Beyond is the most spectacular alpine scenery, with snowfields and cliffs of Kaleetan, Chair, and Bryant Peaks rising above the little lake, one shore in forest, the other in rocks and flowers.

Drive Interstate 90 to Exit 47. Go off onto the Denny Creek road, turn right, and continue 3 miles to Denny Creek Campground. Just past it turn left on a road over the river and follow it ¼ mile, passing private homes, to the road-end parking area and trailhead, elevation 2300 feet. (On busy summer weekends it may be necessary to park before crossing the Snoqualmie River bridge.)

The trail ascends moderately along Denny Creek in forest, passing under the Interstate 90 freeway, crossing the stream on a bridge at ½ mile and recrossing at 1 mile, 2800 feet, below water-smoothed slabs of a lovely cataract. The way leaves forest and strikes upward in avalanche greenery to Keekwulee Falls, 1½ miles.

The next ½ mile of tight switchbacks ascends around cliffs past Snowshoe Falls. By this time the majority of Sunday strollers have found precisely the perfect spot for a picnic.

The next rewards comparably rich are a good bit farther on. At 2 miles, 3500 feet, the path flattens out into the upper basin, shortly crosses the creek, goes from trees to low brush to trees again, and switchbacks to wooded Hemlock Pass, 3½ miles, 4600 feet. From here the trail drops a bit in forest to the outlet of Melakwa Lake, 4½ miles, 4550 feet.

Enjoy views of talus, snowfields, and cliffs falling abruptly from the 6200-foot summits of Kaleetan and Chair. The basin is so heavily pounded it's really best not to camp in it at all—at least until a management plan is completed, specifying permitted sites (if any). To avoid disappointment, check with the Forest Service in advance—or come prepared to continue on to camps elsewhere.

For explorations, roam meadows and boulders to tiny Upper Melakwa Lake and 5300-foot Melakwa Pass. Experienced cross-country travelers can descend past

Keekwulee Falls

Iceberg (Chair Peak) Lake to intersect the Snow Lake trail (Hike 25) for an alternate return to the highway.

For another way back to the highway, and for lonesome walking, take the 3-mile trail from Melakwa Lake to Pratt Lake (Hike 21).

Annette Lake and cliffs of Abiel Peak

SOUTH FORK
SNOQUALMIE RIVER

24 Annette Lake

Round trip 7¼ miles
Hiking time 4 hours
High point 3600 feet
Elevation gain 1400 feet
Best June through November
One day or backpack
USGS Snoqualmie Pass

A very popular and often crowded little subalpine lake, with cliffs and talus of Abiel Peak above the shores of open forest. For lonesome walking here, try early summer or late fall, in the middle of the week, in terrible weather.

Drive Interstate 90 to Exit 47. Go off the freeway and turn right .1 mile, then left on road No. 55 for .6 mile to the parking lot, elevation 2200 feet.

The way starts in an old clearcut, crosses Humpback Creek, and in 1 mile passes under a powerline and enters forest. At 1¼ miles, 2400 feet, cross the Milwaukee (Burlington-Northern) Railroad tracks.

Now comes the hard part, switchbacking steeply upward in nice, old forest on the slopes of Silver Peak, occasional talus openings giving looks over the valley to Humpback Mountain. After gaining 1200 feet in 1½ miles, at the 3600-foot level the way flattens out and goes along a final mile of minor ups and downs to the lake outlet, 3 miles, 3600 feet.

Wander along the east shore for picnic spots with views of small cliffs and waterfalls.

Some cross-country hikers continue to the summit of Silver Peak via the draw between Silver and Abiel Peaks, a good but quite brushy route.

Folks planning to camp do well to call the Forest Service beforehand to learn where and how they can; the lake is so mobbed that great care is being taken to avoid making it a muddy-dusty slum.

	OLD	NEW
Tinkham road	222	55

Snow Lake

**SOUTH FORK
SNOQUALMIE RIVER**

25 Snow Lake

Round trip 8 miles
Hiking time 6 hours
High point 4400 feet
Elevation gain 1300 feet in, 400 feet out
Best July through October
One day or backpack
USGS Snoqualmie Pass and Bandera

The largest alpine lake (more than a mile long) near Snoqualmie Pass. On one side cliffs rise steeply to Chair Peak, and on the other forests fall steeply toward the broad, deep gulf of the Middle Fork Snoqualmie River. The trail and lake are overwhelmingly popular—some 14,000 visitors a year, 500 and more on a fine summer Sunday. If it's the sound of silence you're seeking, be warned.

Drive Interstate 90 to Exit 52 at Snoqualmie Pass and go off left 2 miles on the Alpental road through the ski area and subdivision to the parking lot and trailhead, elevation 3100 feet.

The trail climbs a bit in forest to intersect the generations-old hiking route from the pass, obliterated by the Alpental subdividers, and ascends gradually, sometimes in cool trees, sometimes on open slopes with looks over Source Lake (the source of the South Fork Snoqualmie River) to Denny Mountain, now civilized, and to The Tooth and Chair Peak, still wild.

The way swings around the valley head above the 3800-foot droplet of Source Lake and switchbacks a steep ½ mile in heather and flowers and parkland to the saddle, 3½ miles, 4400 feet, between Source Creek and Snow Lake. Day hikers may well be content with the picnic spots in blossoms and blueberries and splendid views.

The trail drops sharply ½ mile from the saddle to meadow shores of Snow Lake, 4 miles, 4016 feet, rounds the north side, and descends Rock Creek valley to the Middle Fork Snoqualmie.

To get away from overpopulation, follow a path west from the trail, over the Snow Lake outlet, and up to 4800-foot Gem Lake. This is alpine roaming at its best. With map and compass and a sharp eye, experienced wanderers can find easy routes to Upper and Lower Wildcat Lakes, summits of Wright Mountain and Preacher Mountain. And more.

Now, about the camping . . . To provide the highest possible quality of experience without limiting the number of visitors, the Forest Service has devised a management plan for Snow Lake—a plan that informs hikers about "The Responsibility of Freedom." Within a "day use area" along the shore where first reached by the trail, hikers are asked not to camp. In the adjoining "heavy use area," camping should be at **established sites only**. So you want to camp free, and lonesome? Well, all around the basin, away from the lake, are private nooks. Get off the trail. Snoop around. Learn how to hide.

SOUTH FORK SNOQUALMIE RIVER

26 Kendall Catwalk-
Alta Pass-Spectacle Point

Round trip to Catwalk 10½ miles
Hiking time 7 hours
High point 5400 feet
Elevation gain 2700 feet in, 300 feet out
Best July to mid-October
One day
USGS Snoqualmie Pass

Round trip to Spectacle Point 31 miles
Allow 3-4 days
High point 5700 feet
Elevation gain 5500 feet in, 3000 feet out
Best July to mid-October

The bag of superlatives is quickly exhausted on this, one of the most spectacular parts of the Cascade section of the Pacific Crest Trail, and the most accessible and popular.

Drive Interstate 90 to Exit 52 at Snoqualmie Pass. Go off the freeway on the Alpental road several hundred feet to the Pacific Crest Trail parking lot, elevation a bit above 3004 feet.

The trail ascends forest 2 miles, loses 250 feet to negotiate a boulder field, and at 2¾ miles passes the Commonwealth Basin trail (Hike 27). Flattening briefly, the way switchbacks endlessly upward, at 4300 feet crosses an all-summer creek that may be the last water until Ridge Lake, and at 4700 feet attains the wooded crest of Kendall Ridge. On a long traverse around the mountain the path opens out in Kendall Gardens, the start of alpine color that is virtually continuous to Spectacle Point. At 5¼ miles, on a 5400-foot bump, is a happy turnaround for a day hike.

To continue involves stepping carefully along the Kendall Catwalk, blasted across a cliff in solid granite. When snowfree it's safe enough. When snowy, forget it. The mountainside then moderates to heather meadows. At 6¼ miles is the 5270-foot saddle between tiny Ridge Lake and larger Gravel Lake, the last trail camp until Mineral Creek Park.

Overnighters based here typically daytrip to Alaska Mountain, 7¾ miles, 5745 feet, or to Huckleberry-Chikamin saddle, 10¼ miles, 5520 feet (due to ups and downs, a gross elevation gain of 1100 feet from Ridge Lake). On the way the trail swings around the basins of Alaska Lake and Joe Lake, both 1000 feet below and without recommendable sidetrails. The saddle is a precinct of heaven, but is so fragile that to camp here would be a sin, if not a capital crime.

Pacific Crest Trail and Kendall Peak

The upsy-downsy trail swings across the magnificent cliff-and-meadow face of Chikamin Peak and Four Brothers to Alta Pass, on the Cascade Crest at 5700 feet, 14 miles. The path descends the alpine basin of Mineral Creek Park to an established camp at 5200 feet, 14½ miles, dips farther to a 4970-foot pass near Park Pond and a junction with the Park Lakes trail (Hike 31). A final ascent of benches and swales tops out at 5475 feet, 15½ miles, on a shoulder of Three Queens Mountain. Southward ¼ mile along a meadow vale is an all-year creek that waters the grandest trail camps of the area. Sit on the prow of Spectacle Point jutting out in the sky and watch the sun go down. And come up. Beneath your feet sprawls Spectacle Lake (4350 feet, 2½ miles down the Crest Trail and then a sidetrail; Hike 33). Across the valley Glacier Lake snuggles in a cirque. Above rises the long rough wall of Four Brothers, Chikamin, Lemah, Chimney Rock, and Summit Chief.

SOUTH FORK
SNOQUALMIE RIVER

Round trip to pass 10 miles
Hiking time 5 hours
High point 5400 feet
Elevation gain 2700 feet in, 250 feet out

27 Commonwealth Basin- Red Pass

Best mid-July through October
One day or backpack
USGS Snoqualmie Pass

Hikers who have sorrowed for the degradation of Snoqualmie Pass over the past third of a century tend not to go there anymore, because of the pain. However, those diehards who clenched jaws and toughed it out in the legislative battleground saved Commonwealth Basin, the heart of the matter, for wilderness. Here are a peaceful subalpine forest, pure and rippling creeks—an enclave of Olden Days perfect for taking the family on a picnic or experimental backpack.

Drive Interstate 90 to Exit 52 at Snoqualmie Pass. Go off the freeway on the Alpental road and within several hundred feet find the Pacific Crest Trail parking lot, elevation something above 3004 feet.

The ancient and honorable trail got to the basin in merely 1 mile, but on private land that ultimately was clearcut, causing the old path to erode so severely it was abandoned. The new way takes 2¾ miles to make the same distance and in the process gains 700 feet of which 250 are lost. That's progress for you.

Follow the Pacific Crest Trail (Hike 26) 2¾ miles, to where it dips near the valley floor before starting up Kendall Peak. A signed sidepath drops to the old Commonwealth Basin trail. Go left or right or straight ahead off the trail for picnics—or for camps to try out brand-new gear, or new kids.

The basin trail turns upstream 1 mile to the valley head and ascends the crest of an open-forested spur in many, many short switchbacks. At last the way flattens out in

Blueberries

Picking blueberries at Red Pass; Mt. Thompson, center

heather gardens and alpine trees of a cirque basin at the foot of Red Mountain. A few steps away on a sidetrail is Red Pond, 4½ miles, 4900 feet. Eat lunch, tour the bouldery and flowery shores, listen for marmots whistling, walk to the edge of the cirque and look over the valley and the rimming peaks and south to Mt. Rainier. Campsites are overused but pleasant; carry a stove and don't hack the shrubbery.

The trail swings up talus and rock buttresses almost but not quite to the saddle and follows the ridge west to Red Mountain Pass, 5 miles, 5400 feet, and views to the deep Middle Fork Snoqualmie valley, the sharp tower of Mt. Thompson, the rugged Chimney Rock group, and far horizons.

SOUTH FORK
SNOQUALMIE RIVER

28 Cold Creek-Silver Peak Loop

Loop trip 6 miles
Hiking time 3½ hours
High point 4200 feet
Elevation gain 1300 feet
Best July through October
One day
USGS Snoqualmie Pass

Sidetrip up Silver Peak 2 miles
Hiking time 2 hours
High point 5603 feet
Elevation gain 1400 feet

Grand trees, a mountain lake, and a mountain top with great views south over rolling green ridges to Rainier, west to the Olympics (Annette Lake directly below your feet), north to Snoqualmie Pass peaks, and east across Keechelus Reservoir to Mt. Margaret, so heavily patched by clearcuts it looks as if it had a bad case of the mange.

Though much of the old beauty remains, long gone are the challenge and the remoteness that until a quarter-century ago made this one of the most popular hikes near Snoqualmie Pass. This is in the checkerboard dating from the Big Steal, the Northern Pacific Land Grant, and logging roads are built at the whim of private owners, heirs of the thieves. Despite management problems the Forest Service has made a sincere effort at true multiple-use—which means trails, too.

Drive Interstate 90 east from Snoqualmie Pass 2 miles and go off on Hyak Exit 54. Turn right, and right again. In .1 mile turn left on road No. 2236 and climb .4 mile to a junction. Keep straight ahead under a chairlift, ignore spur roads, and follow No. 2236 3½ miles from Interstate 90 to Cold Creek trailhead, signed "Twin Lakes," elevation 2900 feet.

(If your sole interest is the ascent of Silver, stay on No. 2236 another 2 miles to where it crosses the Pacific Crest Trail at Olallie Meadow, 4200 feet. Walk the Trail south 1½ miles to Gardiner Ridge trail, as noted below.)

Alternating between clearcuts and forest, Silver Peak standing 2300 feet above it all, Cold Creek trail No. 1303 attains lower Twin Lake at about ¾ mile. Here is a junction. Go either direction—the loop has as much uphill one way as the other. We describe it clockwise because that's how we happened to do it.

Cross the outlet stream and grind out 1200 feet in 1¾ miles to the Pacific Crest Trail

Mt. Rainier from Silver Peak, Abiel Peak on right

and turn right (north). For the sidetrip ascent of Silver Peak, in an up-and-down ½ mile watch carefully for the sign marking Gardiner Ridge trail, an old route to Hanson Creek that was abandoned because part is in the Cedar River watershed. Easy to miss, the sidetrail gains 600 feet in a short ½ mile that seems a long 1 mile to heather-and-shrub parklands. The mountainside is broken by a large talus; some hikers go straight up the rocks but skirting them left or right is easier. Above the talus follow the flowery ridge crest, then 200 feet of steep, shattered rock to the 5603-foot summit.

Returned from the sidetrip ascent to the Pacific Crest Trail, continue northward to road No. 2236 at Olallie Meadow, turn right on it about 400 feet, find trail No. 1348, and follow it 1 mile back to Twin Lakes and so home.

LAKE KEECHELUS

29 Mount Margaret-Lake Lillian

Round trip to Mt. Margaret 6 miles
Hiking time 5 hours
High point 5520 feet
Elevation gain 1500 feet
Best late June through October
One day
USGS Snoqualmie Pass

Round trip to Lake Lillian 9 miles
Hiking time 6 hours
High point 5200 feet
Elevation gain 1300 feet in, 500 feet out
Best July through October
One day or backpack

A short climb to a little mountain with big views, then onward in meadows to a secluded alpine lake, a fine basecamp for highland roaming on Rampart Ridge.

Drive Interstate 90 east from Snoqualmie Pass 2 miles to Hyak Exit 54 and find the Forest Service road on the north side of the highway. This road parallels Interstate 90 for 2½ miles to Rocky Run and then climbs another 1½ miles, passing several well-marked intersections to a large parking lot, elevation 3800 feet. Walk the road a few hundred feet farther and take a steep abandoned logging track which eventually turns into a trail and enters forest. The trail climbs, with numerous switchbacks, to the ridge top at 5000 feet, a few hundred feet below the summit of Mt. Margaret. From here the Margaret Lake trail drops over the far side of the ridge and descends to the lake 300 feet below. For a view of forest and three or four small lakes, step a few feet over the crest of the ridge and look down. Besides Margaret, there are Stonesthrow, Swan, and Rock Rabbit Lakes.

From the ridge the trail climbs a bit then contours around the west side of Mt. Margaret. (For more views, scramble to the summit. One place is as good as the next—there's no trail.) On the north side of the mountain the trail descends meadows to shallow Twin Lakes at 3 miles, 4700 feet; the campsites aren't at all bad but the water may be—boil it.

Now the trail becomes more difficult. The tread is rough and at times steep as it loses another 200 feet and then climbs back up 300 feet. At 4½ miles, 4800 feet, is

Lake Lillian and Rampart Ridge

lovely Lake Lillian amid glacier-polished rocks and heather and flowers and alpine trees. The shore slopes are so steep that flat space for sleeping is very scanty.

For wandering, climb from the lake to lonesome little basins or to broad views atop Rampart Ridge.

LAKE KACHESS

30 Rachel Lake- Rampart Ridge

Round trip to Rachel Lake 8 miles
Hiking time 6 hours
High point 4700 feet
Elevation gain 1900 feet
Best mid-July through October
One day or backpack
USGS Snoqualmie Pass

Round trip to Rampart Lakes 11 miles
Hiking time 8 hours
High point 5200 feet
Elevation gain 2400 feet

A cool and green valley forest, a large alpine lake walled by glacier-carved cliffs which drop straight to the water, and a heaven of rock-bowl lakelets and ponds, gardens of heather and blossoms, and ridges and nooks for prowling. On summer weekends hundreds of hikers throng Rachel Lake and dozens are in every pocket and on every knob of the high ridge, where hikers have stomped out a spiderweb of paths.

The trail, posted "hikers only," was never built but simply beaten into existence by thousands of feet. The way goes around, up, or down to avoid obstacles and hardly knows how to switchback. But bad is good—if the route were built to freeway standards the highland would be visited not by regiments but swarming hordes.

Drive Interstate 90 east from Snoqualmie Pass 12½ miles, take Lake Kachess Exit 62, and follow signs 5 miles to Kachess Lake Campground. Turn left 4 miles on Box Canyon road No. 2214 to a junction. Turn left ¼ mile and hope to find space for your car in the enormous parking lot at the Rachel Lake trailhead, elevation 2800 feet.

The hike begins with a mile of moderate ascent to a mandatory cold drink and rest stop by water-carved and pot-holed and moss-carpeted slabs. The trail levels out along the creek for 1½ miles. In an open swath of avalanche greenery, look up to 6032-foot Hibox Mountain. At 2½ miles the valley ends in an abrupt headwall and rough tread proceeds straight up, rarely bothering to switchback, gaining 1300 feet in a cruel mile, suffering alleviated by glories of cool-breeze rest-stop waterfalls. Suddenly the angle eases and forest yields to meadows and at 4 miles, 4700 feet, is Rachel Lake.

Follow paths around the lake, admiring blue waters ringed by trees and cliffs—and numerous campsites. Go left past the narrows to the secluded south bay.

To visit higher country, turn right at the shore on a boot-built path climbing above the cirque, with views down to the lake and out Box Canyon Creek. After a steep ½ mile

Lila Lake and Hibox Mountain

the trail flattens in a wide parkland saddle, 5200 feet, and reaches an unmarked junction offering a choice.

Go right 1 mile to 5200-foot Lila Lake (actually **two** lakes, or maybe six, plus ponds, scattered about a variegated basin) or walk a meadow tightrope in the sky to (or near) the summit of 6240-foot Alta Mountain.

Go left an up-and-down mile to 5100-foot Rampart Lakes. Examine in detail each of the little lakes and tiny ponds, the surrounding buttresses, waterfalls, and peaceful mountain homes. Note the mixture of basalts, conglomerates, and rusty mineralized lobes. Snoop into a flowery corner, climb a heather knoll, think about roaming the short but rough way south to Lake Lillian (Hike 29), and before you know it, arrive on the crest of 5800-foot Rampart Ridge and enjoy views down to Gold Creek, west to Snoqualmie Pass, south to Rainier and Adams, east to Stuart, and north to Three Queens and Chimney Rock.

Camping . . . This is one of those areas where popularity is forcing out waterside camps, wood fires, dogs, horses, fish . . .

Chikamin Ridge from slopes above Park Lakes

LAKE KACHESS

31 Mineral Creek Park

Round trip from Cooper Pass road 10 miles
Hiking time 8 hours
High point 4700 feet
Elevation gain 2300 feet
Best July through October
One day or backpack
USGS Snoqualmie Pass and Kachess Lake

Round trip from Kachess Lake
  Campground 20 miles
Allow 2 days
Elevation gain 3300 feet

Heather and huckleberry meadows surrounding alpine lakes, mountains to climb, and views. The trail is tough and not many fish are in the lakes, so the area currently offers more solitude than nearby Spectacle and Rachel Lakes.

Once upon a time—until 1968, in fact—the trip began with a lovely walk along Kachess Lake. Now, in the name of progress, a logging road has intersected the route right in the middle, cutting the hike in half. Since the challenge and satisfaction of traveling the entire distance in unmarred wilderness have been lost, the most practical plan probably is to use the new road as an approach to the upper half and maybe some other day walk the lower half.

To reach the halfway point, drive to Cooper Lake (Hike 33) and keep left on road No. 229 climbing over Cooper Pass and dropping into the Kachess valley. At 11 miles from the Cle Elum River road, at the road-end, find the trailhead, elevation 2400 feet, amid on-going logging by Burlington-Northern.

Just in case there are die-hard hikers willing to ignore the new road to recapture a semblance of the old wilderness experience, the trip will be described here from Kachess Lake.

Drive Interstate 90 east from Snoqualmie Pass 12½ miles, take the Kachess Lake exit, and follow signs 5 miles to Kachess Lake Campground. Inside the campground proceed .7 mile to the northernmost (uplake) section and follow signs to the trailhead, elevation 2254 feet.

Little Kachess trail No. 1312 follows the lake more than 3 miles to its head, never over 200-400 feet above the water, but seldom level and with so many ups and downs that about 1000 feet of elevation are gained and lost. At the end of the lake the footpath merges into a mining road built in the days of the Model T and now abandoned. At about 4½ miles the route turns up Mineral Creek trail No. 1331, climbing steeply; here is the junction with the logging road, the beginning of the short version of the trip.

The mining road continues 1¼ mile to an end at a group of dilapidated buildings; until the Alpine Lakes Wilderness boundary is crossed, expect complications from Burlington-Northern. From here on the tread mainly just grew, going up and down and around, never flat, often very steep. Most of the way is brushed out—thankfully so, for much of the route is on slopes of slick alder and vine maple. Beyond the mine buildings ¼ mile the trail crosses Mineral Creek, and at about 3¾ miles from the Cooper Pass logging road, crosses the outlet stream from lower Park Lake. At about 5 miles the path reaches upper Park Lake, 4700 feet, and the edge of meadow country. Excellent camps here; more are ½ mile to the west up a small stream.

Actually, the lakes are nice but not exceptional, not for **this** area. For the truly memorable trip continue ¼ mile up to intersect the Pacific Crest Trail at 4970 feet. Climb left to Alta Pass or right to Spectacle Point for great views (Hike 26). Or leave the trails and roam hillocks and vales of the headwater basin, and maybe find the goat path over Box Ridge to Lila Lakes.

CLE ELUM RIVER

32 Kachess Ridge

Round trip 9 miles
Hiking time 7½ hours
High point 5850 feet
Elevation gain 2750 feet in, 600 out
Best July to November
One day
USGS Kachess Lake

Magnificent trail country of forest ridges and green meadows climaxing at Thorp Mountain Lookout. Views—Rainier, Stuart, Daniel, and the Dutch Miller Gap peaks. Other views, less esthetic—Kachess Lake (reservoir), powerlines, logging roads (which have shrunk the wildland and brought the ridge in easy reach of a day hike).

The Kachess Ridge trail extends 15 miles from road No. 2105 near Easton to Cooper Pass. The shortest route to Thorp Mountain is Knox Creek trail No. 1315A, starting at 4000 feet and meeting the Kachess Ridge trail in 1½ miles; the total distance to the lookout is 2½ miles, gaining 1800 feet. The way is fairly straightforward, climbing almost entirely in meadows of blueberries and flowers.

Described here is the French Cabin Creek trail, longer and with more ups and downs but giving views of the French Cabin Mountains, a panorama of the Knox Creek trail country, and eventually winding up in the same place.

Drive the Salmon la Sac road 12 miles from the City Hall, First and Dakota, in Roslyn. Just past the end of Cle Elum Lake (reservoir) turn left on French Cabin Creek road No. 2211 and drive 7 miles to the trailhead. On the way pass Knox Creek road No. 2211B at 5 miles (Knox Creek trail starts 2 miles up this road) and at an unmarked junction at 6 miles keep to the right side of the stream. The actual trailhead is up a short, rough spur; it may be best to park on the road, elevation 3700 feet.

French Cabin Creek trail No. 1305 starts in a clearcut and continues in an old burn. At spots very steep, at 1 mile it reaches a campsite with a good spring, then enters forest and at 1½ miles joins the Kachess Ridge trail (at 6½ miles from road No. 2105 near Easton). The ridge trail now grows extremely steep as it ascends a 5700-foot hump at 2 miles. The south side of this high point has great views back over the French Cabin peaks, Kachess Lake, and Rainier. At the start of the descent of the north side is a view down on Knox Creek trail.

French Cabin Creek trail

From the high point the trail drops steeply 400 feet, contours a peak, passes Knox Creek trail at 3¾ miles, climbs, drops 200 feet, climbs another high point, and comes out atop a ridge bump 500 feet directly above Thorp Lake. At 4½ miles is a junction with the Thorp Mountain trail, which switchbacks 400 feet to the lookout at 4½ miles. The ridge trail proceeds 6½ more miles to road No. 2218 near Cooper Pass.

Three Queens Mountain and Spectacle Lake

CLE ELUM RIVER

33 Spectacle Lake

Round trip 20½ miles
Allow 2 days
High point 4350 feet
Elevation gain 1500 feet
Best August through October
USGS Snoqualmie Pass and Kachess Lake

Only a scattering of miniature glaciers remain of the huge frozen streams that gouged out the Alpine Lakes region of the Cascades. However, the handiwork of ancient ice lies everywhere, and is beautifully exhibited by this delightful lake in a basin of glacier-polished rock.

84

Drive Interstate 90 east from Snoqualmie Pass about 27 miles and take the Salmon la Sac-Roslyn exit, following Highway 903 through Roslyn and Ronald and along Lake Cle Elum. At 15 miles from Roslyn and 1 mile short of Salmon la Sac turn left on Cooper road No. 229. At 4.7 miles from the junction turn right on Cooper Lake road No. 235, go by the recreation area, and cross the river on a wooden bridge to the trailhead, elevation 2788 feet.

The trail begins along shores of Cooper Lake, a joy, and then follows the Cooper River, rippling beautifully through virgin forest, 6½ miles to Pete Lake, 2980 feet, and much-used and often-crowded campsites. Unravel a confusion of paths at the shelter cabin and find the main trail, which climbs slightly over a rocky rib and drops to a double crossing of two swift creeks at about 8 miles. Both must be crossed. Footlogs may be available; if not, the boulder-hopping can be difficult in high water of early summer. When the water is impossibly high, follow Lemah Meadow trail No. 1323B some ¾ mile to the Pacific Crest Trail, which crosses the creeks on bridges; the detour adds 1 mile each way.

Shortly beyond the two creeks join the Pacific Crest Trail and switchback up toward Chikamin Ridge, mostly in forest, views scarce. At 9¾ miles the Crest Trail proceeds onward toward Spectacle Point and Park Lakes and the Spectacle Lake trail branches right and climbs straight up the hillside with trees and roots for footholds. This is a hikers-only path; horses are not allowed at the lake.

The steep ascent is difficult but only ½ mile long, soon passing a lovely waterfall spilling from the lake, 4350 feet. For the best camps cross the outlet just above the falls and walk the south shore. The lake is like an octopus with a half-dozen arms, which makes the shoreline difficult to traverse but provides many glorious camps. To the south rises Three Queens, about 6800 feet. To the northwest is Chikamin Peak and to the north the spectacular spires of 7512-foot Lemah Mountain.

Simply poking about on slabs and buttresses of the lakeshore, admiring polishings and groovings done by the ice and picturesque groupings of trees, can fill out a leisurely visit. But one really ought not miss the smashing views from Spectacle Point. Thread through the maze of upsy-downsy paths south, eventually ending up on the sidetrail that ½ mile from the lake outlet hits the Pacific Crest Trail. Climb 2 miles to the high-in-the-sky viewpoint, 5475 feet. If ambition continues, proceed to Alta Pass. (See Hike 26.)

CLE ELUM RIVER

34 Polallie Ridge

Round trip to ridge top 11 miles
Hiking time 7 hours
High point 5300 feet
Elevation gain 2500 feet
Best late June through November
One day
USGS Lake Kachess

One-way trip from Cooper Lake to Salmon
  la Sac 12 miles
Hiking time 6 hours
High point 5547 feet
Elevation gain 2700 feet, not counting
  sidetrip to ridge crest
Best July through November
One day or backpack

A splendid hike to a high ridge overlooking Cooper Lake, with spectacular views of Dutch Miller Gap peaks, Mt. Hinman, and Mt. Daniel. An 11-mile round trip to the ridge top can be made, or if transportation can be arranged, a one-way trip for miles along the open crest, then more miles down through forest. The trail can be very hot and dry in sunny weather; be sure to carry water and start early.

Drive Cooper Lake road (maybe signed Cooper Pass) 4.7 miles, turn right toward Cooper Lake, cross Cooper River, and park at the road-end near the campground, elevation 2788 feet. (To do the one-way trip a party must first leave a car in the Salmon la Sac Campground.)

Hike the abandoned logging road 2½ miles to the Tired Creek trailhead, elevation about 3300 feet. Tired Creek trail No. 1317 starts on a bulldozed fire trail climbing steeply around a clearcut and at the top joining the old trail, a rough but adequate path ascending steadily with many switchbacks. Views begin at the road and get better as elevation is gained. At about 1¾ miles two switchbacks on the edge of a ridge offer a look west to Pete Lake. At 2 miles forest yields to meadowlands as the trail traverses under the ridge and aims for a wooded pass at the head of Tired Creek.

The best views are from the top of this ridge, a logical turnaround for day hikers and an absolutely mandatory sidetrip for those continuing on. Leave the trail at any convenient spot, scramble to the crest, and walk to the highest point, 5300 feet, a

Pete Lake, Lemah Mountain, left; Chimney Rock, right; from Polallie Ridge

great place to soak up scenery and spend the day watching shadows move along distant mountains.

Many goodies remain in store for hikers choosing the one-way trip. Descend from the view crest to regain the trail and contour to the wooded pass, 5400 feet, 3 miles from the abandoned road. Here is a junction. The left fork drops 2 miles to Waptus Pass; for a 15-mile loop trip, return to the car via this pass and Pete Lake (Hike 33). For the best views turn right from the junction on Polallie Ridge trail, in less than ¼ mile reaching the site of the Polallie Ridge Lookout. Continue on the ridge, traversing the crest a mile, then going onward in high forest, meadows, and marshes to a possible campsite at tiny Diamond Lake, 8 miles from Cooper Lake, 5200 feet. The lake is mostly surrounded by trees but there is a good view of the rounded top of 5295-foot Cone Mountain. At about 8½ miles the ridge starts dropping rapidly. The trail more or less keeps on the crest, joining the Cooper River trail at 11 miles and at 11½ miles reaching recreation homes and the road near Salmon la Sac Campground.

Mt. Stuart from Jolly Mountain

CLE ELUM RIVER

35 Jolly Mountain

Round trip from Salmon la Sac 12 miles
Hiking time 7-8 hours
High point 6443 feet
Elevation gain 4043 feet
Best July through September
One day
USGS Kachess Lake

An eastern outpost of the Alpine Lakes Cascades with 360-degree views east to Mt. Stuart and the freeway leading into Ellensburg, north to Mt. Daniel, west to Pete Lake and the Dutch Miller Gap peaks, south to Mt. Rainier, and directly down to Cle Elum Lake.

Drive Interstate 90 east from Snoqualmie Pass about 27 miles and take the Salmon la Sac-Roslyn exit, following Highway 903 through Roslyn and Ronald, beside Lake Cle Elum, and at 16 miles from Roslyn reaching the community of Salmon la Sac. Shortly before an historic old log building turn right on a road to the trailhead parking area by the Forest Service horse barn, elevation 2400 feet.

Go to the left side of the barn and find the trailhead at the edge of the public corral. In ¼ mile briefly touch a service road and then return to trail, which climbs steeply with many switchbacks to a difficult crossing (easier by late July) of Salmon la Sac Creek. Fill canteens, since this is the only certain water on the entire route. At 3½ miles is a junction with the Paris Creek trail; keep right. The way ascends the valley a bit farther and then starts a series of switchbacks up the hillside. At 4½ miles is a junction with the Sasse Mountain sheep driveway (to use this as an alternate approach, see below). Keep left ¼ mile to a junction with the unmarked Jolly Creek trail. Go right, climbing steeply amid growing views for the final 1¼ miles to the 6443-foot summit, site of a fire lookout removed in 1968.

A jolly place to sop up panoramas. Carry a state road map to identify landmarks far out in Eastern Washington and a Forest Service map to name the innumerable peaks.

Though there may be snowfields to traverse then and the creek is difficult to cross, a magnificent time for the trip is June, when the way lies through fields of glacier lilies, spreading phlox, and lanceleaf spring beauty. Unfortunately, a band of sheep summers in the area and some of the meadows may be close-cropped.

An alternate approach saves about 1500 feet of climbing—at the cost of ½ mile or more of off-trail travel. Just .6 mile south of Salmon la Sac find Little Salmon la Sac road No. 2216 and drive 4½ miles to an elevation of about 4500 feet. Park on a turnout near the road-end. It is best to walk the road near its end and then climb straight up the hill to intersect the Sasse Mountain sheep driveway on the crest of Sasse Ridge. The forested slopes are steep but mostly brushfree. Be sure to mark the spot where the ridge is reached in order to retrace steps on the return. Follow the sheep trail north a little over a mile to the junction with the Salmon la Sac trail and proceed to the top of Jolly Mountain.

If transportation can be arranged, a good loop trip can be made by going up the Little Salmon la Sac road and down the Jolly Mountain trail.

Yellow bell

CLE ELUM RIVER

36 Spade and Waptus Lakes

Round trip to Spade Lake 28 miles
Allow 3 days
High point 5400 feet
Elevation gain 3400 feet
Best mid-July through October
USGS Mt. Daniel

Round trip to Waptus Lake 18 miles
Allow 2 days
Best mid-June through October

Hike to Waptus Lake, largest in the Alpine Lakes Wilderness, lying in a broad glacial trough, its waters reflecting the spectacular spire of 7197-foot Bears Breast Mountain and snowfields on Summit Chief Mountain. Then climb to a cirque of glacier-scoured rocks holding lovely Spade Lake.

Though the trail makes a net gain of only 400 feet from road to Waptus Lake, there are many ups and downs, and as is typical of routes heavily used by horses, the tread alternates between powdery dust and cobblestones and seldom is as soft and smooth as a hikers-only path.

Drive to Salmon la Sac (Hike 35) and cross the Cle Elum River bridge. Just beyond, at the edge of the campground, find the head of Waptus River trail No. 1310, elevation 2400 feet.

The route starts on a private road past a group of summer homes, then begins a gradual ascent, first on remnants of a road used years ago for selective logging, soon becoming genuine trail. At 2 miles, 3000 feet, top the low divide and drop to the Waptus valley floor at the ford (a footlog upstream when needed) of Hour Creek, about 3 miles. The camp here is rather horsey; hikers will be happier in any of the numerous small riverside sites up the valley.

The trail now climbs 300 feet, again drops a little, and at about 4 miles touches the bank of the Waptus River. Views here of 5295-foot Cone Mountain rising above the route ahead. The way henceforth remains close to the river, whose clear waters sometimes dance over boulders, other times flow so quiet and smooth they seem not to move at all.

At about 6 miles the trail rounds the base of Cone Mountain, opening views toward the head of the valley, and at 8½ miles reaches a junction. The left fork leads along the west shore of Waptus Lake and climbs Polallie Ridge (Hike 34) to Waptus Pass and Pete Lake (Hike 33).

The Waptus trail goes right, turning downvalley ¼ mile to a steel-and-wood bridge

Glacier-carved rock at the outlet of Spade Lake

over the river, then heading upvalley again to cross Spinola Creek and join Spinola Creek trail No. 1310A coming from Deep Lake (Hike 39). At 9 miles the path arrives at Waptus Lake, 2963 feet, and a wonderful campsite with the best views of mountains reflected in water. However, this is also the most crowded camp; for other lakeside sites follow the trail 1½ miles along the shore.

The trail continues up the Waptus valley, ascending moderately for 3½ miles; along the way, at Spade Creek, it joins the Pacific Crest Trail and the two proceed as one to the Upper Waptus River Bridge. Here the gentle climbing ends. As the Crest Trail goes off left to switchback up Escondido Ridge, Dutch Miller Gap trail No. 1369 goes right, switchbacking 1400 feet in 2½ miles to Lake Ivanhoe at 4652 feet, 15 miles from the road. At 16 miles the trail reaches the 5000-foot summit of Dutch Miller Gap (Hike 17).

The best and worst is yet to come. From the Waptus outlet follow the lakeshore a short mile and find Spade Lake trail No. 1337, one of the lousiest trails in the Cascades because until a few years ago sheep and horses were allowed, making it just one steep rut. The way is mostly dry and hot but is forgiven for the pain when after 4 strenuous miles it reaches Spade Lake, 5210 feet. Campsites are located all around in meadows ribbed by outcrops of ice-polished rock. Don't camp on the heather— once broken down it takes many years to regrow.

Jack Creek Valley from Scatter Creek Pass

CLE ELUM RIVER

37 Scatter Creek Pass-Paddy-Go-Easy Pass Loop

Loop trip 23 miles
Hiking time 2-3 days
Elevation gain 4800 feet
Best mid-July through October
USGS The Cradle and Chiwaukum
   Mountains

The two passes have meadows and views, one has a small lake, and both may have people. Between them, though, is just about guaranteed solitude, miles and miles of it along streams through forests, rewarding hikers who do them in a loop rather than separately.

Due to routefinding problems (including the fact that the usually accurate USGS and Forest Service maps show the trail where it isn't) it's best to start on the Scatter Creek end.

Drive 15½ miles from Roslyn City Hall to Salmon la Sac. Just before the road crosses the river turn right on road No. 2405 and continue 9 miles to Scatter Creek Crossing (the creek is underground most of the summer). Find Scatter Creek trail No. 1328, signed "County Line Trail 2 miles." Elevation, 3320 feet.

Obscure at the start, the trail soon becomes evident as it ascends with virtually no switchbacks 1500 feet to a junction. Go left over Scatter Creek, the trail again evasive and easily lost in sheep-trampled meadows. Several campsites are passed—delightful if the sheep haven't been there lately—as the way generally follows the creek upward to Scatter Creek Pass at 6200 feet, 4½ miles. (Some maps call it "Fish Eagle Pass" but the Forest Service says that's someplace else.) If returning this way make careful note of where the creek was crossed; miss that spot and you may be in trouble.

Obvious trail switchbacks down Solomon Creek to Jack Creek trail No. 1558, 8 miles, 4000 feet. Go downstream through forest 2½ miles to a junction, 10½ miles, 3800 feet. Turn left on Meadow Creek trail No. 1559, which climbs gently (mostly) 4½ miles to a wooded pass at 5400 feet and drops 1 mile in French Creek drainage to the junction, 16 miles, 4750 feet, with Paddy-Go-Easy Pass-French Creek trail No. 1595. Go left, zigzagging up 1400 feet in 2 miles to Paddy-Go-Easy Pass, 6950 feet. Here you may encounter the first other hikers of the trip. Views are fine out to Mt. Daniel. Flowers bloom in mid-July, even though Sprite Lake, nestled in a small cirque, may be frozen until August. No firewood remains at the lake. Thanks (no thanks) to the archaic 1872 Mining Laws, both the pass and the lake are private land, a good reason to abolish the rotten old law.

From the pass drop 2700 feet in 3 miles to the Cle Elum River road and walk 2 miles on the road past Tucquala (Fish) Lake to Scatter Creek.

CLE ELUM RIVER

38 Tuck and Robin Lakes

Round trip to Robin Lakes 14 miles
Allow 3-4 days
High point 6250 feet
Elevation gain 3200 feet
Best August through mid-October
USGS Mt. Daniel and The Cradle

The "Little Enchantments," they've been called, for the glory of lakes, splendor of granite, deliriums of meadow nooks and broad views—and what often seems the largest alpine population this side of the winter Olympics. The Forest Service tried to hold down use by not building a real trail. We cooperated by removing the trip from the previous edition of this guidebook. But a hiker returns starry-eyed and gasping, friends pry the secret out of him, and there goes the neighborhood. The new management goal is not to hide the place but keep it from being pounded and burned and polluted to death.

Drive from Salmon la Sac to the Hyas Lake-Deception Pass trailhead, elevation 3350 feet (Hike 39).

Walk the valley trail to Hyas Lake at 1½ miles, 3448 feet. The mile-long lake ringed by forest and reedy marsh, dominated by the tower of 6724-foot Cathedral Rock, has many pleasant camps and is popular among novices trying out new gear and families trying out new kids. Beyond the lake, at a scant 4 miles, the trail turns steeply up, switchbacking. At some 4½ miles, 4300 feet, while still a long ½ mile from Deception Pass, the way gentles. Watch for an arrow and an "X" carved in a tree, spot tread going off downhill right, and in a few steps find a small trail sign.

An ancient fireman's track, unbuilt, unmaintained, dips to cross two small creeks, bumps against the forest wall, and begins a fascinating alternation of contours to get over or under cliffs and straight-up scrambles to get through them.

A short bit past a rock promontory in an old burn (stunning views) at 6 miles, 5628 feet, the path levels out to Tuck Lake, surrounded by cliffs. Every square foot of flat ground is an "established camp"—and is in the middle of a path to somewhere—and on a fine weekend is occupied. Except for the small area in the woods where the trail first touches the lake, firewood is zero. For peaceful and neat camping you'll do better in a zoo.

From the lake outlet take any of the paths along the divider ridge and when it leaps

Robin Lake and Mt. Daniel

upward ascend to the crest at 5800 feet. Cairns and tread lead along the crest, down and up the side of the ridge to its merger into the mountainside at 6000 feet, then up heather and slabs to a 6250-foot shoulder, and at 1 mile from Tuck, down to Lower Robin Lake, 6163 feet, which connects to Upper Robin, 6178 feet.

Roam as you please in the wide-open parkland. With USGS map in hand, go either way around Upper Robin to easily ascend 7144-foot Granite Mountain. Ramble the up-and-down ridge to 6650-foot Trico Mountain. Gaze down upon and/or prowl around nearly two dozen lakes.

Now, the reason we put the trip back in the book: the sermon. What's good for the Enchantments (see Hike 8) is good for the Robins — and maybe not good enough, the area being smaller and more easily accessible. Campers absolutely **must not** initiate new patches of bare dirt or heaps of charcoal. Camp on established patches of dirt. Carry a stove. Do not camp in the middle of the zoo — find privacy in countless nooks on ridges or in adjacent basins. We further have suggested to the Forest Service that (1) privies be strategically located; (2) the lake vicinity be declared a "no fire" zone; (3) a "day use only" zone on the Snow Lake pattern (Hike 25) be established; and (4) the lakes be allowed to be fished out and go barren.

CLE ELUM RIVER

39 Deep Lake

Round trip 14½ miles
Hiking time 9 hours
High point 5500 feet
Elevation gain 2150 feet in, 1200 feet out
Best July through October
One day or backpack
USGS Mt. Daniel and The Cradle

Climb in forest to beautiful meadow country at the base of Cathedral Rock. Look in one direction down to the Cle Elum River and beyond to Mt. Stuart, second-highest nonvolcanic summit in the Cascades and highest in the eastern section of the Alpine Lakes Wilderness, and in the other to 7960-foot Mt. Daniel, highest summit in King County and the western section of the Alpine Lakes. Look below to the green valley of Spinola Creek and, at its head, under the slopes of Daniel, the blue waters of Deep Lake.

Drive to Salmon la Sac (Hike 35). Just before crossing the Cle Elum River turn right on road No. 2405, signed Fish Lake Guard Station. Drive 12½ miles, passing Fish Lake (Tucquala Lake) and the guard station, to a junction near the road-end. The right spur goes a few dozen yards to the Hyas Lake-Deception Pass trailhead. Take the left spur a similar distance to the Deep Lake trailhead, elevation 3350 feet.

Cathedral Peak trail No. 1345 (the official moniker) crosses the Cle Elum River on a bridge and ascends steadily but moderately in cool forest, at 2 miles passing a junction with Trail Creek trail No. 1322. At 2½ miles the new trail emerges into marshy meadows around the shores of little Squaw Lake, 4841 feet, a pleasant picnic spot and a good turnaround for an easy afternoon.

The way continues up in alpine forest and patches of flowers and growing views, traverses heather gardens along the ridge slopes, and at 4¼ miles, 5500 feet, reaches Cathedral Pass nearly at the foot of Cathedral Rock, at this point intersecting the new Pacific Crest Trail coming from Deception Pass.

To descend or not to descend—that is the question. The views from the saddle make it a satisfying destination, and parkland on the crest of the ridge invites wandering; in early summer, snowmelt ponds permit delightful camps.

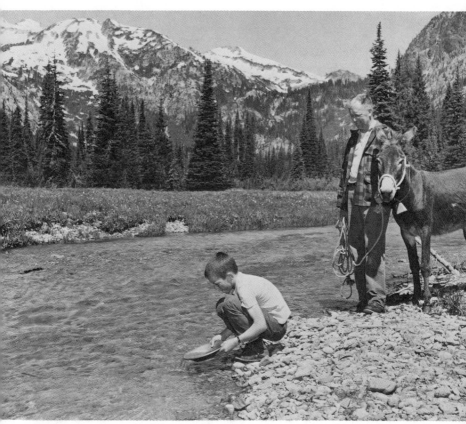

Spinola Creek and shoulder of Mt. Daniel

If the lake is chosen, descend 1200 feet on the Crest Trail, which drops into forest in a long series of switchbacks, at 7¼ miles from your trailhead arriving on the east side of Deep Lake, 4382 feet. Campsites here and elsewhere along the shores. If time allows, explore to broad meadows at the lake outlet and to flowers and waterfalls at the inlet.

The Crest Trail proceeds down the lake to the broad meadows. It and the Spinola Creek trail (former Crest Trail) both end up at Waptus River and Lake.

CLE ELUM RIVER

40 Marmot Lake

Round trip 17 miles
Allow 2 days
High point 4900 feet
Elevation gain 2400 feet
Best July through October
USGS Mt. Daniel and The Cradle

Sample the variety of the Alpine Lakes: begin with a close-to-the-road and extremely-popular valley lake, climb to a cirque lake ringed by cliffs and talus parkland and fishermen, and wander on to a lonesome off-trail lake colored jade green by meltwater from a small glacier. Go from forests to heather meadows to moraines. Look up at the peaks from below, then out to the peaks from high viewpoints.

Drive from Salmon la Sac to the Hyas Lake-Deception Pass trailhead, elevation 3350 feet (Hike 39). Hike to Hyas Lake at 1½ miles, 3448 feet. The occupants of most of the scores of cars typically parked at the road-end stop here, content with the wading, swimming, fishing, camping, and scenery-watching.

Continue past the lake and along the river bottom, then up switchbacks with views back down to Hyas Lake and across the valley to Mt. Daniel and Mt. Hinman. At 5 miles the trail tops 4475-foot Deception Pass and turns north toward Deception Lakes. Turn left on trail No. 1066, signed "Marmot Lake, 3½ miles."

The path ascends gently in parkland, by small ponds (camps), crosses a 4760-foot swale in Blue Ridge, and wends down through the meadow basin of Hozzbizz Lake, 4520 feet, beneath scenic cliffs and waterfalls of Peak 6556. The camps here tend to be horsey but several nice sites are in the woods a short way down Hozzbizz Creek. The trail drops to 3840 feet and resumes climbing, crossing a nameless creek from Marmot Lake and at 3 miles from Deception Pass coming to a Y. The right fork leads 1 mile to Lake Clarice, 4530 feet. Switchback left, climbing in a final ½ mile to Marmot Lake, 4930 feet, 8½ miles. The best camps (usually horsey, fishy, and garbagey) lie ¼ mile south along the shore. Until the Forest Service installs privies, watch where you throw down your sleeping bag.

The lake is pleasant to gaze upon, its broad waters mirroring Terrace Mountain, but due to cliffs isn't much for easy exploration. If feeling doughty, carry on. A rough, tricky, awkward path goes up and down around Marmot Lake to the inlet and leads steeply and treacherously up a rocky gully, at a long, slow 1 mile leveling out in the

No Name Lake and Lynch Peak

meadow draw of No Name Lake, 5600 feet. A few steps more and—wow!—a bit below, at 5442 feet, lies the miracle of Jade Lake, colored by rockmilk from the little Jade Glacier between 7250-foot Lynch Peak on the left and 7960-foot Diptop Peak on the right. A path drops to the lake but to proceed to the far shore and upward on the peaks entails travel beyond what the ordinary hiker should try.

Deception Pass and Marmot Lake also can be approached from the north via Surprise Lake (Hike 6).

Mt. Stuart from County Line Trail

NORTH FORK TEANAWAY

41 County Line Trail

One-way trip from Highway 97 to
   Teanaway River road about 24 miles
Allow 3-4 days
High point 6300 feet
Elevation gain 3500 feet
Best mid-June through October
USGS Mt. Stuart, Liberty

The Wenatchee Mountain crest, boundary of two counties, offers two sets of spectacular views: from the Chelan County side, to rugged peaks of the Stuart Range; from the Kittitas County side, to foothills and farmlands. Presently the trip offers solitude, at a price—about half the trail, built in the 1920s for patrol work and abandoned prior to World War II, has totally vanished and most of the rest is sketchy. This therefore is not truly a trail walk but rather a cross-country venture to be attempted only with the aid of Forest Service and USGS maps. It's not tough for experienced wilderness navigators to follow in clear weather, but a party engulfed in clouds had best beat a quick retreat.

—That's the **good** news. The bad news is that by 1984 the Forest Service, using state Off-Road-Vehicle ("ORV") funds, will have rebuilt the eastern section as far as Miller Peak as a motorcycle raceway. When **that** problem is solved and the County Line Trail is rebuilt the entire distance, it will form part of a splendid long journey from Blewett Pass to Stevens Pass. Keep the faith.

From north or south drive Highway 970 (old US 97) toward Swauk Pass. Turn off on the old Blewett Pass highway, now road No. 2208, signed "Scotty Campground" at the north end and "Park Campground" at the south. Near the pass turn off northwest on a logging road about 1 mile to a trailhead parking lot, elevation 4300 feet.

Intermittent ridgetop tread of Blewett Summit trail No. 1226 (shown as 1225 on some maps) ends (1981) 5 miles from the pass, just short of 6400-foot Miller Peak.

Scramble over the peak and follow ups and downs of the ridge crest toward Navaho Peak, sometimes on surviving bits of the County Line Trail. At approximately 10 miles from Blewett Pass, on slopes of Navaho Peak, intersect Fall Creek trail and follow it westward a short mile to a saddle under Earl Peak and an intersection with trails from Stafford and Cascade Creeks.

For the next 3 air miles the trail is plainer on maps than on the ground, but even where tread is utterly gone the walking is not all that difficult. At the intersection with Fourth Creek trail the County Line Trail is maintained ½ mile to the intersection with Beverly-Turnpike trail (Hike 42).

Descend the Beverly Creek trail a short bit and find Iron Peak trail, a long-abandoned route reopened in 1977 by the Youth Conservation Corps, climbing over a saddle and dropping 4 miles to the Teanaway River road.

Walk the road upvalley 1½ miles to the road-end and take the trail up Esmerelda Basin (Hike 43) to Fortune Creek Pass—or near. At ¼ mile short of the pass, at a little creek, the old trail route turns up right into a small basin and climbs to a divide on the ridge of Ingalls Peak. Drop to tiny Lake Ann, at the foot of the peak's walls, and follow an old sheep trail to Van Epps Pass, thence go via North Fork Fortune Creek to Scatter Creek trail, which descends to the Cle Elum River road (Hike 37).

NORTH FORK TEANAWAY

42 Beverly-Turnpike

Round trip to Ingalls Creek 14 miles
Allow 2 days
High point 5800 feet
Elevation gain 2000 feet in, 1000 feet out
Best mid-July through October
USGS Mt. Stuart

Cross a high pass from the Teanaway River valley to Ingalls Creek. Climb through open forests, flower fields, rock gardens, and views, including 9415-foot Mt. Stuart, second-highest nonvolcanic mountain in the state. In proper season the flowers begin at the trailhead and never quit, climaxing in the weird, desert-like serpentine barrens for which the area is famed among botanists. A number of stream crossings can give bad trouble in high water—an argument for not doing the hike in early summer, since a little while later when the flowers are best the creeks are easy.

Drive North Fork Teanaway River road (Hike 43) 16½ miles to Beverly Creek. Just before crossing the creek, turn right on Beverly Creek road No. 232A and proceed 1.6 miles to the end and trailhead, elevation 3800 feet.

Trail No. 1391 starts steeply up a clearing, quickly passing a junction with the Bean Creek trail, and then facing the first of the high-water challenges, the crossing of Bean Creek. For ½ mile the trail sidehills high above Beverly Creek, then drops to make the first of five crossings of the stream. Some of these may have footlogs, but don't count on it. Past the fourth crossing the way switchbacks high up a rocky hillside, brilliant at the right time with the yellow of buckwheat and the scarlet of gilia, and at 2½ miles meets Fourth Creek trail, a possible alternate return. Beverly Creek is crossed the last time and switchbacks climb to 5800-foot Beverly-Turnpike Pass.

The north side of the pass is thick-forested, so if one is not going on, for views of Stuart climb the hill to the left (west) of the pass. But the really terrific sidetrip from here is on the Iron Peak trail, hit just before the pass, leading up to the serpentine barrens and a superb ridge-crest stroll in crazy rocks and violent flowers and big views down to and across the Teanaway River.

From the pass the trail drops through woods, then switchbacks steeply down a barren avalanche slope to the valley bottom and a pleasant forest walk along Turnpike Creek. At 6 miles, by a nice campsite, is a crossing of the creek (again, possibly difficult). The way then climbs a bit and drops to a crossing of Ingalls Creek—unless a log (scarce) can be found, this is impossible at high water. On the far side is the Ingalls Creek trail (Hike 12). For a loop trip, follow the Ingalls Creek trail downstream 1½ miles to the junction with Fourth Creek trail, recross Ingalls Creek, and follow Fourth Creek up to its source, cross the ridge, and rejoin the Beverly-Turnpike trail.

Mt. Stuart from Beverly-Turnpike Pass

Harebell   Elephant's head   Scarlet gilia

NORTH FORK TEANAWAY

43 Esmerelda Basin

Round trip to Fortune Creek Pass 7 miles
Hiking time 5 hours
High point 6000 feet
Elevation gain 1750 feet
Best late June through October
One day or backpack
USGS Mt. Stuart

Loop trip around Esmereldas 15 miles
Hiking time 8 hours
High point 6000 feet
Elevation gain 3000 feet
Best July through October
One day or backpack

Pass through a slot between craggy peaks into a peaceful basin of forests, streams, and wildflowers the more vivid for rockslide barrens. Climb to wide views at "Fortune Cookie" (Fortune Creek) Pass. —Or descend through the basin from Fortune Cookie, returning from a loop trip that completely encircles Esmerelda Peaks.

Esmerelda Basin is splendid for day and weekend hikes, particularly when the Cascade Crest is misty-dripping and the sun is (maybe) brilliant here in the rain-shadow. Close-to-road camps are ideal for families introducing small children to backpacking.

Drive Interstate 90 east of Cle Elum, go off on Exit 85, proceed north toward Wenatchee on Highway 970 (old US 97) 5 miles, and turn west on Teanaway River road. At all junctions follow signs for "North Fork Teanaway" and/or "Beverly Creek

Camp." At 23 miles from SR 970 the road ends in a trailhead parking lot, elevation 4243 feet.

The hike starts on a mining road built in 1910; periodically the ancient Mining Laws are abused by a sorry bunch for whom institutionalization would be a mercy, but the entire basin is closed to public motor vehicles and the road now is merely a nice wide trail. Ascending within sight and sound of the creek-size river, in ¼ mile the old road passes the trail to Longs Pass and Ingalls Lake (Hike 44). Soon the way flattens in streamside greenery and rock gardens. Good campsites hereabouts, above and below the road; by late summer this may be the last water of the trip.

The way traverses a rocky avalanche slope, brilliant in late July with scarlet gilia and buckwheat, skirts marshy meadows covered with pink elephanthead and white bog orchid and crosses creeks lined by violet shooting stars and blue butterwort.

At 2 miles, near fallen-down cabins of Esmerelda, the trail diverges from the old mine road and ascends to Fortune Cookie Pass, 6000 feet, 3½ miles. For bigger views climb the righthand (north) skyline to a 6500-foot hilltop. Or, drop back down from the pass ¼ mile to the last creek and ascend it to a hidden basin and a pass overlooking Lake Ann, a delightful tarn (Hike 41).

Now, to get to Fortune Cookie via the loop:

At 1½ miles short of the road-end, park where the sideroad drops left to what used to be De Roux Forest Camp. Elevation, 3750 feet. In the camp find the De Roux Creek trail and follow it over the creek and up a spectacular gorge; in 1 mile keep right at a junction. The way passes lewisia rockeries and levels out in a meadow basin with delightful camps. Switchbacks climb to the broad green vale between crags of Esmerelda Peaks and Hawkin Mountains; there, at 5600 feet, **bad news**: The Forest Service has left open to jeep jockeys the old mining track that comes up Boulder Creek and goes down Fortune Creek. In a few yards, 4 miles from the road, emerge in emerald lawns around pretty little Gallagher Head Lake—and see wheel tracks trenching marshy meadows. Follow the road down from the lake 1 mile, at about 5050 feet spot the path taking off uphill right, and switchback 1 mile to Fortune Cookie. On the survey day in late July more than 150 species of flowers were in bloom on the loop.

Round trip to Ingalls Lake 8 miles
Hiking time 8 hours
High point 6500 feet
Elevation gain 2600 feet in, 600 feet out
Best mid-July through October
One day or backpack
USGS Mt. Stuart

44 Ingalls Lake

A rock-basin lake at the foot of rugged Ingalls Peak, at the top of waterfalls plunging to Ingalls Creek, and directly across the valley from the massive south wall of 9415-foot Mt. Stuart, the highest peak between Glacier Peak and Rainier. The blend of blue lake, snowfields, ice-polished slabs of brown rock, lush green meadows, a glory of flowers, and groves of whitebark pine, larch, and alpine fir is magical. From a basecamp one can spend days of happy alpine wandering.

Drive to the end of the North Fork Teanaway road, elevation 4243 feet, and hike to Esmerelda Basin (Hike 43). At ¼ mile turn right on the trail signed for Longs Pass and Ingalls Lake. Carry a loaded canteen; the climb can be hot and often is waterless.

The path ascends steadily in fields of grass and blossoms, patches of small trees. Nearby ridges are a startling blend of gray and brown and rusty-red rocks. South beyond Esmerelda Peaks appear Mt. Adams, the Goat Rocks, and Mt. Rainier. At about 5600 feet is a junction; the right fork climbs a scant ½ mile to 6250-foot Longs Pass and famous views of Mt. Stuart. Go left, swinging around the mountainside into a small valley, winding through buttresses and flowers, joining an older and steeper trail. Just below the pass is a small green bench with snowmelt (and camps) in early summer. The final stretch is a short crawl up outcrops to Ingalls Pass, 6500 feet, 3 miles, and a grand view of Mt. Stuart. The way to here is mostly free of snow in late June, while slopes to the north are still white. The ridge can be scrambled in either direction for higher views.

Drop abruptly into Headlight Creek Basin, a parkland with cold streams and delightful camps, and traverse northward, losing 300 feet or so. Meager trail regains the 300 feet in climbing a low ridge of polished brown buttresses — and at last, below, is the lake. The way down to the 6463-foot shore is short and easy, but getting around the west (lefthand) side to the outlet requires a ticklish scramble up and down slabs and huge boulders. Don't try the righthand side — it's strictly a rock-climbing route.

From the outlet one can explore to Stuart Pass (Hike 12). From the trail one can roam to private meadow basins and wide-horizon ridges.

Camping is very limited at the lake and firewood nonexistent; anyhow, the lake basin is best considered a "day use zone." Camp either in Headlight Basin or below the lake in meadowy headwaters of Ingalls Creek.

Ingalls Lake and Mt. Stuart

CARBON RIVER

45 Summit Lake

Round trip to Summit Lake 5 miles
Hiking time 3 hours
High point 5400 feet
Elevation gain 1200 feet
Best July through October
One day or backpack
USGS Enumclaw

An alpine lake, but don't be misled by the name—it isn't on the summit of anything. However, there are flower fields and a fabulous view of Mt. Rainier.

Drive US 410 to a complicated intersection at the southwest corner of Buckley, turn south on Highway No. 162-165 for 1½ miles, and turn left on Highway 165 and proceed 18 miles, passing Wilkeson and Carbonado, following signs to Ipsut Creek and Fairfax. Just before the entrance to Mount Rainier National Park, turn left on road No. 7810, cross the Carbon River on a wooden bridge, and drive 5.3 miles uphill to a junction with road No. 7820. Keep left on No. 7810 and at 6.9 miles reach the road-end and the trailhead, 4200 feet, to Twin Lake, Bearhead Mountain, and Summit Lake.

Going steadily east and constantly climbing, the trail starts up through a clearcut, makes a big switchback, and enters thick forest which cuts off sights and sounds of encroaching logging and automobiles. At 1 mile, 4800 feet, is wooded Twin Lake; keep left here at the junction with Carbon trail No. 1179.

The path rounds the lake and heads uphill, passing subalpine ponds or marshes, depending on the season. Nearly at the top of the ridge the way turns west and traverses the slopes on a fairly level grade, at one point emerging from timber into a small meadow with a view of Rainier. At 2½ miles, 5400 feet, Summit Lake is attained. Bordering the shores are open fields covered with beargrass. On the west side is an old burn. The best camps are on the east side where the trail reaches the lake. To preserve the vegetation hikers are asked to camp 100 feet from the shore.

For the first and most essential sidetrip, follow the trail around the lake, leave tread, find an easy route to the top of the 5737-foot hill, and look down at Coplay, Coundly, Lily, and Cedar Lakes. The view is grand of Mt. Rainier above—and equally broad of the network of logging operations below.

For another wandering, hike the trail past the lake a mile to the end, climb Rooster

OLD	NEW
1811	7810
1848	7820

Summit Lake and Mt. Rainier (John Spring photo)

Comb Ridge, and follow the crest down to boggy meadows; if ambitious, join Clearwater trail No. 1178 and go ½ mile to 4700-foot Celery Meadows.

For an alternate trip, turn right at Twin Lake on the Carbon trail, keep right at all old trail junctions, and in 2½ miles from Twin Lake reach the 6089-foot summit of Bearhead, former site of a lookout, and a magnificent panorama of Rainier and the hinterland.

WHITE RISER

46 Naches Wagon Trail

Round trip to Government Meadows
  from west side 10½ miles
Hiking time 5 hours
High point 4800 feet
Elevation gain 2200 feet
Best late June through November
One day or backpack
USGS Lester

One-way trip from east side 9½ miles
Hiking time 5 hours
High point 4900 feet
Elevation gain 1500 feet

Walk the pioneer wagon route across Naches Pass and see blazes cut by emigrants, logs they rolled out of the way, dirt they shoveled, and trees they chopped. Unfortunately, you will see more tracks of vandals than pioneers, because the Forest Service inexcusably permits motorbikes and jeeps on the route. These adventurers seeking a mechanical challenge have obliterated much of the pioneers' trail which should have been preserved for more respectful travelers with an appreciation of history. This may be the only pioneer trail left in the 48 states that hasn't been paved over or bulldozed. Yet Weyerhaeuser has cut the trail with roads at four places, the Forest Service at two others, and the Forest Service has shortened the trail on the east side.

Highlights can be enjoyed in a day hike to Government Meadows from the west side, but for a better appreciation of the trek of 1853, start from the east side, camp overnight at Government Meadows (where the pioneers spent months), and next morning descend the west side, over "The Cliff" where wagons were lowered on rawhide ropes. In either case, allow plenty of time for leisurely exploration.

For a day hike from the west, drive US 410 east from Enumclaw 20 miles to a log-trestle overpass, turn left on road No. 70, and go 8 miles to the Greenwater River bridge. About ¼ mile beyond turn right on a spur road, cross Pyramid Creek, and park, elevation 2560 feet. The trail (track) takes off up the timbered ridge to the left. Ascend 3½ miles through forest to Government Meadows, 4800 feet.

For an overnight hike, leave one car at the west trailhead and drive a second over Chinook Pass and 23.5 miles east from the summit. Turn left 14 miles on Little Naches

	OLD	NEW
Greenwater road	197	70

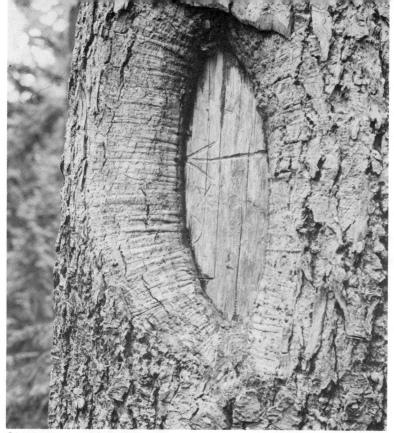
Old blaze made by pioneers

road No. 197, then turn right on road No. 1923 and go .3 mile to the trailhead, elevation 3200 feet.

The first wagon train crossed Naches Pass in 1853. One or two others followed, but the route proved so difficult it was abandoned. In 1910 the Forest Service reopened the way for foot and horse travel. To "celebrate" the centennial of the first crossing, a group of jeepsters hacked and gouged over the pass in 1953, and since then the trail has been heavily used by motorbikes and four-wheel vehicles which have rutted the forest. Thanks to the vehicles, the trail is impossible to miss, but finding remnants of the original wagon road requires imagination. Two clues are useful:

For one, the pioneers took the line of least resistance by detouring around big trees and logs; the jeepsters use chainsaws to make a more direct line, and thus in many places the old track is several hundred feet from the jeep ruts and relatively well-preserved. For a second clue, the wagons were top-heavy and to save shoveling on sidehills the pioneers frequently followed the ups and downs of a ridge crest; particularly on the west side, jeeps have contoured around some ridge tops.

In 6 miles from the east trailhead, reach the wooded, 4900-foot summit of Naches Pass, and in another ¾ mile the Pacific Crest Trail junction and campsites at Government Meadows. The next day cross six roads on the way down; at ½ mile from the west trailhead descend "The Cliff," where pioneers lowered their wagons.

Footbridge over Greenwater River

WHITE RIVER

47 Echo Lake

Round trip 14 miles
Hiking time 7 hours
High point 4100 feet
Elevation gain 1640 feet
Best May to mid-November at lower
  elevations
One day or backpack
USGS Lester

Long one of the most famous cathedrals of old-growth Douglas fir outside a dedicated wilderness or national park, among the greatest valley forests in the state, the Greenwater greenery now is being whacked down by Weyerhaeuser and shipped overseas. A last-ditch effort is being made to preserve a sample by placing it in the proposed Cougar Lakes (William O. Douglas?) Wilderness. Amid the lingering trees are sparkling forest lakes and a lovely subalpine lake.

Drive US 410 east from Enumclaw and take the Greenwater road to the Naches Wagon Trail trailhead (Hike 46), elevation 2560 feet. Take Greenwater trail No. 1176 through a clearcut and soon enter climax forest where the magnificence of trees competes with the rich understory of devil's club, vanilla leaf, trillium, and moss, much much moss. Sad to say, Weyerhaeuser won't let the Forest Service close the trail to motorcycles, so there is that irritation as well as the debris from ongoing logging operations on both sides of the valley.

At ¾ mile the trail crosses Greenwater River, a limeade joy, and at 1½ miles recrosses at the first of the two little Meeker (Greenwater) Lakes. The second is at 2 miles. At 4 miles the trail reaches a junction with Lost Creek trail No. 1185, a 3-mile sidetrip to Lost Lake. So far the trail has gained only 200 feet a mile, but near the 5-mile mark it leaves the valley bottom and starts climbing in earnest. At 5½ miles pass a junction with trail No. 1186. At 6½ miles cross a 4100-foot high point and drop 200 feet to the edge of 3819-foot Echo Lake, surrounded by wooded hills with a glimpse of meadows and craggy peaks of Castle Mountain.

The trail continues 6 miles to Corral Pass. The entire route, near lakes and along river, offers numerous campsites. At Echo Lake campers are asked to keep 100 feet from the water; the west shore is closed.

OLD	NEW
197	70

113

White River and Mt. Rainier from Crystal Ridge

WHITE RIVER

48 Crystal Ridge

Round trip to viewpoint 6 miles
Hiking time 3½ hours
High point 5500 feet
Elevation gain 1300 feet
Best July to October
One day
USGS Bumping Lake and White River Park

Loop trip 13 miles
Hiking time 7 hours
High point 6600 feet
Elevation gain 2400 feet
One day

Along the Crystal Mountain ridge, boundary of Rainier National Park, a Forest Service trail wanders through a series of striking views of Rainier and the White River. Flowers in one season, great huckleberries in another. Hikers who get up early enough in the morning have a good chance of seeing elk.

The trip comes in two versions, one using the feet only for a standard uphill-downhill walk, the other using the Crystal Mountain chairlift for the uphill, a trail-road combination for the downhill. Both will be described here, the "normal" version first.

From US 410 at the Park boundary near Silver Springs, turn left on the Crystal Mountain Highway. Drive 4½ miles to an unmarked logging road on the right and follow it ¼ mile to the trailhead and horse-unloading ramp, elevation 4200 feet.

Trail No. 1163 begins as a service road under a powerline but soon becomes legitimate, climbing gently through clearcuts, then an old burn, in loose, dusty, pumice soil. Shade is scarce and water non-existent (did you remember to fill the canteen?). Heat and thirst are forgotten when, in 3 miles, at 5500 feet, the crest of Crystal Ridge is attained and Mt. Rainier overpowers the horizon.

The ridge varies from narrow, with a cliff on the Park side, to broad and rounded meadows. Below the crest are vast fields of huckleberries. And the views! Chances are a party will find ample rewards long before completing the 3 steady-climbing ridgecrest miles to the top terminal of Chair No. 2.

For a loop trip with an interesting variety of lakes, meadows, and huckleberries, descend on a service road that starts near the terminal. In ⅓ mile find a legitimate trail switchbacking down through Silver Queen Basin, past Henskin Lakes, to a junction with Silver Creek trail No. 1192. Follow it 1 mile to road No. 7190410, then go by road to the ski area parking lot, 4½ miles from the top terminal. From there walk the paved road 2½ miles back to the starting point; alternately, follow the old mine road, No. 7190410, to Crystal Mountain Highway, cross, and return on the trail.

Now for the all-downhill tour. (Let it be noted this version is no good for elk-watching—by the time of day the chairlifts start running, the animals have finished eating and retired to the forest to chew their cuds.) Drive to the ski area parking lot, elevation 4200 feet, ride Chair No. 2 to the top, elevation 6600 feet, and find the Crystal Ridge trail and hike either way. Both ways are so interesting and different that you may want to go back a second time for the other direction or, as we did, start early in the morning so you can see the elk and hike the whole loop at one time.

	OLD	NEW
	184	7190410

49 Big Crow Basin- Norse Peak

Round trip to Norse Peak 8½ miles
Hiking time 6 hours
High point 6856 feet
Elevation gain 2900 feet
Best late June through early November
One day
USGS Bumping Lake

Lovely alpine meadows, one with a small lake, offering a wonderful weekend of wandering. However, the shortest way to the basin involves climbing nearly to the top of 6856-foot Norse Peak—an arduous backpack. Most hikers therefore settle for a day trip to the summit, an abandoned lookout site, and enjoy the views down to the inviting gardens and all around to panoramas extending from Snoqualmie Pass peaks to Mt. Adams, from golden hills of Eastern Washington to green lowlands of Puget Sound. The trail to Norse Peak usually is open for walking in late June; the meadow country remains under snow until mid-July.

Drive US 410 east 33 miles from Enumclaw to Silver Springs summer homes. A bit beyond, just before the Rainier National Park boundary, turn left toward the Crystal Mountain ski area. At 4 miles, 3900 feet, park.

Find the old mine-to-market road, No. 7190410, walk it about 1000 feet, and go off left on trail No. 1191—making sure before that to fill canteens at a spring, the only sure water. The original path to the lookout was short and steep; the Forest Service recently improved the route, which now is somewhat gentler but considerably longer.

Very soon the tip of Mt. Rainier appears over the ridge to the west and every additional step reveals more of the mountain. By 2 miles the whole summit is in sight and the scene steadily expands as more elevation is gained. The route is confused here and there by crisscrossing of the old tread—take the path of least resistance, which generally is the new trail. At 4 miles, 6600 feet, the summit ridge is topped and a junction reached.

The right fork follows the ridge crest ¼ mile to Norse Peak. Look northeast into Big Crow Basin and east to Lake Basin and appealing Basin Lake. Look down to the Crystal Mountain ski area, one of the finest ski developments in the Northwest; unfortunately, winter doesn't last all year and the summer view is a hodgepodge of bulldozer tracks.

OLD	NEW
184	7190410

Mt. Rainier from Norse Peak

The left fork drops eastward 1 mile to join the Pacific Crest Trail, which descends ½ mile to Big Crow Basin; at about 5700 feet are a shelter cabin and good camping, though water may be scarce in late summer. Partway down find a sidetrail leading over a low green ridge to Basin Lake, 6200 feet.

The meadows and peak also can be approached by intersecting the Crest Trail at Bullion Basin, or by taking the trail starting at Corral Pass, 5600 feet. The latter long and scenic route includes two descents and ascents of 800 feet each in 4 miles before joining the Crest Trail near Little Crow Basin (camps and water).

AMERICAN RIVER

50 Crow Lake Way

Round trip to Grassy Saddle 8 miles
Hiking time 7 hours
High point 6200 feet
Elevation gain 3000 feet in, 600 feet out
Best early June to hunting season
One day or backpack
USGS Bumping Lake

An extemely steep trail, with no water except that carried in canteens, climbs from valley forests to high meadows, compensating for the sweat and struggle by offering exciting views of the needle-like spires of Fifes Peaks and the meandering course of the American River. The route can be continued past pretty little Grassy Saddle to the large, boggy meadows surrounding Crow Creek Lake, a favorite haunt of throngs of elk and deer. The animals are fun to watch in summer but are best steered clear of in that season when hunters outnumber the huntees.

Drive US 410 east of Chinook Pass to 1.2 miles east of Pleasant Valley Campground and find the trailhead, elevation 3400 feet.

Crow Lake Way No. 953, steep from the start and gaining 2200 feet in the first 2½ hot, dry miles, begins with ¼ mile of jeep track before turning into true trail. The way climbs 1¼ miles through forest to a hogback, which then is followed, by glimpses of Fifes Peaks, past dramatic dropoffs overlooking American Ridge, the views growing step by step, to a 5800-foot high point at 3 miles, a good turnaround for day-trippers.

The trail then descends 200 feet into Survey Creek drainage and at 3½ miles crosses a broad divide, 6000 feet, to Crow Creek drainage. West are rolling green meadows inviting a tour. At about 4 miles, 5600 feet, the trail enters Grassy Saddle with a small creek and, half-hidden in trees, a very small lake. Campsites nearby are great bases for explorations.

For the first, roam the basin at the head of Falls Creek. The unmarked trail starts at the far end of the lake, skirts a rockslide, and climbs to the basin edge at 6400 feet. The basin rim can be followed like the lip of a cup in a semicircle to cliffs of Fifes Peaks. Other explorations are the 6400-foot hill to the west and, longer, the 3 miles along Crow Lake Way, in green meadows, to Crow Creek Lake.

Fifes Peaks from Crow Lake Way

51 Sourdough Gap

Round trip 6 miles
Hiking time 4 hours
High point 6400 feet
Elevation gain 1100 feet in, 200 feet out
Best July through October
One day or backpack
USGS Mt. Rainier and Bumping Lake

A delightful bit of the Pacific Crest Trail (probably the easiest meadow walk in this entire book) through flower gardens and grassy fields to a high pass. A good overnight hike for beginners, except that camping space is limited and very crowded on weekends. Do the trip in early August when flowers are at their peak.

Drive US 410 east from Enumclaw to the summit of Chinook Pass, 5432 feet. Find the first available parking lot—which may be around the bend in the highway. (The shortage of parking space is a serious problem on fine summer weekends. So is the vandalism of cars left overnight.) The trailhead (Pacific Crest Trail No. 2000) is near the wooden overpass.

The trail goes north, paralleling the highway, dropping slightly in the first mile, at times on cliffs almost directly above the road. At about 1½ miles the way rounds a ridge, leaves the highway, and starts a gentle climb to Sheep Lake, 2½ miles, 5700 feet—a great place to camp if not crowded. But it almost always is, and the meadows have been badly damaged. Find better camping on benches a few hundred feet away.

The moderate ascent continues through flowers, with a final long switchback leading to Sourdough Gap, 3 miles, 6400 feet. (About 500 feet below the gap the summit of Mt. Rainier can be seen briefly between two peaks to the west.)

Views from the gap are limited. For broader vistas, continue on the trail another ⅓ mile, descending a little to a small pass with looks down Morse Creek to Placer Lake, an artificial lake made by miners years ago.

For really wide horizons, ascend the 6734-foot peak west of the gap—not a difficult climb by mountaineering standards, but steep with a loose scree slope near the top. Drop a few feet north from the gap and start up along the base of cliffs, following a well-worn path. For the best footing stay off the scree. From the summit admire the huge white bulk of Mt. Rainier, peaks south to Mt. Adams, and north along the Cascade Crest. A vertical cliff falls to Crystal Lakes 900 feet below, seemingly only a swandive away.

Sheep Lake

52 American Ridge

Round trip from Goose Prairie to viewpoint
12 miles
Hiking time 7 hours
High point 6310 feet
Elevation gain 2900 feet
Best June through November
One day or backpack
USGS Bumping Lake

One-way trip from Goose Prairie to Pacific
Crest Trail 19 miles
Allow 3 days
High point 6946 feet
Elevation gain 5500 feet
Best late July through October

As the crow flies, American Ridge is 17 miles long, but with twists, turns, and switchbacks, the trail takes 27 miles to complete the traverse. The way is mostly rough and sometimes steep, but the meadowlands are beautiful and lonesome. Flowers are in full bloom at the east end of the ridge about Memorial Day (the usual time that Chinook Pass opens) and at the west end in early August. The east end makes an excellent early-season trip when other high trails are still snowed in. Look for avalanche and glacier lilies and a rare pink-and-purple flower called steer's head.

The entire ridge is worth hiking, but only the east end is free of snow in June, and by August it is dry and hot. Therefore the recommendation is to hike from Goose Prairie to an intersection with the American Ridge trail and then go east (in June) or west (in August) along the ridge crest.

Drive US 410 east from Chinook Pass 18.5 miles and turn right on the Bumping River road. In .6 mile is the eastern trailhead, elevation 2900 feet, signed American Ridge trail No. 958; if a complete traverse of American Ridge is planned, start here.

At 9.3 miles from US 410 find Goose Prairie trail No. 972 on the right side of the road, elevation 3360 feet. Parking space in a small camp on the left.

The Goose Prairie trail is in woods all the way, beginning in fir and pine forest typical of the east slopes of the Cascades and ascending into Alaska cedars, alpine firs, and wind-bent pines. The route climbs steadily but never steeply. At 1½ miles the path crosses several small streams and begins a series of nine switchbacks, at 2 miles recrossing the same streams, the last reliable water for a long stretch. At 4¾ miles is a spring which runs most of the summer; possible camping here. At 5 miles the ridge top is attained and the intersection with American Ridge trail No. 958, elevation 6200 feet.

Day hikers (any season) should follow the ridge west, climbing ½ mile to a point

Nelson Ridge, left, and Bumping Lake, right, from American Ridge

where the trail starts down into Kettle Creek drainage. Leave the trail and continue ¼ mile more up the ridge to a 6310-foot knoll with fine views of Mt. Rainier, Mt. Aix, and miles of ridges north and south.

Early-season overnight hikers should turn east, following the ridge through forest and meadows to Goat Peak at 11 miles, site of the former American Ridge Lookout, elevation 6473 feet, and a view of the spectacular cliffs of Fifes Peaks. If transportation has been arranged, a party can continue 7½ miles down to the Bumping River road and the previously-mentioned American Ridge trailhead, completing a one-way trip of 18½ miles with an elevation gain of about 3600 feet.

Midsummer and fall overnight hikers should turn west, climbing near the top of the 6310-foot knoll, then descending to campsites at shallow Kettle Lake, 6 miles, 5650 feet. (Below the lake is a small spring.) The trail contours around the head of Kettle Creek, climbing to the ridge crest at 10 miles, 6900 feet, dropping again to Big Basin at 11 miles, 6300 feet, a cirque with good campsites, bands of elk, and glorious scenery.

With some ups and more downs, the trail follows the ridge top from meadows back into alpine forest at a low point of 5500 feet, then up to meadowland at 6000 feet and a campsite near Mud Lake at 13½ miles. At 16½ miles in a junction with Swamp Lake trail No. 970, a popular route leading to Cougar Lakes in 1 mile and a steep way trail that joins the Crest Trail; No. 958 goes right, reaching American Lake at 18 miles and the Crest Trail at 19½ miles.

If transportation can be arranged, a one-way trip can be made via the Crest Trail to Chinook Pass, a total distance of 26.5 miles, or via the Swamp Lake trail to Upper Bumping road, a total of 21 miles.

Looking south along Nelson Ridge

BUMPING RIVER

53 Nelson Ridge- Mount Aix

Round trip to Mt. Aix 12 miles
Hiking time 10 hours
High point 7766 feet
Elevation gain 4000 feet
Best mid-June through October
One day
USGS Bumping Lake

High gardens in the blue sky of the rainshadow, amid views east to the brown vastness of the heat-hazy Columbia Plateau, west to the shimmering white hugeness of Mt. Rainier, and south along the Cascade Crest to the Goat Rocks and Mt. Adams. Plus closer looks over meadows and forests of the proposed Cougar Lakes Wilderness. This is not a beginners' trail—the way is steep, hot, and dry.

Drive US 410 east from Chinook Pass 18.5 miles and turn right on the Bumping Lake road 11 miles to a junction. Take the left fork, signed road No. 162, 1½ miles and just before a bridge over Copper Creek turn left up a steep road signed "Mt. Aix Trail." Park in a few yards, elevation 3700 feet. The rude road continues ¼ mile but this final stretch is best walked to the trailhead. Fill canteens at a creek not far from the beginning; the climb is long and can be thirsty.

The merciless trail attains highlands with minimum delay. For openers, the path ascends deep forest nearly to a branch of Copper Creek, but never gets to the water, instead switchbacking up a steep hillside. (Across the Copper Creek valley, above Miners Ridge, Rainier appears, and grows with every step.) At 2¼ miles the trail swings into open subalpine forest at the lip of a hanging valley but again never gets to the water. Switchbacks now trend out from the valley into open forest distinguished by superb specimens of whitebark pine.

At nearly 4 miles, 6400 feet, is a grassy promontory with views of Rainier, Adams, and the Goat Rocks. A nice campsite here in early summer, when snowmelt is available. This far makes a satisfying destination for a day hike, especially when slopes above are snowy or the party is pooped.

From the promontory the trail traverses shrubby forest and scree southward and upward to the wide-open crest of Nelson Ridge, 7100 feet, and a choice of wanderings. The up-and-down crest cries out for rambling in either or both directions. The trail contours and climbs a final rocky mile to the summit of 7766-foot Mt. Aix, one-time site of a fire lookout.

Because of their position on the east slope of the Cascades, and the mostly southwest exposures of the trail route, Nelson Ridge and Mt. Aix are free of snow weeks earlier than country a few miles distant. And if the tread at the hanging valley of Copper Creek is all white, as it may be through June, a short and simple detour up amid trees leads back to clear ground. Actually, the maximum flower display comes when patches of snow still linger. The locals consider this trail—whether to the promontory at 4 miles, to Nelson Ridge at 5 miles, or Mt. Aix at 6 miles—the best early-summer hike in the entire Bumping River area.

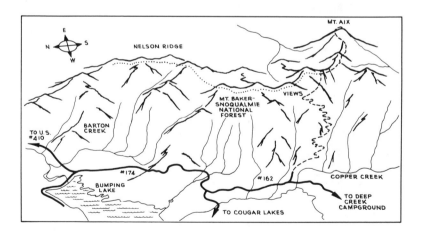

54 Cougar Lakes

Round trip to Cougar Lakes 12 miles
Hiking time 8 hours
High point 5300 feet
Elevation gain 1700 feet in, 300 feet out
Best mid-July through October
One day or backpack
USGS Bumping Lake

Two alpine lakes, a big one and a little one, surrounded by generous flower fields in late July and early August, blueberries in early September, and fall colors in October. From ridges above, wide views of Mt. Rainier and the Cascade Crest country.

Drive US 410 east from Chinook Pass 18.5 miles and turn right 10.8 miles on the Bumping River road to the end of pavement at Bumping Lake. Continue on road No. 174 to a junction at 2½ miles and turn right on the Upper Bumping road 3.6 miles to the road-end and trailhead, elevation 3600 feet.

The flat forest way leads in ½ mile to a ford of the broad and shallow Bumping River, which has very cold water and sharp rocks, so wear wool socks or tennis shoes — or boots without socks, which thus are kept dry for redonning. A bit farther is a junction with the Bumping Lake trail. Go straight ahead, climbing moderately and steadily in woods and occasional openings to the outlet of Swamp Lake, 3.7 miles, 4800 feet; campsites at and near the shelter cabin.

The trail ascends several hundred feet in ¾ mile to an indistinct divide and a junction with the American Ridge trail (Hike 52). Go left ¼ mile to another junction. The righthand trail climbs past American Lake to the Cascade Crest; go left instead, rounding a ridge spur at 5300 feet and dropping into the lake basin, at 6 miles, 5015 feet, reaching the isthmus between the Cougar Lakes.

To the right is Little Cougar Lake, at the foot of the basalt cliffs of House Rock. To the left is Big Cougar Lake. The shores offer numerous camps but the sites with the most privacy and largest views are in meadows along the inlet stream feeding Big Cougar Lake. (Be sure to camp a distance from lakeshore and streams.)

For extended horizons, climb a steep and perhaps very muddy mile on the boulder-strewn path leading from the inlet of Big Cougar to the Cascade Crest at 6000

Little Cougar Lake and House Rock

feet. Look for mountain goat, marmots, and rock conies (pikas). For maximum scenery and garden walking, wander north on the Pacific Crest Trail and in about 1½ miles turn right on the trail down to American Lake and back to Cougar Lakes, completing a 5-mile loop.

To preserve the vegetation, camp at least 100 feet from the lakeshores.

Beargrass on top of Tumac Mountain

BUMPING RIVER

55 Tumac Mountain

Round trip 10½ miles
Hiking time 5 hours
High point 6340 feet
Elevation gain 2100 feet
Best July through October
One day or backpack
USGS Bumping Lake and White Pass

Hike through alpine meadows by myriad lakes and ponds to the most varied view of vulcanism in the Washington Cascades. Tumac itself is no simple cone but rather, built of both cinders and lava and having two craters (both lake-filled), an infant stratovolcano standing on a broad lava plateau. This is how mighty Rainier began.

The summit presents a panorama of stratovolcanoes of other ages: Spiral Butte, another infant, at the south end of the lava plateau; youthful St. Helens, expected by geologists to grow a lot more; bulky, mature, deeply-dissected Rainier and Adams; and the old old Goat Rocks, remnant of a once-mighty volcano now reduced to mere roots. Do the climb in mid-July when upper slopes are covered with red and white heather plus a peppering of bright red paintbrush. The trip can be one day or overnight, camping at one of the lovely Twin Sisters Lakes. Carry water; except for the lakes, the way can be quite dry.

Drive US 410 east from Chinook Pass 18.5 miles and turn right 10.8 miles on the Bumping River road to the end of pavement at Bumping Lake. Continue on road No. 174 to a junction at 2.5 miles and turn left on road No. 162, going 7 miles to the road-end at Deep Creek Campground, elevation 4300 feet.

Find Twin Sister trail No. 980 on the north side of the campground. The way gains 800 feet in 2¼ miles (all in woods) to Little Twin Sister Lake, 5100 feet.

The "little" lake (only a comparison, for both are quite large) has numerous bays and rocky points. To see it at its best, climb open slopes of the 5733-foot hill rising above the shores. To reach Big Twin Sister Lake, follow trail No. 980 westward ½ mile. Both lakes are outstanding and have beautiful campsites. They have many delightful sand beaches, the more so since the replenishment of May 18, 1980.

From Little Twin Sister Lake turn left on trail No. 1104, which in ½ mile turns toward Blankenship Meadows. Keep straight ahead on Tumac Mountain trail No. 44, which aims at the peak. The way climbs steadily in open meadows 1 mile. Note how small trees are taking over the meadowland, a phenomenon which only recently has received attention. Are the trees just now growing after the Ice Age, or are they returning after catastrophic forest fires, insect invasion, or uncontrolled stock grazing of years ago? Whatever the reason, alpine meadows all over this portion of the Cascades are rapidly changing to forest, especially here and at Mt. Rainier.

The final mile is steep and badly chewed up by horses, but the views get steadily better and become downright exciting on the 6340-foot summit. The most striking is northeast, down to Blankenship Meadows and the three Blankenship Lakes (Hike 58). To the west are many tree-ringed lakes, a few of which can be seen, including Dumbbell Lake (Hike 56). Mt. Aix and neighbors dominate the northeast horizon. In other directions are the volcanoes.

To protect the vegetation, campers are asked to use sites at least 100 feet from the lakeshores. At Big Twin Sister, the only permitted camps are on the north side.

TIETON RIVER

56 Dumbbell Lake

Round trip to Sand Lake 6 miles
Hiking time 4 hours
High point 5295 feet
Elevation gain 900 feet
Best mid-July through November
One day
USGS White Pass

Round trip to Dumbbell Lake 13 miles
Hiking time 7 hours
High point 5600 feet
Elevation gain 1200 feet in, 500 feet out
Best mid-July through November
One day or backpack

If you like alpine lakes, this is certainly the trail—there are dozens of them, large and small. If you like tall, picturesque alpine trees, this is the trail—there are thousands of lovely specimens. And if you like fall hiking through the bright red leaves of huckleberry bushes, this is the trail—there are miles of color. The hike along a delightful section of the Pacific Crest Trail can be done as a day trip to Sand Lake or an overnight to Dumbbell Lake.

Drive US 12 east from White Pass .7 mile, turn left into White Pass Campground, and continue about ¼ mile to the trailhead near Leech Lake, elevation 4412 feet. This is Pacific Crest Trail No. 2000. A new and very confusing system of signing gives trail numbers rather than destinations. There is no problem so long as a party stays on the Crest Trail but any deviation requires a Forest Service map to decipher the signs.

The trail starts in forest, climbing 800 feet in 2½ miles to Deer Lake, 5206 feet, still in woods. At 3 miles is Sand Lake, 5295 feet, with numerous arms surrounded by meadows and alpine trees. Though the water is very clear, the shallow lake seems to have neither inlet nor outlet, so the water should be boiled before drinking. Sand Lake is an excellent turnaround for day hikers. (Many a person who long had wondered why the lakes hereabouts are so sandy understood after St. Helens lost its head.)

Now the trail wanders past numerous small lakes, climbing to 5600 feet at 4 miles.

130

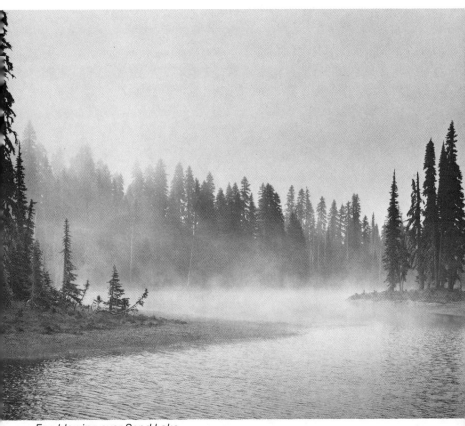

Fog blowing over Sand Lake

Several places offer glimpses southward of Mt. Adams and the Goat Rocks; Spiral Butte can be seen through the trees to the east.

At about 5 miles the trail switches from the east side of the crest to the west and descends in forest, losing 500 feet in ¾ mile. Now and then Mt. Rainier can be partly viewed through trees; for a better look walk off the trail 100 feet onto a low, rocky knoll located on the left side of the path soon after passing two small ponds.

At 6 miles the way skirts Buesch Lake, 5081 feet, and reaches a junction with Cramer Lake trail No. 1106. Follow this a short ¼ mile to Dumbbell Lake, 5091 feet. Much of the lake is shallow; the rocky shoreline is very interesting. To appreciate its unusual shape, beat through a patch of brush and scramble to the bald summit of 5992-foot Cramer Mountain—and views much broader than merely the lake.

For an alternate return, follow Cramer Lake trail No. 1106 down to within ½ mile of Dog Lake, turn west on Dark Meadow trail No. 1107, and finish with a last mile on the Crest Trail. The distance is about the same but most of the way is in forest.

Shoe Lake from Pacific Crest Trail

TIETON RIVER

57 Shoe Lake

Round trip from trailhead east of White
    Pass 14 miles
Hiking time 7 hours
High point 6600 feet
Elevation gain 2200 feet in, 500 feet out
Best mid-July through October
One day
USGS White Pass

Round trip from top of White Pass chairlift
    8 miles
Hiking time 4 hours
Elevation gain 900 feet in, 600 feet out
Forest Service wilderness permit required

Meadows and parklands along the Cascade Crest, grand views of the Goat Rocks and Mt. Adams, and a beautiful lake in a green basin. All this on an easy day from the road.

Drive US 12 east from White Pass .7 mile to the parking lot and trailhead (Pacific Crest Trail) opposite Leech Lake Campground, elevation 4400 feet.

(Alternately, for a shorter hike, park at White Pass ski area, 4400 feet, climb the ski hill 1½ miles, and take a short path which intersects the Pacific Crest Trail at a point 3 miles from the trailhead described above. For an even quicker trip, some hikers ride the chairlift to the top.)

From the formal trailhead east of White Pass, the way traverses and switchbacks open forest, touching a ski run at one point, and at 3 miles, 5900 feet, intersects the ridge crest and the path from the top of the chairlift.

Now the trail ascends into gardens and scattered alpine trees on the slopes of Hogback Mountain and swings onto the west side of the crest, with a great view of Mt. Rainier. Attaining a 6400-foot saddle, the route contours steep, broad shale slopes on the east side of 6789-foot Hogback (an easy scramble from the trail to the summit) above the basin containing little Miriam Lake, and climbs to a 6600-foot saddle, 6½ miles, in a spur ridge—and commanding views of the Goat Rocks and Mt. Adams. And below, the bright waters of Shoe Lake.

Drop ⅓ mile to the lake, 6200 feet, and fields of flowers. However, due to damage done by past overuse, camping has been banned in the entire basin so that meadows may have a chance to recover. Camping is permitted ½ mile beyond the lake at Hidden Springs.

133

TIETON RIVER

58 Blankenship Lakes

Round trip to Blankenship Lakes 12 miles
Hiking time 6 hours
High point 5200 feet
Elevation gain 2000 feet in, 200 feet out
Best mid-July through October
One day or backpack
USGS White Pass

Pocket-size meadows, vast grasslands, and beautiful mountain lakes make this country unique in the Cascades. The map calls the area "Mosquito Valley," and rightly so. Though the meadows are magnificent when bright green, the bugs are then numbered by the billions; the hike is much more enjoyable in late summer and fall.

Besides a USGS map, a party **must carry** a Forest Service map, because the local signing system gives only trail numbers instead of place names, guaranteed to confuse and lose anyone who forgets his map.

Drive US 12 east from White Pass 8.3 miles. A few hundred feet before Indian Creek Campground, turn left on road No. 1410, signed "Bootjack Summer Homes." Drive .8 mile to a junction and keep left, still on road No. 1410; at 3 miles from the highway is the parking lot by the trailhead sign, Indian Creek trail No. 1105, elevation 3400 feet.

The first 2 miles of "trail" lie along a very rough mining road best walked. Just before the end of the road, find the start of true trail, which drops steeply 200 feet into a canyon, crosses Indian Creek, and climbs very steeply out of the canyon. At about 2½ miles listen for a waterfall; the canyon edge and a view of the lovely falls are just a few feet off the path, though one may have to try a couple spots before finding the only really good vantage point.

The trail crosses Indian Creek again at about 3 miles, recrosses at 4 miles, and at 4½ miles enters the large (⅓-mile-long) Indian Creek Meadows. Stay on trail No. 1105, passing trail No. 1148 to Pear and Apple Lakes. The tread is faint as it traverses the meadow and heads west, but becomes distinct again beyond the grass. At 5 miles pass trail No. 1148 to Apple Lake, and at just under 6 miles take a short sidetrail to the first of the three Blankenship Lakes, 5200 feet, a fair spot for a basecamp.

The first thing to do is explore the other two lakes, a stone's throw from each other. Next comes the ascent of 6340-foot Tumac Mountain, a small volcano rising over the lakes and offering superb views; two trails lead to the top from other sides (Hike 55)

Blankenship Lake and Tumac Mountain

but a path really isn't needed. Follow trail No. 1104B between the lakes, climbing to its junction with the Sand Ridge trail. Continue uphill, off-trail, to the summit, avoiding soft cinder slopes.

Another ½ mile along trail No. 1105 are Blankenship Meadows—many little clearings and one huge expanse. As is true of many other meadows in this portion of the Cascades, young trees are invading the grass. There are strangely few flowers in the meadows, but beargrass and lupine grow in the woods, and bog orchids and elephantheads in wet places. (Blankenship Meadows can also be reached by a 4-mile hike from road No. 162, near Bumping Lake.)

A 2-mile sidetrip to Pear and Apple Lakes is a must. This can be done as a one-way walk, going first to shallow Apple Lake on trail No. 1148, then continuing on the same trail to deep Pear Lake, and returning to the main route on trail No. 1148.

Good camps at Indian Creek Meadows, Blankenship Lakes, and Pear Lake.

59 Bear Creek Mountain

Round trip 7½ miles
Hiking time 4 hours
High point 7335 feet
Elevation gain 1400 feet
Best mid-July to mid-October
One day or backpack
USGS White Pass, Forest Service Goat
Rocks Wilderness

Amble through flowers and lawns and subalpine trees on slopes of a high ridge. Then shift down and ascend lava rocks of the old Goat Rocks Volcano to the summit of Bear Creek Mountain, 7335 feet, onetime site of a fire lookout with fabulous views up and down the Cascades.

When the St. Helens cannon went off it was pointed right at this spot; a month later the surveyor climbed from Conrad Meadows in gray ash that was inches thick atop the snow. Wind, water, and gravity are mingling the Event of 1980 with the many prior Events, but for years the hiker will find stretches of soft "beach."

The flowers are at their best in late July and early August, which is nice timing, because the road to the trailhead usually is snowbound until early July; if visiting before then, approach from Conrad Meadows (Hike 60).

Drive US 12 from White Pass and before reaching Rimrock Reservoir turn right on the paved road signed "Tieton Road" and "Clear Lake." Instructions in case some of the signs are missing, stolen by local fun-seekers: at 3.2 miles cross North Fork Tieton River, at 5.3 miles turn right on gravel road No. 1311, at 7.9 miles go straight on No. 1311A, at 10 miles go left on No. 1311B, at 10.9 miles go right (uphill) on No. 1314, at another junction at 12.2 miles go right (uphill) on non-gravel and maybe rough and rude road. At 14.8 miles heave a sigh at the road-end and trailhead a few feet from the pond humorously called Section 3 "Lake," elevation approximately 6000 feet.

Trail No. 1130 is a dream, traversing wildflowers and Christmas trees and creeklets and many a lovely camp. At 2¼ miles is a junction with the trail from Conrad Meadows. From here the way winds up through gaudy rocks and cold-snowy nooks with a different array of flowers and still more possible camps and at 3¾ miles attains the summit. Look out to the great volcanoes of Rainier and Adams. Look around you, back down Pinegrass Ridge and to Devils Horns, Tieton, Old Snowy, and Gilbert and realize you are smack in the middle of a volcano that was worn out and broken down eons before St. Helens was so much as a puff of steam in a lowland swamp.

Mt. Rainier from lookout site on Bear Creek Mountain

60 Meade Glacier- Conrad Glacier

Round trip to Tieton-Conrad divide
  16 miles
Allow 3 days
High point 6000 feet
Elevation gain 2100 feet
Best July to October
USGS White Pass (part only), Forest
  Service Goat Rocks Wilderness
Forest Service wilderness permit required

Two glaciers on 8201-foot Gilbert Peak are sublimely scenic. So are black and gray and brown cliffs of Gilbert and Moon Mountain and yellow and red cliffs of Tieton Peak and brick-red spires of Devils Horns. But first the hiker must pass through miles and miles of cow pies and horse apples, an experience that on a hot day requires a stiff upper lip. Moreover, this area was directly in the mainline of 1980 ashing and for years the lower trails will be stirred to clouds of dust by passage of feet and hooves and the camps will be sandy.

Drive US 12 east from White Pass 19 miles, to just short of Hause Creek Campground, and turn right on South Fork Tieton road No. 143, heading back westward along Rimrock Lake. At 4½ miles turn left on road No. 133 and stay with it at

A shoulder of Gilbert Peak

all junctions. At 18 miles the road is gated at the edge of private property. Park here, elevation 3900 feet.

South Fork Tieton trail No. 1120 passes the gate, fords Short Creek and Long Creek, at a junction with Tenday trail goes right, and enters Conrad Meadows, one of the largest subalpine valley-bottom meadows in the Cascades. In the summer after The Blast, when ash kept out the cows, the vastness of lush, table-flat greenery glowed with approximately 17½ googols of flowers. However, except after eruptions this Paradise is closely cropped and reekingly flopped. Additionally, in the late 1970s some of the stupidest logging in the history of the world commenced in scraggly forests edging the meadows. The entirety of the valley ultimately must be added to the Goat Rocks Wilderness.

At 1¼ miles trail No. 1120 (beware of misleading cow paths and cat roads) hits the logging road, turns left, and crosses the South Fork Tieton on remnants of a truck bridge; when this is finally gone, expect a ford that in early summer will be quite formidable. Where the road heads uphill (a private section was logged in the early 1970s by Boise Cascade) the trail goes off right. At 2 miles it fords the South Fork, here a mere creek. The way alternates between open forest and small meadows to enter Goat Rocks Wilderness at 3 miles and at 4¼ miles, 4250 feet, reach a junction in a hellebore meadow. Campsites here.

Goat Rocks trail No. 1132 goes right, across the meadow, ascends steeply and roughly to the crest of the divide ridge between the South Fork Tieton and Conrad Creek, and proceeds gently to a 6000-foot saddle about 3 miles from the junction; here it drops off the ridge to headwaters of the South Fork.

From the junction, trail No. 1120 fords the South Fork and switchbacks steeply to Surprise Lake, 5300 feet, 6 miles, a fishy hole in the woods stomped and fouled by horses whose owners don't give a darn. Nicer camping is a bit beyond the lake, where the trail opens out in meadows on its ascent across the valley head to the 6000-foot saddle, attained at about 8 miles.

The saddle is the end of trail-hiking, the start of off-trail roaming in all directions: to the Meade Glacier, to Warm Lake, to the Conrad Glacier, to Cold Lake.

Many fine and private camps are scattered about. However, the fragile meadows are so readily churned by hooves that the Forest Service **must** ban horses; it should build a corral at the 6000-foot saddle and tell all comers that to go beyond they must park and walk.

COWLITZ RIVER

61 Trails End
(Purcell Mountain)

Round trip via Purcell Mountain trail
　16 miles
Allow 2 days
High point 5442 feet
Elevation gain 4500 feet
Best July through November
USGS Randle

Round trip via lookout trail 7 miles
Hiking time 6 hours (unless maintained)
Elevation gain 2600 feet
Best mid-June through November
One day or backpack

A basin of subalpine trees and a large flower-covered meadow, topped by 5442-foot Purcell Mountain, site of Trails End Lookout. Nothing remains except melted glass, nails, a few bits of rusty iron, a heliport, and a panorama of the South Cascades.

A few years back the Forest Service built a logging road to the 3500-foot level. Hikers complained but it did no good—or did it? Since then a switch has been made

Whalehead Ridge from Purcell Mountain trail

from roading to helicopter logging, small solace for the trees but it does preserve the trail system.

There are two approaches, the long Purcell Mountain trail which traverses the entire length of the mountain, and the lookout trail climbing directly to the summit. Snow remains on the longer route until early July but the direct route can be hiked in mid-June, with only a few snowpatches up high.

Drive US 12 east from Randle toward Packwood. For the Purcell Mountain trail, at 5.6 miles, where the highway skirts the mountain, find the trailhead, elevation 920 feet. Park on the south side of the highway 75 yards east of the trailhead. The way crosses private land; if the owners say NO TRESPASSING, take the other trail, described below.

The trail starts from the valley bottom and switchbacks upward in a 160-year-old stand of timber, gaining 2500 feet in 3 miles. The trees provide shade but the slope faces south and has no dependable water, so carry loaded canteens. At 3 miles the trail passes "The Gate"—a local landmark though the gate has been gone a long time—and makes a big switchback. The way is still up, but the views improve. At 3½ miles is a junction with a path to springs and open meadows, 4400 feet, under Cockscomb Mountain. Now the trail levels off, still in timber, ascending slightly under 5065-foot Prairie Mountain. At approximately 5 miles is Little Paradise, 4800 feet, a small meadow surrounded by tall trees; water and camps can be found a bit below the meadow.

What to do now? One choice is to wander the short distance up Prairie Mountain; all but the summit and steep south side are wooded. The other choice is to continue 3 more miles to the top of Purcell Mountain and the panoramas.

For the lookout trail, continue .3 mile past the Purcell Mountain trailhead, turn left on an unmarked paved road (the old highway), and in 1 mile turn left on road No. 63. In a mile look over the side of the Davis Creek bridge into a spectacular canyon. At 4½ miles from the paved road (11½ miles from Randle) bear left onto road No. 6310 and in ½ mile cross Davis Creek and a short distance farther find the trailhead, elevation 2800 feet.

The route follows an abandoned road. In about ¹⁄₃ mile the trail doubles back to the right off the road and zigzags upward through a clearing, then forest. At 2½ miles the way reaches meadows and continues upward. At 3 miles, 5000 feet, just before the junction with the Purcell Mountain trail, is a possible camp. A final ½ mile climbs to the summit.

	OLD	NEW
Davis Creek road	1303	63
Spur road	1303C	6310

COWLITZ RIVER

62 Klickitat Trail

One-way trip 16 miles
Allow 2-3 days
High point 5400 feet
Elevation gain 4000 feet
Best mid-July through October
USGS Tower Rock

Tradition says this is part of the trail followed by the Klickitats on trading excursions from their homes east of the Cascades, climbing from the Klickitat River to Cispus Pass (Hike 66), then descending to Puget Sound country.

But the European has come, and though the trail is lonesome, seldom is it beyond sight or sound of logging. The way is paralleled by logging roads, cut once by a road (near Jackpot Lake), and hacked by several clearcuts. Only time will tell whether the Forest Service will adopt true multiple-use and preserve this rewarding trail.

To reach the west terminus of the trail, turn south in Randle, cross the Cowlitz River, and in 1 mile keep left on road No. 23. At 6 miles turn left on road No. 55 and in 15 miles (from Randle) turn left on road No. 5508.024 and in 1 mile find the trailhead on the left side of the road, elevation 4000 feet.

To reach the east terminus, drive State Highway 12 south from Packwood 2½ miles, turn east on Johnson Creek road No. 21, and in 16½ miles (from Packwood), just beyond Hugo Lake, turn right on road No. 22 and in 3½ miles reach the trailhead, elevation approximately 4000 feet.

Signs at both ends call it "Klickitat Trail No. 7." By consulting a current Forest Service map, hikers can intersect the trail by climbing clearcuts from logging roads, but in doing so would lose a lot of the fun. The mileages and elevations given here are estimates; there are some mile markers along the route, but no indication where the counting starts.

From the west terminus, the trail climbs 500 feet, follows the ridge top, and in a bit more than a mile drops steeply to a clearcut. Once beyond this, the way passes under

OLD	NEW
121	55
123	23
1302	21
1111	22
1216B	5508.024

Mt. Rainier from Cispus Point

5805-foot Twin Sisters and at about 4 miles, 5200 feet, comes to a junction with the Pompey Peak trail.

The next 1½ miles are a glorious combination of alpine meadows and forest groves. Castle Butte towers above. At Cispus Point, 5½ miles, are campsites. An absolute must is the ½-mile sidetrip to the site of the old lookout and wide views of Rainier, Adams, St. Helens, Hood, and ridge upon forested ridge.

Now the trail descends into timber, dropping almost 1000 feet to Jackpot Lake, 6 miles, 4500 feet, and another logging mess. A traverse near the top of a 5500-foot butte offers more views. At 8 miles the route drops into headwaters of Deception Creek, crosses clearcuts, and at 9 miles contours under Horseshoe Point and gradually ascends to a saddle below 5733-foot Cold Springs Butte. Along here the tread is particularly faint and appears unwalked in years. The short sidetrip to the summit of the butte is well worth the effort.

The path drops through forest to campsites at St. Michael Lake, 10½ miles, 4700 feet, contours past tiny St. John Lake, climbs nearly over the top of 5683-foot Mission Mountain, and goes downward in trees, passing a junction with the Elk Peak trail at 15¾ miles and at 17 miles reaching the east terminus on road No. 22.

COWLITZ RIVER

63 Packwood Lake

Round trip to Packwood Lake 9 miles
Hiking time 5 hours
High point 3100 feet
Elevation gain 400 feet, loss 300 feet
Best June through November
One day or backpack
USGS Packwood

Round trip to Lost Lake 18¼ miles
Allow 2 days
High point 5165 feet
Elevation gain 2300 feet
Best July through October

A tree-ringed lake on the edge of the Goat Rocks Wilderness. From the outlet, look up to 7487-foot Johnson Peak. From the inlet, look back to Mt. Rainier. A wooded island punctuates the picturesque waters.

Unfortunately, man has left his disastrous mark on this scenic treasure. Washington Public Power Supply System was allowed to dam the outlet to gain a small amount of "peaking" power and the Federal Power Commission mysteriously gave permission for the dam to be built 3 feet higher than specified in the agreement with the Forest Service. So far the power company has not been permitted to raise the lake above the natural level; if it ever is, the shore will be ruined.

Additionally, the trail was built so wide and flat and easy that every weekend the lake is overwhelmed by little children, old folk, motorbikers, horsemen, all jumbled together. Near the outlet are a small resort and a few campsites—terribly overcrowded. To avoid standing room only, visit the lake on a weekday; otherwise, pause amid the crowds to enjoy the view, then hike onward to Lost Lake.

Thanks to an easy trail, the lake is heavily used by hikers and horses. Though motorcycles are forbidden on the trail, they race up and down the adjoining pipeline road.

From Packwood, next to the Packwood Ranger Station, drive east on road No.

	OLD	NEW
	1320	1260

1260, in 6 miles coming to a steel tower and, nearby, a large parking lot and the trailhead, elevation 2700 feet.

Trail No. 78 goes gently through big trees with occasional views over the Cowlitz valley toward Rainier, passing several springs in the first half—but the second half is dry, so carry water. As the lake is neared, the snowy, craggy Goat Rocks can be seen at the valley head. With ups and downs grossing 400 feet but netting only 167 feet, at 4¼ miles the trail reaches Packwood Lake, 2867 feet.

For less jammed-up camping continue 4¾ miles to tiny Mosquito Lake, 4800 feet, or Lost Lake, 5165 feet, surrounded by alpine trees and flowery meadows.

For an extra-special treat, do a 12½-mile loop from Packwood Lake. Hike to Lost Lake and contour airy miles along 6700-foot Coyote Ridge on trail No. 79 to Packwood Saddle, 5520 feet. Return to Packwood Lake on Upper Lake trail No. 81. About half the distance is in steep meadows high above timberline. The way is little traveled, very odd considering the number of people at the lake and the superb scenery of the loop.

Packwood Lake and Johnson Peak

64 Lily Basin-Heart Lake

Round trip to viewpoint 8 miles
Hiking time 5 hours
High point 5700 feet
Elevation gain 1300 feet
Best late July to mid-October
One day
USGS Packwood

Round trip to Heart Lake 13 miles
Hiking time 8 hours
High point 6100 feet
Elevation gain 1700 feet in, 400 out
Backpack

Hike a forest ridge to a spectacular view of Packwood Lake and Mt. Rainier, then contour Lily Basin, a high cirque under Johnson Peak, and continue to Heart Lake and views of Mt. Adams. Logging roads to 4500 feet have ripped up the wildland and taken most of the work out of visiting this once-remote corner of the Goat Rocks.

Drive US 12 from Packwood Ranger Station west toward Randle 1.6 miles, passing the Packwood Lumber Company, and approximately opposite a small power substation turn left on road No. 48. Follow it 9 miles and turn left and stay on No. 48 another 1.2 miles to the trailhead, on the right side of the road. Park on a wide shoulder just beyond, elevation about 4400 feet.

The trail is signed "Lily Basin Trail No. 86." Climbing through timber to an old burn, at ½ mile the way enters Goat Rocks Wilderness and at 1½ miles reaches the crest of a wooded ridge, 4900 feet. The path follows ups and downs of the crest, more ups than downs, occasionally contouring around a bump. At 4 miles, 5700 feet, begin heather and flower meadows with a spectacular view of Packwood Lake and Rainier. At 4½ miles the trail dips under cliffs and regains the ridge top, following to its very end at Johnson Peak.

Now a mile-long contour around the head of Lily Basin leads over several creeks (the first water of the trip) and a large rockslide. At 6 miles, 6100 feet, the path tops a ridge with magnificent views of Mt. Adams. Here, joined by the Angry Mountain trail, it contours a steep slope and drops to Heart Lake, 5700 feet, 6½ miles, the first logical campsite.

The trip can be extended—trail No. 86 continues to Jordan Basin, Goat Lake, and Snowgrass Flat (Hike 66).

OLD	NEW
132	48
1323	48

Packwood Lake and Mt. Rainier from Lily Basin trail

Tatoosh Lake and Mt. Rainier

COWLITZ RIVER

65 Tatoosh Ridge

Round trip to viewpoint 6 miles
Hiking time 4 hours
High point 5400 feet
Elevation gain 2600 feet
Best July through September
One day; possible camping at lake
USGS Packwood

A long ridge with flower meadows and a beautiful lake lies under the dominance of Mt. Rainier, giving views not only of The Mountain but the backside of the Tatoosh Range, whose peaks are familiar as seen from Paradise but except for Pinnacle are difficult to recognize from here. On the highest point is the site of the Tatoosh Lookout made famous in the 1940s by Martha Hardy's bestselling book, **Tatoosh**, the story of her years as a fire lookout. (The book was reprinted in the 1980s.) "Belonging" to Rainier National Park but outside the boundaries, the ridge has been proposed for addition to the Park by both the Forest and Park Services, but to date nothing has been done about it.

The trail covers the full length of the ridge, starting in the south near Packwood and ending in the north on a logging road near the Park boundary. If transportation can be arranged, the entire distance can be done on one trip. It is described here from a north-end start because that way has 1000 feet less elevation gain.

From Packwood Ranger Station at the north end of Packwood, drive west on Skate Creek road No. 52. In ½ mile cross the Cowlitz River. (To start on the south end of the ridge, cross the bridge and turn right on Cannon road which eventually becomes road No. 5290. Follow this upriver 9 miles and turn right on road No. 5292 for 1.2 miles to the trailhead.) For the north end continue on Skate Creek road 4 miles from the ranger station (sign says 3), turn north on road No. 5270, and drive 5.8 miles to a junction, and there continue ahead on No. 5272 for 1.5 miles to the trailhead, elevation 2800 feet.

Trail No. 161 sets off at a steep grade, gaining about 1800 feet in 2 miles, climbing from Douglas fir forest to Alaska cedar and mountain hemlock. At about 2½ miles begin steep alpine meadows, covered in season with colorful blossoms. The trail makes three short switchbacks up a small stream, the only water on the main route—and maybe none here late in summer. Shortly beyond is an unmarked junction. Proceed straight ahead but keep the junction in mind for later reference. Tread may be lost in lush greenery and soft pumice; just keep going and eventually gain a ridge shoulder, 5400 feet, and a spectacular view of Mt. Adams, St. Helens, and the Cowlitz valley. To the north Mt. Rainier looks down like a benevolent old lady, very fat.

After soaking up views, there are things to do, more to see. For one, continue on the trail another 1½ miles and find the mile-long spur trail climbing to the Tatoosh Lookout site at 6310 feet, highest point on the ridge outside the Park. Second, retrace steps to that unmarked junction and follow an old trail to the Park boundary. Or, if experienced in wildland navigation and possessed of the USGS map, try to find Tatoosh Lakes, a small one and a large one, on the east side of Tatoosh Ridge. From the aforementioned junction an unmarked trail of sorts switchbacks up, crosses a 5500-foot saddle, and drops to the lakes near the outlet. But the trail can be hard to follow and cliffs make cross-country travel tricky.

	OLD	NEW
Skate Creek road	152	52
	1412	5290
	1412A	5292
	1411	5270
	1411B	5272

Mt. Adams and Pacific Crest Trail near Snowgrass Flat

CISPUS RIVER

66 Snowgrass Flat

Round trip to Snowgrass Flat 8 miles
Hiking time 5 hours
High point 5700 feet
Elevation gain 1100 feet
Best July through November
One day or backpack
USGS Walupt Lake
Forest Service wilderness permit required

One of the most famous meadows in the Cascades, a riot of color during flower season. But when the flowers are gone the vast parklands higher up, with views of Adams, St. Helens, and of course, the Goat Rocks, still make the trip a genuine spectacular.

Drive US 12 south from Packwood 2.5 miles and turn east on Johnson Creek road No. 21. At 15.7 miles turn left on road No. 2150 and at 18.5 miles keep right on road No.

2150-014, in 19 miles from Packwood coming to Berry Patch and the trailhead, elevation 4600 feet.

Set out in the woods on Snowgrass Flat trail No. 96A, contouring the slopes of Goat Ridge to a junction with trail No. 96 and then a crossing of Goat Creek, 4700 feet. Especially in early summer, stop at the bridge to apply insect repellent, lots of it, because from here the trail passes for ¼ mile through marshy forest where one may expect heavy attack by swarms of mosquitoes.

At 2 miles the trail begins climbing from the valley bottom, leaving behind the hordes of hungry bugs. At Bypass Camp, 3½ miles, cross Snowgrass Creek and continue up, emerging occasionally from trees into small meadows, and at 4 miles finally entering the open expanse of Snowgrass Flat, 5700 feet.

Because of overgrazing by horses and punishment by heavy foot traffic, and to give nature a chance to repair the damage, camping is no longer permitted in the Flat; however, Bypass Camp is only minutes below and, alpine camps a short way above, either makes a fine base for exploratory walks. From the Flat hike another ½ mile and about 400 feet higher to join the Pacific Crest Trail. Campsites in the meadows here offer wide views, including all three southern volcanoes.

What to do now? For one choice, hike 2 miles south on the Crest Trail into the vast meadows of Cispus Basin and to Cispus Pass, 6473 feet, and superb views down the Klickitat River and out to 8201-foot Gilbert Peak.

Alternately, hike the Crest Trail north to its 7600-foot high point on the side of Old Snowy (Hike 68). Or, for a loop trip back to Berry Patch, total distance 13 miles, traverse to 6500-foot Goat Lake (sitting in a cold cirque and frozen most of most summers) and return by way of Goat Ridge.

The heaviest ashfall in an alpine area except on St. Helens itself buried the Snowgrass Flats vicinity in 1980. Few flowers bloomed that summer and much of the heather was killed. Paintbrush and lupine made a great show in 1981. It will be interesting to watch the meadows recover from the blast—as they have from many others of the like—and worse—over the centuries and eons.

OLD	NEW
1302	21
1104	2150
1118	2150-014

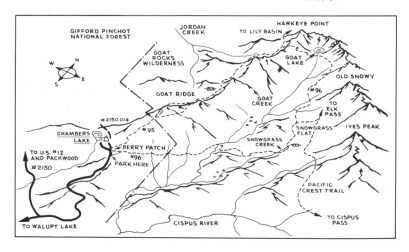

CISPUS RIVER

67 Nannie Ridge

Round trip to Nannie Peak 7 miles
Hiking time 4½ hours
High point 5800 feet
Elevation gain 1800 feet
Best July to October
One day
USGS Walupt Lake

Round trip to Sheep Lake 12 miles
Hiking time 8 hours
High point 5700 feet
Elevation gain 2300 feet
Best late July through September
One day or backpack
Forest Service wilderness permit required

A long hike through meadowland to a small lake, then on to views into the head of the Klickitat River and up to the rugged pinnacles of 8201-foot Gilbert Peak, highest in the Goat Rocks; or an easy day hike to Nannie Peak, overlooking meadows and summits of the Goat Rocks.

Drive US 12 south from Packwood 2.5 miles and turn east on Johnson Creek road No. 63. At 18.5 miles (from Packwood) turn left on road No. 2160. At 20.5 miles the good logging road turns off and the No. 2160 continues to Walupt Lake at 24 miles, elevation 3927 feet. Find the trailhead in the Walupt Lake Picnic Area.

Start on trail No. 101 and in a few yards turn left on Nannie Ridge trail No. 98 and begin to climb. The first 1½ miles are through timber, passing two small streams—the last water for 3 miles. At about 2 miles the trees thin out; the next mile is miserably rutted. At about 3 miles the way tops a 5600-foot ridge. On the very crest an unmarked, unmaintained, but quite decent trail climbs in ½ mile to Nannie Peak, 6106 feet, site of a former lookout. The summit is a ¼-mile ridge of heather, grass, alpine trees, and rocks. Be sure to explore the full length—from the south end are views of Adams and St. Helens and from the north end views of Gilbert Peak and vast meadows.

	OLD	NEW
Johnson Creek road	1302	63
	1114	2160

152

Sheep Lake and Mt. Adams

Those who choose the longer trip now must lose a discouraging 300 feet as the main trail drops under cliffs. At 3½ miles is a pond (which may dry up in late summer) and another trail, also unmarked, switchbacking to the summit of Nannie Peak. A short bit beyond the pond look down on a small lake, about 500 feet below the trail, a tempting place to camp. After passing below more cliffs of Nannie, the way regains the ridge and meadow country and follows ups and downs of the crest to lovely little Sheep Lake, 5¾ miles, 5710 feet, surrounded by grass and flowers, an ideal camp. The best sites are on the ridge to the west beside a row of protecting trees. Walk around the shore for views of Adams and St. Helens.

A visit to a viewpoint above the Klickitat River is mandatory. There are two choices. For one, hike the ridge almost directly north a long mile to its summit at 6512 feet. The other alternative is to find the Pacific Crest Trail on the north side of the lake and follow it northward 1½ miles to where it crosses a small pass into Klickitat drainage. For a return follow the Crest Trail south and take trail No. 101 back to the starting point.

Gilbert Peak from the Pacific Crest Trail

CISPUS RIVER

68 Goat Rocks Crest

One-way trip 30 miles
Allow 3-4 days
High point 7600 feet
Elevation gain 5300 feet
Best July through September
USGS White Pass
Forest Service wilderness permit required

Walk a rock garden between heaven and earth on a narrow, 7000-foot ridge dividing Eastern and Western Washington. This spectacular section of the Pacific Crest Trail is popular with horseriders, so try it in the first half of July, when the tread is free enough of snow for safe hiking but not yet passable to horses; tiny alpine flowers are then in bloom, too. The climax portion can be done as a round trip of about 8 miles from Snowgrass Flat (Hike 66), but the route is described here in its full length from White Pass to Walupt Lake.

Drive to White Pass, elevation 4400 feet, and hike 7 miles south on the Pacific Crest Trail to Shoe Lake (Hike 57).

From Shoe Lake the trail crosses a low ridge and drops 900 feet into forest, then ascends and contours to Tieton Pass, 12 miles, and a junction with the North Fork

Tieton River trail. Going only slightly up and down, the way proceeds on or near the crest to a Y at 13½ miles. The left (the old Crest Trail) contours 1 mile to a dead-end in McCall Basin, 5200 feet, with overused camps and much good off-trail exploring. The new Crest Trail steeply ascends 2 long miles to Elk Pass, 6600 feet. One great compensation for the energy output is that the entire way is in open country with views of Mt. Rainier and miles of meadowland on the slopes of Coyote Ridge to the west. The last campsites for 3½ miles are in flat meadows before the final drag to the pass, at which is a junction with the Coyote Ridge trail (Hike 63).

Views broaden at the pass—down to Packwood Lake and across the immense depth of Lake Creek to rugged Johnson Peak. The trail follows the ridge several hundred feet higher and then descends. From here one senses the quality of the route ahead. The tread can be seen—blasted out of cliffs, gouged in scree slopes; in some places the crest of the ridge has actually been leveled off to give walking room.

The next 2 miles are mostly above 7000 feet, the highest Washington section of the Crest Trail and also the most dangerous. Meeting a horse party is bad business, because the horses cannot be turned around and thus hikers must backtrack to a safe turnout. Snowstorms can be expected in any month. Two parties of recent years have lost a member from hypothermia and there have been several narrow escapes. Don't attempt this section in poor weather.

The trail first contours and climbs to a 7100-foot point with a view of weird-shaped towers and small glaciers on 8201-foot Gilbert Peak, highest in the Goat Rocks. There is also a fine view of Old Snowy, 7930 feet. Nooks and crannies hold the superb rock gardens, which are in full bloom during early July.

The way now follows ups and downs of the narrow crest, sometimes on the exact top and other times swinging around small knobs. From a spot a little beyond the lowest portion, it is possible to avoid a climb by contouring across the Packwood Glacier and rejoining the trail where several signs can be seen in a saddle on the skyline. The glacier crossing is easy in July, but by late August may involve hard ice; the best plan is to stay with the trail on its ascent to the highest elevation at 7600 feet on Old Snowy, a short sidetrip away from the 7930-foot summit.

The trail now descends. At 6900 feet is a rock shelter built by the Bellevue Presbyterian Church in memory of Dana May Yelverton, who died of exposure on the crest August 4, 1962. Winter snows have been hard on the building, which seems fated for early collapse.

From the cabin the path drops into parkland, at 21 miles intersecting the Snowgrass Flat trail (Hike 66), then contouring into the glory of Cispus Basin. The route continues in meadows to the Nannie Ridge trail at 24 miles, and then by this trail 6 miles to Walupt Lake, as described in Hike 67.

CISPUS RIVER

69 Adams Glacier Meadows

Round trip 11 miles
Hiking time 7 hours
High point 6900 feet
Elevation gain 2300 feet
Best mid-July through mid-October
One day or backpack
Forest Service Mt. Adams Wilderness
Forest Service wilderness permit required

Parklands, meadows, waterfalls, and moraines, close views of lava cliffs, cinder cones, and glaciers, distant views of St. Helens and Rainier, all this and more in a paradise for wandering high on the slopes of Mt. Adams. The hike leads to a magnificent alpine camp used by summit climbers, a place variously called Mountaineer Camp, Adams Glacier Camp, or High Camp. Snow still covers some of the meadows in early July, but tiny alpine flowers are then blooming in the highest gardens and beargrass down lower. Later in the summer more of the meadows are open for roaming and the country is superb in every month on through autumn.

Drive south, then east from Randle 32 miles on road No. 23 and turn left on road No. 2329. In 2 miles from the junction pass Taklakh Lake and at 5.7 miles (37.7 miles from Randle) find the parking area and trailhead, elevation 4600 feet.

Killen Creek trail No. 113 ascends toward the mountain in subalpine forest on a wide ridge. Occasionally the crest steepens and the path does likewise. At about 3 miles, 5800 feet, the way enters meadowland with the first dependable creek and remains of an old cabin. The camping here, just inside the Mt. Adams Wilderness, is wonderful, but there is better to come. In 3½ miles cross abandoned tread of the Pacific Crest Trail; a short bit farther is a reflecting pond and a junction with the new Crest Trail, elevation 6100 feet.

Beyond the junction the trail continues upward sometimes in alpine trees, sometimes in grassy meadows dotted in season by paintbrush, hellebore, and avalanche lilies, generally following slopes of a prominent ridge trending toward the peak. The tread soon becomes faint and in ½ mile one may be tempted by the wide-open terrain to forget the sketchy path and roam at will. Do so if desired, but be sure to take careful visual "fixes" on landmarks so the trail can be found again on the way out—from up high one ridge looks like the next and it's easy to get confused.

At 5½ miles the trail ends at High Camp, 6900 feet, near a saddle in the main ridge

OLD	NEW
101	2329
123	23

Mt. Adams and meadow

and not far above the green flats and meandering streams of Adams Glacier Meadows. The camp area lies along a snowmelt stream bubbling through gardens decorated with lava boulders and wind-sculpted clumps of trees. And the views! St. Helens, Rainier, and the Goat Rocks rise above forests and ridges of the Cispus River. Look north into the crater of Potato Hill, an old cinder cone, and out over ancient lava flows covered by scrubby trees. Especially look up to steep ice of the Adams Glacier cascading from the summit. Sunsets from this camp are beyond words—and also the dawns.

Spend a day or weekend or longer. Follow a waterfall down to the delights of Glacier Meadows. Follow the ridge up past lava cliffs, waterfalls, meadows, moraines to the edge of the Adams Glacier. Climb higher onto the crest of the northwest ridge of Adams and look down to the Lava Glacier, and look up to the summit of the great volcano and out to far horizons.

Much of the way back to the road the trail points straight at Rainier, some compensation for having to leave these heavenly meadows.

CISPUS RIVER

70 Juniper Mountain

Round trip to Juniper Peak 8 miles
Hiking time 5 hours
High point 5593 feet
Elevation gain 2000 feet
Best mid-June through November
One day
USGS McCoy Peak

Round trip to Boundary Trail 26 miles
Allow 3 days
High point about 5788 feet
**Elevation gain 2300 feet, plus ups and
    downs**
Best July through October

Dramatic views up the Cispus River to Mt. Adams, out to Mt. Rainier and Mt. St. Helens, and over endless forested hills and valleys—all while walking a long ridge, sometimes on open hillsides covered with huckleberries, sometimes in young forest just getting established after the tremendous Cispus fires of 1902 and 1929. The route provides a variety of trips: an easy afternoon stroll to a 4500-foot saddle (the trail this

Beargrass on Juniper Peak, Mt. Adams in distance

far generally is free of snow in early or mid-June); a day hike to Juniper Mountain; an overnight backpack; or a long approach to the Boundary Trail (Hike 71). Warning: The prospecting underway along McCoy Creek holds the possibility of wrecking the trail.

Turn south in Randle, cross the Cowlitz River, and drive 1 mile. Turn left on road No. 23 and in 9 miles (from Randle) turn right on road No. 28. At 10 miles leave pavement and keep straight ahead on road No. 29. In 14 miles turn left on road No. 2904 and at 18 miles find the trailhead, elevation about 3500 feet.

The trail goes a few hundred feet through a clearcut, enters second-growth forest, and climbs under two prominent knolls, ascending steadily, with frequent views, 2¼ miles to a 4500-foot saddle. The trail continues climbing, gaining 1100 feet to within a few feet of the top of 5593-foot Juniper Peak (4 miles, a good turnaround for day hikers), then, dropping about 400 feet, goes under cliffs. At 5½ miles is a super-great huckleberry patch—outstanding even in an area famous for huckleberries. At 5¾ miles pass a tiny lake and campsites.

At 7 miles is the Sunrise Peak trail, a ¼-mile sidetrip up a steep stairway with handrails to the 5880-foot site of a former lookout; by the junction is a fair camp. At 7¾ miles, on a big saddle in the ridge, is Old Cow Camp with water and scenic camping. The trail again drops several hundred feet and passes under cliffs of 5788-foot Jumbo Peak, 9 miles, then descends to Dark Meadows, 12 miles, 4300 feet, offering plenty of water and campsites. From here a trail drops 3½ miles to road No. 23.

From Dark Meadows the trail proceeds ¾ mile to good campsites in a large basin and in ¼ mile more reaches the Boundary Trail at a point 2 miles from the road at McCoy Pass.

Note the many sawn stumps along the ridge to Juniper. These are not from logging but the cutting of old snags, which in the old Smoky Bear Dogma had to be eliminated lest they draw lightning and flame like torches. Contemporary foresters know that snags are the feeding and nesting headquarters of many important birds.

OLD	NEW
123	23
112	28
111	29
1106	2904

CISPUS RIVER

71 Boundary Trail

One-way trip 37 miles
Allow 4-6 days
High point 5000 feet
Elevation gain about 4700 feet
Best July through October
USGS Spirit Lake, French Butte, McCoy
    Peak, and Steamboat Mountain

A National Scenic Trail (so designated in 1979) that eventually will start at Mt. Adams, follow the crest of the Lewis River-Cispus River watershed, and finish at Mt. St. Helens. Currently, part of the way near Adams lies along roads, but 37 miles are complete. At six places roads cut the route, which therefore can be traveled in small sections if desired. The final stretch suffered a serious accident in 1980. For a good sample of the country, hike from McCoy Creek to Elk Pass.

The hike can be taken in either direction, depending on whether one prefers to watch Adams or St. Helens grow larger and the other smaller. The east-to-west direction is described here.

Turn south in Randle, cross the Cowlitz River, and drive 1 mile. Turn left 33 miles on road No. 23 to Council Lake, 4200 feet, and find the head of trail No. 1.

The way starts with a steep climb up the abandoned Council Bluff road, then gradually drops to a stream crossing at 4½ miles and again goes up. At 6¾ miles round Table Mountain, at 8½ miles pass Prairie Mountain and a good camp, climb a few hundred feet, and drop to campsites at Dark Meadows. Climb again to a 4000-foot saddle at 12 miles and descend to McCoy Creek road No. 29, 14½ miles, 3800 feet. At 15½ miles are more camps in a basin south of the trail, which then rises steadily to 16½ miles. A bit beyond, keep left on new tread ascending to a 4800-foot viewpoint, 17 miles, then skirting below impressive cliffs of Hat Rock while dropping to 4000-foot Yellowjacket Pass; campsites here a few feet to the south.

At 21½ miles pass under 4800-foot Craggy Peak, next under Shark Rock, and with little change in elevation contour slopes of 5659-foot Badger Peak to Badger Lake, 25½ miles; numerous good camps. At 29½ miles reach Mosquito Meadows. The trail continues, crossing road No. 25 at Elk Pass, 3900 feet, 30½ miles.

OLD	NEW
123	23
111	29
125	25

Mt. Adams from side of Hat Mountain

In case the way is legal when you arrive: The trail enters timber but soon emerges into a clearcut and follows a spur road ¼ mile before reverting to footpath and trees. At 33½ miles the route again strikes a road and goes along it almost 2 miles, partly on forest road and partly on a jeep track, crossing a stream at 34½ miles and at 35½ miles intersecting Spirit Lake road and traversing a large clearcut. At 36½ miles re-enter forest; the tread here is cut into soft pumice — easy on the feet but slow walking, like mushy snow. (Note: this comment predates the Great Blast of 1980!) At about 37 miles the way vanishes in the explosion area.

For nostalgia's sake, here's how the route used to conclude: ". . . pass three small streams (but no possible camps) and at 38 miles reach a ridge. There switchback up a slope burned in 1961, and at 39½ miles cross road No. 100 and pass an undeveloped path to Ghost Lake, a ½-mile sidetrip. At 40 miles top the ridge and start down into Green River drainage, at 41½ miles reaching Meta Lake, 3600 feet, and campsites. At 42½ miles reach Independence Pass, 4000 feet, from which the trail drops to Spirit Lake, 3188 feet, 44½ miles. Walk the lakeshore trail 1 mile to Duck Bay boat launching area and the road."

Cultus Lake and Lemei Rock

TROUT LAKE

72 Indian Heaven

Short loop trip 10 miles
Hiking time 6 hours
High point 5237 feet
Elevation gain about 1700 feet
Best July through October
One day or backpack
USGS Lone Butte and Wind River

A fascinating portion of the Pacific Crest Trail, with 17 lakes big enough to have names, 6 more on a short sidetrail, and almost 100 smaller lakes, ponds, and tadpole pools, all in an area of around 5000 feet elevation, a mixture of forest, groves of alpine trees, and flat, grassy meadows, the foregrounds complemented by occasional glimpses of glaciered volcanoes. The Forest Service is contemplating designating the country from Red Mountain to the Berryfields as a wilderness area.

The region can be sampled by taking a one-day, 10-mile loop hike (described here), an overnight 18-mile loop, or by spending several days in order to include a visit to the Indian Race Track, where the rut made by racing horses still indents a meadow used for centuries as a gathering place. The lakes melt free of snow early in July, but since Indian Heaven has been appropriately called "Mosquito Heaven," the trip is recommended for late August or September when the bugs are gone, and incidentally, the blueberries are ripe.

The starting point is Cultus Creek Campground, elevation 3988 feet, reached from the Randle-Trout Lake road No. 24. Follow signs to the Berryfields. The campground is 3 miles south of the Berryfields on road No. 2400181. The trailhead is in the back of a camp with no provision for hikers' cars, so park either at the guard station or the woodshed, making sure to leave the Forest Service access to its buildings.

Whatever the chosen trip, start on trail No. 33, thus avoiding a very steep and hot ascent of 1200 feet on trail No. 108, which is better used for the return leg of the loop.

Trail No. 33 begins in forest, climbing 600 feet in the first mile. At 1¾ mile make the short sidetrip on trail 33A to Deep Lake with a view of Mt. Adams rising over tree tops, then on to Cultus Lake at 2 miles, 5050 feet, a body of water typical of many of the lakes, having trees around half the shore, meadows around the rest. To the southeast is 5925-foot Lemei Rock, and the northwest, 5706-foot Bird Mountain; one or the other of these peaks can be seen from a number of the lakes. The way climbs 100 more feet, then descends in ½ mile to meet Lemei Lake trail No. 179. Keep right, staying on trail No. 33; in ½ mile pass within a few yards of Clear Lake, coming to Bear Lake at 4 miles. Cross the outlet (no problem) to join the Crest Trail on the far side, the return route for the longer loop. Head north on the Crest Trail, passing Deer Lake and numerous ponds. At about 7½ miles turn right on trail No. 108, climb 100 feet over a 5237-foot saddle in Bird Mountain, and drop steeply 1½ miles to Cultus Creek Campground.

Don't be fooled by the seemingly-flat terrain—the paths have many short ups and downs. Campsites are numerous, some by lakes and others by streams. The pumice soil is very fragile, so camp in the forest or in already established campsites. The lakes and streams have a very small flow of water so to avoid contamination keep camps far away from the water's edge.

OLD	NEW
123	24
N707	2400181

73 Mount Adams Highline

One-way trip from Cold Springs Camp to
  Avalanche Valley 27½ miles
Allow 3-4 days
High point 7760 feet
Elevation gain approximately 4000 feet
Best mid-July through September
Forest Service Mt. Adams Wilderness
Forest Service wilderness permit
  required

Round trip from Killen Creek road to
  Avalanche Valley 26 miles
Allow 3-4 days
High point 7760 feet
Elevation gain 4200 feet

The 34-mile timberline circuit of Mt. Adams is one of the greatest highland walks in the Cascades. Foregrounds of parkland and flowers and waterfalls rise to lava jumbles that look like yesterday's eruptions to a succession of glaciers tumbling from the 12,326-foot summit. By day the hikers look out to miles of forested ridges and three other massive volcanoes. By night they gaze to megalopolitan skyglows of Puget Sound City, Yakima, and Portland.

However, you can't hardly do it. The Great Gap, the 4½ miles between Avalanche

OLD	NEW
FH 17	FH 17
N700	82
N80	80
N81	8051

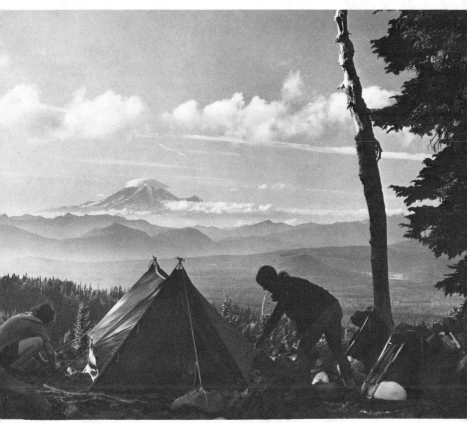

Camping near Foggy Bottom, Mt. Rainier in distance

Valley and Bird Creek Meadows, has a half-dozen major glacial torrents to cross; one, the main branch of the Big Muddy, often requires a dangerous bypass high on the Klickitat Glacier. There never has been and never can be a trail—not without huge expenditures and a miles-long detour down the valley to where bridges could be built (and annually rebuilt).

Moreover, 8 miles of the circuit—including the Gap—lie in the Yakima Indian Reservation and require obtaining a permit from the Yakima Indian Tribal Council in Toppenish, a process as complicated as the Big Muddy. For reasons of safety and politics we advise starting the journey not at Bird Creek Meadows, in the reservation, but at Cold Springs Campground.

From Highway 141 at Trout Lake drive north on road No. FH17, signed "Mt. Adams Recreation Area." Follow signs to Morrison Creek Campground and the end of road No. 8051 at Cold Springs, elevation 5600 feet. Hike 1 mile up abandoned road to Timberline Campground (often with no water) and at 6200 feet intersect the Mount Adams Highline (or Round the Mountain) Trail.

To the right the trail contours 2 miles to the reservation boundary and legendary Bird Creek Meadows; the Yakimas allow day use here for $3 a day. An off-trail, meadow-

Mt. Adams from near Foggy Bottom

contouring mile leads to a viewpoint at 6512 feet, an overlook of Hellroaring valley, this end of the Great Gap.

To the left the trail goes upsy-downsy, mainly in subalpine forest but with many meadow interludes and many vistas and many tempting sidetrips up to moraines and glaciers. Creeks and camps are frequent, though some of the glacial torrents are muddy, requiring the water to be settled in a pot to become palatable; a little milk never hurt anyone and adds body to the drink. At 6½ miles from Timberline Camp the Pacific Crest Trail is joined at Horseshoe Meadow, 5900 feet; a promontory just beyond gives a four-volcano vista, including the trip's last look at Hood.

Sidetrips continue to beckon as the Crest Trail proceeds below little Crystal Lake and above little Sheep Lake, across the awesome Mutton Creek lava flow. At 14½ miles, 6100 feet, is the headwater creek of Lewis River; for a supreme basecamp, amble up the slope to meadowlands and settle down for days of exploring country below the Pinnacle and Adams Glaciers. At 17 miles, 6084 feet, is a junction with Killen Creek trail No. 113 (Hike 69), 3½ miles from the road; for hikers wishing to focus on Avalanche Valley this is the proper approach.

At 18 miles Killen Creek is crossed (camping) and in ¼ mile more Highline Trail No. 114 departs to the right from the Crest Trail, at 20½ miles entering the green flat of Foggy Bottom, 6000 feet, a lovely meadow traversed by a clear brook. Now a stern uphill commences, from forest to the lava chaos below Lava Glacier—whose meltwater torrents may be impossible to cross—and at last tops out in the vast tundra barrens of Devils Gardens, 7760 feet. What a spot! Above are icefalls of Lyman and Wilson Glaciers, below is the volcanic vent of Red Butte. The winds they do howl up here, and the clouds do roll—though giant cairns mark the route, to attempt this saddle in a storm is to court hypothermia. Here, too, the reservation is entered.

The way drops to fine campsites in meadows of the Little Muddy, 7000 feet, 24½ miles, contours to a saddle between Mt. Adams and another volcanic vent, Goat Butte, and drops to Avalanche Valley, 6600 feet, 26½ miles, and trail's end. What's to say about this green vale where cold springs gush from lava tubes and meander through the flowers beneath cold walls of the Wilson and Rusk Glaciers, beetling crags of Battlement Ridge, Victory Ridge, The Spearhead, The Castle, Roosevelt Cliff? Well, when good little hikers finally check in their boots, this is where they go.

Bad little hikers spend eternity in the 4½ miles of The Gap, staggering from moraine boulder to boulder, leaping Big Muddy and Hellroaring, trying to find the one and only semi-easy way over the Ridge of Wonders, never quite attaining Bird Creek Meadows at 34 miles to complete the circuit.

Avalanche Valley in the Yakima Indian Reservation

Mount
St. Helens

On May 18, 1980, Mt. St. Helens ceased to be the "Mt. Fuji of the West," one of the most graceful peaks in the nation. However, it did not stop being—as it long has been—one of the most photographed peaks in the nation. In fact, after explosively lowering its summit from 9677 to 8364 feet, it became almost a bore on television and in the newspapers, magazines, and bookstores. But not in person—the new St. Helens is as awesome and exciting a mountain as there is in the nation, and thousands of Americans have gathered to gape. Among hikers, the eruption was watched with a mixture of dismay and excitement to have actually lived during a time of dramatic change in the earth's crust.

The eruption destroyed the 14-mile trail around Mt. St. Helens, the very popular 3-mile trail to the north end of Spirit Lake, and the 5-mile trail to the site of a former lookout on Coldwater Peak. The trails to Strawberry Ridge and Goat Mountain are still usable but buried under a thick layer of soft ash.

For the first two years the Forest Service established a wide safety zone and no one but scientists and loggers could enter. In 1982 the safety zone was considerably

1977 photograph of Spirit Lake and Mt. St. Helens from the shoulder of Mt. Margaret

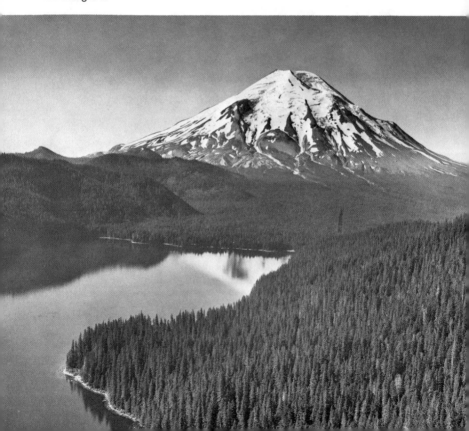

slimmed, thus reopening the Strawberry Ridge and Goat Mountain trails to hikers. The old 100 Road past Meta Lake and Independence Pass was paved, reopened, and renamed Road 99. Future plans call for a trail to Norway Pass giving access to Mt. Margaret. Depending on what the restless volcano is up to, the boundaries of the restricted zone will doubtless be revised many times. This may go on for only another year or two, or 50 years (duration of the last eruption period in the 19th century) or 500 years (duration of the next-to-last eruption period). For the latest information, call either the Randle Ranger Station (206) 497-7565 or the St. Helens Ranger Station (206) 247-5473.

On August 26, 1982, President Reagan signed into law the (too small) 110,000-acre Mt. St. Helens National Volcanic Monument District—to preserve undisturbed an (insufficient) example of nature recovering from the sort of catastrophe that is, in the deep time of the Cascades, a common occurrence, but the only one that has happened in our shallow time, before our very eyes.

1982 photograph of Spirit Lake and Mt. St. Helens from Norway Pass, reached by going cross country from Meta Lake. Note that Spirit Lake is covered with logs.

Observation Peak and Mt. Hood from Sisters Rock

WIND RIVER

74 Observation (Trapper) Peak

Round trip from Government Mineral
  Springs 12 miles
Hiking time 7½ hours
High point 4207 feet
Elevation gain 2900 feet
Best June to October
One day
USGS Lookout Mountain, Wind River

Round trip from road No. 58 6 miles
Hiking time 3 hours
Elevation gain 1600 feet in, 300 feet out

A loop trip through forest from the valley bottom to the 4207-foot summit of Observation Peak, site of the old Trapper Lookout, with a panoramic view of the Wind River valley, or an easier ridge walk with meadows and vistas.

For the loop trip drive Wind River road (county road No. 13) 15 miles north from Carson to Government Mineral Springs. Cross the Wind River and in ¼ mile turn right on road No. 5401 and drive a short distance farther to where the road is gated and find the trailhead, elevation 1300 feet.

Observation Peak trail No. 132 parallels a summer-home road 1 mile to a junction with the Trapper Creek trail. From there the peak trail climbs steeply up the south side of Howe Ridge with fleeting views through trees. At 3 miles cross a small stream which may be the last water. At 4½ miles the way swings around the north side of the ridge. At 6½ miles is a junction with Ridge trail No. 157 (see below). Keep climbing a final ½ mile to the peak and views, views, and more views. For the return go back to the junction with No. 157, follow it west ½ mile, then descend Big Hollow trail No. 158 which runs into Dry Creek trail No. 194, ending at the same trailhead you started from.

For the Ridge Trail drive Wind River road to within ½ mile of Government Mineral Springs, just short of Wind River bridge. Keep right on road No. 30. At 2 miles turn left on Dry Creek road No. 64 for 8 miles, then go left on road No. 58 for 2 more miles and find the trailhead on the east side of the road, elevation 3200 feet.

Ridge trail No. 157 sets out in virgin forest of Sister Rocks Research Natural Area, gaining 800 feet. Then, at about 1 mile, it enters an old burn grown up in huckleberries and flowers and drops 300 feet along the ridge connecting Sisters Rock to Observation (Trapper) Peak. At 1¾ miles is Observation Camp (water is sometimes to be found in a spring on the north side of the ridge). At 2½ miles is the junction with the trail from Government Mineral Springs.

For an interesting sidetrip wander up meadows of flowers and huckleberries to the top of Sister Rocks, 4261 feet. Near the top are traces of an old trail, a few telephone poles, and bits of melted glass, all that remains of Sisters Rock Lookout.

OLD	NEW
30 (county)	13
N73	30
N64	64
N63	58

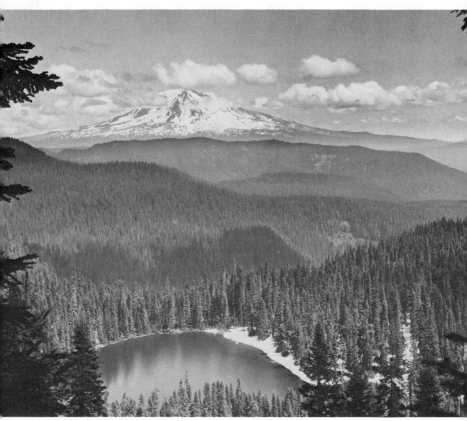

Blue Lake and Mt. Adams

LEWIS RIVER

75 Shark Rock and Craggy Peak

Round trip to Boundary Trail 13 miles
Hiking time 5 hours
High point 5200 feet
Elevation gain 1800 feet
Best mid-July to early November
One day or backpack
USGS Spencer Butte, Quartz Creek, and
   McCoy Peak

Follow a wooded ridge to a mountain lake, 2 miles of alpine meadows, and views, and views, and views. Nowhere else in the State of Washington can one see so vast an expanse of solid virgin forest as in the vista over Straight Creek and Quartz Creek to Mt. Adams; only a few distant clearings far to the south break the solid green. Try this trip early in July; if conditions are right there may be miles of beargrass in bloom.

Note: The Big Show of 1980 dropped 6-8 inches of ash, mostly popcorn size, hereabouts.

The trail is harassed by machines and jeopardized by logging, inclu[...] sale ¼ mile from Blue Lake. That the path has survived until now is due [...] Sierra Club lawsuit. Logging at these high elevations is particularly shocking [...] the timber has relatively little commercial value—a quarter or more of the tr[...] left on the ground to rot after being cut and a new forest may be 150-300 y[...] growing.

From Lewis River Ranger Station on Swift Reservoir, drive north on road No. 2[...] (passing a junction with road No. 92). At 5.6 miles turn right on road No. 9327. Watch all intersections carefully; during logging operations some sideroads are used more than the main road. At 18 miles is a junction with Lewis River road No. 93, with an alternate approach. At 18.7 miles find the trailhead, elevation 3400 feet.

The way starts as trail No. 80, part of the old Spirit Lake—Guler trail. In 1½ up-and-down miles reach an intersection (only ¼ mile from road No. 93, a possible shortcut) with trail No. 3, signed "Blue Lake." Follow this uphill. At 2½ miles pass close to a clearcut which offers another shortcut. (To reach this alternative starting point from the trailhead, drive road No. 9327 another 1.3 miles to an unmarked spur and find your way across the clearing.)

In the next 2 miles the trail climbs gently, eventually ascending a wide ridge. At a little over 4½ miles the ridge becomes quite narrow and at times the route is steep. But the vista begins. At 5200 feet the way contours around a high point and drops to a view of Blue Lake at 5 miles. (To get to 4553-foot Blue Lake hike the trail to the point where the lake comes clearly in sight and find an unmarked way trail down to the shore.)

The timber thins, the trail enters meadows, and at 5½ miles, 5200 feet, is a short sidetrail to a campsite—water is scarce after the snow melts. At 6 miles pass a sidetrail ¼ mile southeast to Basin Camp. After contouring slopes of a knob, at 6½ miles, 5200 feet, join trail No. 1, the Boundary Trail (Hike 71).

For the widest views along the route, wander up either of the grassy knolls at 3½ or 4 miles. Shark Rock at the head of Clear Creek is the most impressive rocky peak on the Boundary Ridge.

	OLD	NEW
	125	25
	N92	92
	N920	9327
Lewis River road	N923	93

One-way trip 9½ miles
Hiking time 5 hours
High point 1600 feet
Elevation gain 1000 feet upstream, 600 feet
    downstream
Best March through November
One day or backpack
USGS Burnt Peak and Spencer Butte

...firs, cedars, and maples serves as a canopy to a green and varied ...pet of Oregon grape, vanilla leaf, moss dotted with oxalis, and shoulder-high brush. The Forest Service has promised to preserve in a natural condition a wide corridor along the Lewis River, keeping this trail, perhaps the last low-elevation valley path remaining in Gifford Pinchot National Forest, as a 9-mile sample and reminder of the many, many miles of such splendor that we inherited and have now mostly squandered.

The trail can be hiked in either direction, and parties which can arrange transportation to allow a one-way trip would be well-advised to start at the top, which is 400 feet higher than the bottom. However, parties making a round trip should start at the bottom and thus be sure to cover at least the lower 3 miles, where the best trees are; for this reason the bottom-to-top direction is described here.

From road No. 25 at the end of Swift Reservoir turn right on road No. 90. At 5.2 miles turn left on road No. 9039, and at 6.2 miles cross the Lewis River bridge. At 6.6 miles find the lower trailhead, elevation about 1100 feet.

To reach the upper trailhead, from the junction of roads Nos. 90 and 9039 continue on No. 90 (avoiding sideroads that may be used more than the main one) to a concrete bridge over the Lewis River at 14.5 miles from the ranger station. A few yards from the west end of the bridge find the trailhead, elevation about 1400 feet.

From the lower beginning, trail No. 31 immediately drops to river level, about 1000 feet, and magnificent forest. The way winds along bottomland flats, climbs a small bank, and emerges into a clearcut at 1 mile. To somewhat beyond 1½ miles the path follows the margin of the logging show before re-entering virgin trees. After a few steep ups and downs, at just under 2½ miles is Bolt Camp; the shelter here is

OLD	NEW
125	25
N90	90
N836	9039

174

Lewis River trail

amazingly well-preserved considering it was built in the early 1930s. (In 1979 a Forest Service employee spent his days off re-shaking the cabin.) At 4 miles the valley narrows to a canyon, a good turnaround for round-trip hikers, since from this point the trail goes up and down a lot but never again reaches river level—though there are several spots where one can easily drop to the stream.

At 7 miles the trail climbs a 300-foot bluff. At 7½ miles find a viewpoint a few feet off the tread and look down to the canyon sliced in columnar basalt. From here on the river is unseen and old forest yields to young forest dating from the Spencer Butte fire which swept the area in the 1920s; because snags were then considered a major fire hazard, most were cut many years ago. At 9 miles cross Cussed Hollow and climb over the last bump to the upper trailhead at 9½ miles, 1400 feet.

LEWIS RIVER

77 Pacific Crest Trail

One-way trip from Columbia River to White
    Pass about 120 miles
Hiking time 13 days minimum
High point 7620 feet
Elevation gain about 18,000 feet
Best in May the first 27 miles, mid-July for
    the rest
USGS Hood River, Wind River, Willard,
    Steamboat Mountain, Mt. Adams, and
    White Pass
Forest Service wilderness permits
    required in Mt. Adams and Goat Rocks
    Wildernesses

The Pacific Crest National Scenic Trail, which extends from Mexico to Canada, is most commonly called in the northernmost 470 miles by its older name, the Cascade Crest Trail. The 286-mile portion between the Columbia River and Stevens Pass traverses highlands past three grand volcanoes and penetrates the heart of two spectacular masses of high alpine peaks. The way isn't all pure fun because it also goes through lower, forested sections of the Cascade Range where logging roads and clearcuts have savaged the wilderness solitude. However, the feeling of accomplishment gained by traveling the full length of the crest cannot be spoiled even by the worst of the messed-up parts.

Few hikers complete the route in a single effort; most do the trail in short bits over a period of years. Those taking the whole trip at once can start at either end; the south-to-north direction is described here.

At many places the trail is being relocated for the sake of easier grades or better scenery. For example, to bring Crest hikers closer to a crossing of the Columbia River, the trail will be re-routed toward the Bridge of the Gods. A temporary starting point has been established at Panther Creek on road No. 65 (near Wind River Ranger Station). Until the trail to the bridge is completed the recommended start is on the Dog Mountain trail.

The following brief summary is intended merely to provide a general impression of the route. For details of mileages and campsites, consult the Forest Service map and log of the Pacific Crest Trail, available from any Forest Service office.

Columbia River to White Pass

Begin beside the legendary "River of the West," skirt the slopes of giant Mt. Adams, enjoy views to what's left of graceful Mt. St. Helens, and walk the airy crest of the Goat Rocks Wilderness—the most difficult, as well as one of the most dramatically beautiful, segments of the entire Crest Trail.

Drive Highway 14 east from Vancouver, Washington to the town of Stevenson and some 9 miles beyond to the parking lot and trailhead (adjacent to small cafe in parking lot) on the north side of the highway, elevation 186 feet.

Hike through forests, lava flows, and occasional views—the route interrupted by logging roads, clearcuts, powerlines, and pipelines. Go steeply up and down several times, passing Dog Mountain, Grassy Knoll, and Big Huckleberry Mountain to road No. 60 near Race Track Campground. **Distance from Columbia River to Race Track Campground about 27 miles; elevation gain about 5500 feet; hiking time 3 days.**

From road No. 60 climb miles of woods to Red Mountain and Blue Lake and the pond-dotted meadows and famous huckleberry fields of Indian Heaven (Hike 72). Pass near Bear Lake, go almost over the top of Sawtooth Mountain, cross road No. 24, and continue through Huckleberry Meadows to Mosquito Creek. Cross the road

Johnson Peak, Egg Butte in lower right

again and traverse the east side of Steamboat Mountain to a third crossing of road No. 24. **Distance from Race Track Campground to road No. 24 about 26 miles; elevation gain about 2900 feet; hiking time 3 days**.

The next stage is climaxed by the alpine gardens and glacial streams on the flanks of Mt. Adams. From road No. 24 cross road No. 88, Trout Lake Creek, and road No. 8810, climb to Dry Meadows and Grand Meadows, cross road No. 23, traverse Swampy Meadows, and at 12 miles join the Mount Adams Highline Trail (Hike 73). At 22 miles leave the Highline Trail and at 23½ miles leave the Mt. Adams Wilderness at Spring Creek and proceed to road No. 2329 at Midway Meadows. **Distance from road No. 24 to Midway Meadows about 29 miles; elevation gain about 3500 feet; hiking time 3 days**.

Now starts the first long stretch of roadless country, most of it in the Goat Rocks Wilderness, including a couple miles which can be dangerous. From Midway Meadows go a short bit along a rough road, round a lava flow, and at 6 miles enter the Wilderness. Proceed past Coleman Weed Patch, intersect the Walupt Lake trail, and pass above Snowgrass Flat (Hike 66). Carefully, bewaring of hazards, climb the ridge above Packwood Glacier and traverse the shoulder of Old Snowy to Elk Pass (Hike 63). The route crosses above to McCall Basin, Tieton Pass, and Shoe Lake (Hike 57), at 34 miles leaving the Wilderness and descending to White Pass. **Distance from Midway Meadows to White Pass about 38 miles; elevation gain about 6100 feet; hiking time 4-5 days**.

Pacific
Crest
Trail
(Cont'd.)

One-way trip from White Pass to Stevens Pass about 166 miles
Hiking time 19 days
High point 6500 feet
Elevation gain about 20,400 feet
Best mid-July through October
USGS White Pass, Bumping Lake, Lester, Snoqualmie Pass, Big Snow Mountain, Mt. Daniel, The Cradle, Scenic, and Stevens Pass

White Pass to Stevens Pass

North from White Pass extend miles of marvelous meadows and lakes and large views of Mt. Rainier, then a lower and more wooded (and road-marred) section of the crest leading to Snoqualmie Pass, and finally the splendid assemblage of forests and cliffs and glaciers and flowers and waters constituting the Alpine Lakes Wilderness. This scenic segment of the Crest Trail is close to population centers and extremely popular.

The first stage rarely leaves meadows and panoramas for long and passes numerous small lakes—too many to name here. From the White Pass Highway at Leech Lake (Hike 56) hike to Sand Lake, Cowlitz Pass, Fish Lake, and the Mount Rainier National Park boundary at 15½ miles. Weave in and out of the Park, following the crest by Two Lakes, Dewey Lakes, and around the side of Naches Peak to Chinook Pass and US 410; here leave the National Park. **Distance from White Pass to Chinook Pass about 25 miles; elevation gain about 2400 feet; hiking time 3 days.**

The opening third of the next part lies in alpine terrain as before, and the remainder in woods broken by roads. Climb from Chinook Pass to Sourdough Gap (Hike 51), traverse to Bear Gap and around Pickhandle Point and Crown Point, with views to the Crystal Mountain Ski Area, ascend the crest, contour below the summit of Norse Peak, and drop into Big Crow Basin (Hike 49). Proceed to Little Crow Basin, a junction with the Arch Rock trail, Arch Rock Camp, and Rod's Gap. Pass Government Meadows and cross the Naches Wagon Trail (Hike 46), contour under Pyramid Peak to Windy Gap. **Distance from Chinook Pass to Windy Gap about 27 miles; elevation gain about 2500 feet; hiking time 3 days.**

Now comes a portion with few views except in clearcuts. From Windy Gap follow the crest nearly to the top of Blowout Mountain, descend in woods and clearcuts to Tacoma Pass and a logging road, and travel onward under Snowshoe Butte to Lizard Lake and the road at Stampede Pass. **Distance from Windy Gap to Stampede Pass about 27 miles; elevation gain about 1100 feet; hiking time 3 days.**

More forest travel—but much of the private land is being logged so the path is not always easy to find and not always pleasant, despite increasingly mountainous views northward. From Stampede Pass hike to Dandy Pass, Mirror Lake, contour Tinkham and Silver Peaks (Hike 28) to Olallie Meadow and Lodge Lake, climb to Beaver Lake, and drop down ski slopes to Snoqualmie Pass Ranger Station. **Distance from Stampede Pass to Snoqualmie Pass about 18 miles; elevation gain about 1400 feet; hiking time 2 days.**

From this point north no roads mar the route, which now traverses the superb Alpine Lakes Wilderness. From Snoqualmie Pass the trail climbs high on Kendall Peak and ridge-runs in meadows to Ridge Lake (Hike 26) at 6 miles, then contours headwaters of Gold Creek under avalanche-scoured walls of Chikamin Ridge to a green pass above Park Lakes (Hike 26) at 14 miles. It enters the Cle Elum River watershed, passes Spectacle Lake junction (Hike 33) at 17 miles, and drops to a crossing of Lemah Creek at 21 miles. It climbs past Escondido Lake at 27½ miles and descends to a crossing of the Waptus River at 32 miles. The trail rounds the shore of Waptus Lake (Hike 36) and climbs Spinola Creek to Deep Lake (Hike 39) at 39 miles. It switchbacks to Cathedral Pass at 42½ miles and proceeds down and up to Deception Pass (Hike 40) at 47½ miles. From there the way is fairly level to Deception Lakes (Hike 6), then up to Peiper Pass, down to Glacier Lake, over another pass to a viewpoint above Lake Josephine, and finally down to Stevens Pass at 68 miles. **Distance from Snoqualmie Pass to Stevens Pass about 68 miles; elevation gain 10,600 feet; hiking time 6 days**.

From Stevens Pass the Pacific Crest Trail continues 185 miles to Allison Pass in Canada. See **101 Hikes in the North Cascades**.

OLD	NEW
N60	60
123	24
N88	88
101	2324

78 Mount Ellinor

Round trip to timberline 3 miles
Hiking time 2 hours
High point 5200 feet
Elevation gain 1700 feet
Best July through October
One day
USGS Mt. Steele and The Brothers

From 1853 to 1857 George Davidson surveyed Puget Sound, working from the brig **R.H. Fauntleroy**, named for his superior, the head of the U.S. Coast and Geodetic Survey. Needing names for the maps he was making, he drew upon the Fauntleroy family, calling the southernmost prominent peak on the Olympic skyline Ellinor, for the youngest daughter, the double-summited peak for her Brothers, and the highest point for her older sister Constance. Later, Davidson and Ellinor were married. However, subsequent mappers shifted Ellinor to a lower peak, replacing her with Mt. Washington.

A century and more later, hikers look from Ellinor over a panorama of the Cascades from Mt. St. Helens to Glacier Peak, and of the Olympics from neighboring Mt. Washington, whose profile can be imagined to resemble that of the general and president, to the distant white mass of Mt. Olympus.

Drive US 101 along Hood Canal to Hoodsport. Turn west 9 miles on the Lake Cushman road to a junction. Turn right 1.6 miles on road No. 2450000, then left 4.9 miles on Big Creek road No. 2419 to the signed trailhead. Though the trail will be kept open from this start, for a shorter hike continue on the road to the first Y, take the left fork to the end, and there find an unsigned trailhead, elevation about 3500 feet. Carry a full canteen; the slopes are dry.

Find a boot-built path climbing to the ridge top. At 1½ miles, about 5200 feet, is timberline and the trail-end, and for inexperienced hikers, the proper turnaround. The vistas of lowlands and Cascades are as good here as from the summit—and there is no danger of getting lost, as there may be on the final slopes.

The temptation to go on is overwhelming; to the inexperienced eye, the gully from

OLD	NEW
245	2450000
2419	2419000

Hood Canal and Mt. Rainier from trail's end on Mt. Ellinor

trail-end to summit looks simple. It's not. The gully is steeper than it appears and the rocks are sometimes slippery and always loose—terrain for an experienced rock-scrambler. Should the fog roll in, one easily can stray into the wrong gully and get lost. If a person wants to go for the top of the mountain, he should choose a quiet weekday rather than a mobbed weekend, or come in early summer when the road is still snowbound.

Upper Mildred Lake and Sawtooth Range

79 Mildred Lakes

Round trip about 8 miles
Hiking time 7 hours
High point 4100 feet
Elevation gain 2300 feet in, 600 feet out
Best mid-July to mid-October
Backpack
USGS Mt. Steel

Three mountain lakes beneath the startling basalt spires of Sawtooth Ridge, well worth a visit—as they'd darn well better be, after the struggle. The trail (way), not recognized by the Forest Service as part of its system, and on certain wooded slopes so obscure the hiker may not recognize it either, has been hammered into hillsides and over countless logs by generations of fishermen, hikers, and climbers. The distance is only 4 miles (or is it 5?), but that doesn't include detours around wooden barricades. Nor does the figure given here for elevation gain include the ups and downs over logs and rocks and bumps. These are just extra dividends. But don't complain—they keep out the motorcycles.

Drive 14 miles up Hamma Hamma road No. 2490000 to the end at a concrete bridge over the Hamma Hamma River, elevation 1900 feet. Find the trail, signed by the Forest Service even if not recognized, at the far side of the bridge.

On the first mile a little work has been done—logs cut, the tread occasionally graded. Such gestures end in the second mile as the way climbs steeply over a 3200-foot ridge and drops 300 feet to a delightful camp beside a brook, approximately 2½ miles. The trail is easily lost here amid false paths made by mixed-up hikers.

Cross the creek, stay level several hundred feet, then climb—and climb, with only an occasional respite, 1000 feet, mostly straight up. At 4100 feet is a ridge top of heather and alpine trees and great views that tempt a party to call it quits. Don't. The end is near. Drop 300 feet to Lower Mildred Lake, follow the shore to the lakehead, and near the inlet find the trail (again, amid many false paths) climbing a bit more than 300 feet in ⅓ mile to the upper lake and great views and great camps.

The third lake, about the same elevation, is off toward Cruiser Peak. The path starts from the outlet of the upper lake.

If time permits, ascend (with some bushwhacking) a 5000-foot knoll below Mt. Lincoln. The effort is repaid with a view of Mt. Washington, Mt. Pershing, and a score of other Olympic peaks.

OLD	NEW
249	2490000

80 Flapjack Lakes

Round trip to lakes 15.6 miles
Hiking time 10 hours
High point 4000 feet
Elevation gain 3100 feet
Best July through October
One day or backpack
USGS Mt. Steel
Park Service backcountry use permit
  required

Two subalpine lakes set side by side like flapjacks in a frying pan. Above the waters and the forests rise sharp summits of the Sawtooth Range, a group of peaks noted among climbers for the odd texture of the rock, which largely consists of "pillow lava" erupted under the surface of an ancient sea and now eroded into weird shapes.

Drive US 101 along Hood Canal to Hoodsport. Turn west to Lake Cushman and follow the North Fork Skokomish River road to Staircase Ranger Station and the trailhead, elevation 800 feet.

The trail follows an abandoned road the first 3.7 miles, then ascends moderately but steadily in cool forest to a junction at 7.2 miles. From here a faint way trail goes left to Black and White Lakes in 1⅓ miles, Smith Lake in 2¼ miles.

The right fork reaches Flapjack Lakes, 4000 feet, in ½ mile. One lake, quite shallow, is well along toward becoming a marsh, while the other is deeper and ringed by rock buttresses; the two are separated by a narrow isthmus. The most striking Sawtooth summit from the lake is The Horn—known to a party of hikers, who saw it on an autumn night years ago with the full moon (made of green cheese, then) touching its yearning snout, as "The Mouse."

Actually, the trip only just begins at the lakes. For high and wide meadows and broad views, walk the Mt. Gladys trail 1½ more miles up a lovely valley of rocks and flowers and bubbling water to Gladys Pass, 5000 feet, between a rounded garden peak and a vicious finger of lava. Roam the gardens to the 5600-foot summit of Mt. Gladys. Stare at the frightening walls of 6104-foot Cruiser ("Bruiser") Peak, whose tower is visible from Seattle, standing like a boundary monument on the southeast corner of Olympic National Park.

Popularity has forced stringent restrictions on camping: a nightly limit of 30 persons at the lakes and above; stoves only at the lakes and above (wood fires permitted below Donahue Creek). Alternative campsites are at Smith Lake.

Upper Flapjack Lake and Mt. Lincoln

185

81 Home Sweet Home

Round trip to Camp Pleasant 13 miles
Hiking time 8 hours
High point 1600 feet
Elevation gain 800 feet
Best May through November
One day or backpack
USGS Mt. Steel

Round trip to Home Sweet Home 26 miles
Allow 2 days
High point 5688 feet
Elevation gain 4000 feet in, 500 feet out
Best mid-July through October
Park Service backcountry use permit
required

In early May, when a small elk herd is still in the Skokomish valley and trillium and calypso orchids are in bloom, walk the gentle trail to Nine Stream. In summer, climb from the valley to First Divide and broad views, then drop to Duckabush River drainage and the lupine meadows of Home Sweet Home.

Drive US 101 to Hoodsport and turn west to the end of the North Fork Skokomish River road (Hike 80), elevation 800 feet.

The North Fork Skokomish River trail follows an abandoned road 3.7 miles, then enters forest to Big Log Camp, 5½ miles, a spacious area beside the stream. At 6 miles the way crosses the river on a bridge over a deep, quiet pool. Immediately beyond is a junction; go right. The trail climbs slightly to Camp Pleasant, 6½ miles, 1600 feet, on a large maple flat. This appropriately-named spot makes a good overnight stop for springtime backpackers.

At 9½ miles, 2091 feet, is Nine Stream and the end of level walking. In the next mile the trail ascends at a comfortable rate through a big meadow, then forest. After that the way is continuously steep and often rough. Flower gardens become more frequent. Mt. Stone appears to the south.

At about 12 miles the trail reaches a meadow below Mt. Steel, turns sharply right, and climbs to the crest of 4688-foot First Divide, 12½ miles, and views across the Duckabush valley to Mt. LaCrosse, White Mountain, and the greenery of LaCrosse Pass.

The path descends ½ mile to Home Sweet Home, 4198 feet. Even from a bunk in

Mt. Steel from near Home Sweet Home. Picture was taken in early July when the meadows were still covered with snow.

the shelter one may enjoy the blossoms of avalanche lilies or lupine, depending on the season. The view is superb of 6233-foot Mt. Steel.

From First Divide a faint way trail goes around the south side of Mt. Hopper, but the route is rough and best left to very experienced travelers.

Many hikers continue from Home Sweet Home to Lake LaCrosse (Hike 99), 7 miles farther, with a loss of 2000 feet followed by a stiff gain of 2500 feet to the lake. From there they either proceed onward around O'Neil Pass to the Enchanted Valley trail or over Anderson Pass to the Dosewallips trail.

A few hikers drop from Home Sweet Home to the Duckabush River, hike 1½ miles downstream, and climb over 5566-foot LaCrosse Pass to Honeymoon Meadows on the Dosewallips (Hike 85). Only the vast meadows at the pass make this grueling 3000-foot ascent on a waterless, south-facing slope worth the effort.

82 Upper Lena Lake

Round trip to upper lake 14 miles
Hiking time 12 hours
High point 4600 feet
Elevation gain 3900 feet
Best to lower lake April through November
Best to upper lake July through October
One day or backpack
USGS The Brothers
Park Service backcountry use permit
required

Hike an easy trail, free of snow most of the year, through splendid forest to popular and often crowded Lower Lena Lake, surrounded by tall trees. Continue on steeper, rougher trail to the subalpine country of Upper Lena Lake.

Drive US 101 along Hood Canal to Eldon. Turn west on the Hamma Hamma River road about 9 miles to Phantom Creek and ½ mile beyond to the trailhead, elevation 685 feet.

The wide "super-trail" switchbacks gently and endlessly in forest shadows, crossing beautiful Lena Creek and soon thereafter reaching Lower Lena Lake at 2¾ miles, 1800 feet. The way passes a popular camp area and rounds the west shore ½ mile to other campsites near the head of the lake.

Shortly beyond the head of the lake is a junction. The path to the right follows East Fork Lena Creek into the Valley of Silent Men, crossing and recrossing the stream many times, toward The Brothers, a principal summit of the Olympic horizon seen from Seattle. This boot-built track is mainly used by fishermen and climbers but is well worth exploration by hikers who enjoy loitering beside cold water frothing and sparkling through rapids, swirling in green pools, all in the deep shade of old forest.

The left fork—no supertrail—follows West Fork Lena Creek, entering Olympic National Park at 4 miles. At approximately 5 miles, 2700 feet, the trail crosses a small creek and becomes steep and badly eroded. The present trail was built in the late 1930s. It was steep then, but the tread was smooth and wide. Subsequently a few windfalls have been cut but otherwise there has been no maintenance. Floods, slides,

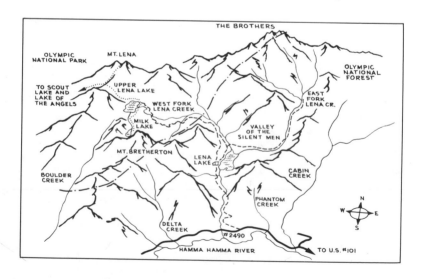

and fallen trees have taken their toll and only remnants of the original tread remain.

As the trail climbs, the vegetation changes from fir to subalpine forest. Heather and huckleberry appear along with Alaska cedar. There are occasional views down the valley toward The Brothers. The steepness ends abruptly at Upper Lena Lake, 4600 feet, 7 miles. A rough up-and-down way trail rounds the north side.

Camps are inviting (no wood fires, stoves only) and the shore demands roaming, as do the meadows and screes ringing the cirque. For more ambitious explorations scramble to the summit of 5998-foot Mt. Lena, or ascend the creek falling from little Milk Lake, tucked in a quiet pocket and generally frozen until late summer, or follow a boot-worn track over a 5000-foot ridge near Mt. Lena to Scout Lake, or follow the ridge with its numerous tarns toward Mt. Stone and Lake of the Angels.

Upper Lena Lake and Mt. Bretherton

The Brothers from Mt. Jupiter trail

83 Mount Jupiter

Round trip 14 miles
Hiking time 10 hours
High point 5701 feet
Elevation gain 3600 feet
Best June through October
One day
USGS Point Misery and The Brothers

Look from Seattle across Puget Sound to the Olympic horizon; right smack between The Brothers and Mt. Constance is Jupiter. Actually, the peak does not deserve inclusion in such distinguished company, but stands so far out in the front of the range as to seem bigger than it really is. And in fact, old Jupe offers unique combination views of lowlands and mountains. The summit ascent, however, is long and strenuous and usually dry and hot. Most hikers are content to climb the trail to the views and leave the summit to peakbaggers.

Drive US 101 along Hood Canal to a short mile north of the Duckabush River bridge. A bit south of the Black Point road, turn west 3½ miles on unsigned Mt. Jupiter road No. 2620012 to a junction. Turn left on the fork (sometimes) signed "Mt. Jupiter Trail" and drive 3 steep and tortuous miles to the trailhead, elevation 2150 feet.

The first mile switchbacks up south slopes of the ridge dividing the Duckabush and Dosewallips Rivers. At 1 mile, 2850 feet, the trail reaches the ridge crest, and here leaves state land and enters Olympic National Forest. The hike to this point, with splendid panoramas, can be done in late May and early June, when the trip is really the most pleasant, especially since rhododendrons are then in bloom along the lower trail.

However, the way goes on for those willing, following the ridge crest up and down, up and down, with more views, and finally climbs a very steep final mile to the summit, 7 miles, 5701 feet.

From the summit, or from the trail, the views are glorious — and thought-provoking. North beyond the Dosewallips is Mt. Constance, and south beyond the Duckabush are The Brothers. See the logging, steadily encroaching on state and Olympic National Forest lands. Westward is the protected grandeur of Olympic National Park. Eastward across Hood Canal and the Kitsap Peninsula are Seattle, the Space Needle, suburbia, smog, civilization.

OLD	NEW
262	2620012

84 Lake Constance

Round trip to the lake 4 miles
Hiking time 7 hours
High point 4750 feet
Elevation gain 3300 feet
Best August through October
One day or backpack
USGS The Brothers and Tyler Peak
Park Service backcountry use permit
required (from Hoodsport Ranger
Station)

A classic tarn, the deep blue waters ringed by alpine trees and heather gardens and sheer cliffs of Mt. Constance. Mountain goats wander the precipices by day—and at night visit campfires to scavenge goodies. But hikers must earn their passage to the secluded cirque the hard way, climbing 3300 feet in only 2 miles. The trail is super-steep, somewhat dangerous in spots, and is not recommended for beginners or small children or the faint-hearted.

Drive US 101 along Hood Canal to the Dosewallips River road just north of Brinnon. Turn west 14 miles to ½ mile inside the Park boundary and several wide spots that serve for the trailhead parking area at Constance Creek, elevation 1450 feet.

The first mile is brutal, virtually without switchbacks, gaining some 2000 feet to a short level stretch, and good forest camp, at the 1-mile marker. The second mile seems even steeper, though this is purely an optical illusion caused by the ladder-ways of tree roots and the short rock cliffs. Feet must be placed with care and hands used for balance. Caution is especially essential on the descent. At 2 miles, 4750 feet, the trail flattens into the cirque. Camping restrictions forced by popularity include a nightly limit of 20 campers (make reservations by calling or visiting the Park Service—Forest Service joint visitors' center at Hoodsport) and a ban on wood fires.

Impressive as is the lake, the truly awesome scenery lies higher, beyond the portals of what oldtime Boy Scouts, feeling spooky, used to call "Dead Man's Gap." Follow a boot-beaten climbers' track above the lake, up talus, through the gap into Avalanche Canyon, a mile-long glacier trough between the east and west peaks of Constance. Solemn and spectacular it is, a place of crags, cliffs, and screes, snowfields and moraines. Hikers can walk safely to the canyon head at about 6000 feet. Those with ice axes and experience in snow travel can climb easily to Crystal Pass and views down the glacier in Tunnel Creek.

The geology adds fascination. The weird, bumpy-looking walls of the canyon

Lake Constance

consist of "pillow lava" formed by molten rock erupting under the sea and cooling into these odd, rounded shapes. Heat and pressure metamorphosed limestone into pastel-colored rocks, often in variegated fault breccias of striking beauty. Hot mineralized solutions deposited green crystals of epidote intermixed with quartz and calcite.

The goats that tour the campsites by night and occasionally by day (such as on a Monday morning, after the weekenders have gone home) often can be spotted on cliffs, little kids gamboling about the airy rocks, older folks moving more deliberately.

85 Anderson Glacier

Round trip to Anderson Glacier 22½ miles
Allow 3 days
High point 5200 feet
Elevation gain 4000 feet
Best mid-July through October
USGS The Brothers and Mt. Steel
Park Service backcountry use permit
   required

Follow a long trail to the edge of one of the largest glaciers in the eastern Olympics. Enjoy glorious views down the Dosewallips River to Mt. Constance, over Anderson Pass to Mt. LaCrosse and White Mountain, down into the Enchanted Valley at the head of the Quinault River, and of course, across the Anderson Glacier to the summits of Mt. Anderson. In early August a wild array of flowers bloom, including small fields of

Anderson Glacier on Mt. Anderson

lupine and paintbrush that stand out dramatically against the rugged background.

Drive US 101 along Hood Canal to just north of Brinnon and turn west on the Dosewallips River road, coming to the end of pavement in 4¾ miles, Elkhorn Campground junction at 10¾ miles, Constance Creek at 13½ miles, and at 15 miles the road-end and trailhead, elevation 1540 feet.

The trail starts in deep forest with a showing of rhododendrons in late June, and after going up and down a bit reaches a junction at 1½ miles. Turn left to Dose Forks Camp and cross the river. At about 2½ miles the way again crosses the river, now the West Fork Dosewallips, this time on a bridge perched spectacularly some 100 feet above the water. The trail climbs steeply to dry forests high above the stream, which flows in so deep a gorge that often it cannot be heard.

The trail descends a bit to a welcome drink of water and campsites at 5 miles, then climbs high again and with minor ups and downs reaches the small opening of Diamond Meadow at 6¾ miles, 2692 feet. Pleasant campsites by the stream. At 7¼ miles the trail once more crosses the river and begins a steady ascent, at about 8 miles climbing steeply beside the raging torrent as it tumbles through a narrow gorge. At 8¾ miles, 3627 feet, the valley opens into the broad, flat expanse and good camps of Honeymoon Meadows, named years ago by a Seattle couple who long since have celebrated their golden wedding anniversary. (Here and above, stove-only camping.) One final time the trail crosses the river, here a jump wide (a big jump), and ascends a rough path to emergency-use-only Anderson Pass Shelter ("Camp Siberia") at 10 miles and Anderson Pass at 10½ miles, 4464 feet.

The Anderson Glacier trail climbs steeply from the north side of the wooded pass, emerging from trees and in ¾ mile ending at a small tarn amid boulders and meadows. A few feet farther lead to the 5200-foot edge of an old moraine and the views.

The West Fork Dosewallips trail to Anderson Pass often is included in longer trips: a 27-mile one-way hike down Enchanted Valley (Hike 98); a 49-mile one-way hike to O'Neil Pass and out the Duckabush River (Hike 99); a 36½-mile one-way hike out the North Fork Skokomish River; and a 41-mile loop trip via O'Neil Pass and the upper Duckabush, returning to the Dosewallips with a grueling 3000-foot climb to LaCrosse Pass.

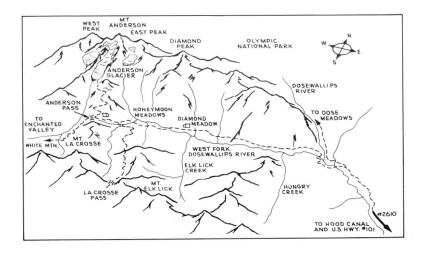

86 Hayden Pass

Round trip to Hayden Pass 31 miles
Allow 3-4 days
High point 5847 feet
Elevation gain 4250 feet
Best July through October
USGS Tyler Peak, The Brothers, and Mt.
   Angeles
Park Service backcountry use permit
   required

Miles of marvelous forest, then alpine meadows waist-deep in flowers, where fragrance makes the head swim on warm days, where a quiet hiker may see deer, elk, marmots, bear, and perhaps a goat on a high ridge. All this and impressive views too, plus numerous fine campsites at short intervals along the trail. The pass makes a superb round-trip destination, or can be included in an across-the-Olympics journey to the Elwha River, or in a 10-day giant loop over Low Divide and returning via Anderson Pass.

Drive US 101 along Hood Canal to the Dosewallips River road just north of Brinnon. Turn west 15½ miles (the final 2 miles in the National Park are steep and rough) to the road-end campground and trailhead, elevation 1540 feet.

A gentle 1½ miles through open forest with a dense groundcover of salal and rhododendron (the latter blooms in early July) lead to Dose Forks. A bit beyond is a junction with the trail to Anderson Pass (Hike 85); take the right fork and start climbing. At 2 miles note animal prints at a soda spring. Cross many little streams, nice spots for resting and drinking. At 2½ miles a sidetrail heads up to supremely-scenic but far-above Constance Pass.

As the path ascends, Diamond Mountain appears across the river; from a well-marked point, see Hatana Falls. At about 8 miles the valley widens and the trail crosses a series of meadows. At 9 miles pass the Graywolf sidetrail and continue in steadily more open terrain, with wider views, to Dose Meadows at 13 miles, 4450 feet; no sign announces where you are, but a sidetrail here ascends rightward to Lost Pass.

Beyond the meadows is a small canyon which used to be crossed on a bridge; the creek-size river has a lion-size roar but makes no major difficulties. At 13½ miles, 4600 feet, the way enters the vast garden basin of the headwaters, surrounded by

Avalanche lilies on Hayden Pass (John Spring photo)

high peaks. The trail crosses the river one last time and switchbacks to Hayden Pass, 15½ miles, 5847 feet. In early summer a large, steep snowbank blocks the tread; be cautious.

Hayden Pass is the low point on the narrow ridge connecting Mt. Fromme and Sentinel Peak. North is Mt. Claywood, east are Wellesley Peak and the Dosewallips valley, south is glacier-covered Mt. Anderson, and west are the Bailey Range and distant Mt. Olympus.

Down from the pass 1 mile on the Elwha River side, just before the trail enters forest, find a delightful campsite by a bubbling creek.

For the across-the-Olympics hike, continue 9 miles and 4200 feet down from the pass to the Elwha River trail and then 17 miles more to the Whiskey Bend road-end (Hike 91).

No woodfires are permitted above 4000 feet; carry a stove or a lot of baloney sandwiches.

Warrior Peak and Mt. Constance from Marmot Pass

HOOD CANAL

87 Marmot Pass

Round trip to Marmot Pass 12 miles
Hiking time 9 hours
High point 6000 feet
Elevation gain 3400 feet
Best July through mid-November
One day or backpack
USGS Tyler Peak

Before World War II, in an era when Boy Scouts were perhaps the principal wanderers of the Olympic wilderness, the "Three Rivers Hike" was among the most popular trips from old Camp Parsons. Thousands of Scouts now getting quite long in the tooth vividly recall their introduction to highlands on the grueling "Poop Out Drag," climbing steeply and endlessly upward along a sun-baked south slope, arriving in late afternoon at Camp Mystery, then taking an after-dinner walk through flower gardens and broad meadows to Marmot Pass and thrilling evening views down to shadowed forests of the Dungeness River, 3000 feet below, and beyond to Mt. Mystery, Mt. Deception, second-highest in the Olympics, and the jagged line of The Needles, all etched in a sunset-colored sky.

Drive US 101 along Hood Canal to ½ mile north of the Quilcene River bridge, .9 mile south of the Quilcene Ranger Station, and turn west on the Quilcene River road, a paved but unmarked county road that soon is numbered road No. 28120. Stay with that number at the many junctions and at 10.7 miles from the highway turn left on road No. 2720000 (no kidding!). At 15.3 miles, just beyond 10 Mile Shelter and Wet Weather Creek, find the start of Big Quilcene trail No. 833, elevation 2500 feet.

The trail follows the river bottom through cool forest, crossing numerous step-across creeks, passing many close-up looks at the lovely river. At 3 miles is Shelter Rock Camp, 3600 feet, and the last water for more than 2 miles.

Now the way turns steeply upward into the hot, dry scree, alternating with flowers, of the famous (or infamous) Poop Out Drag.

At a bit past 5 miles the suffering ends as the trail abruptly turns into Camp Mystery, 5400 feet, with a delightful spring and campsites in alpine trees. Except for snowmelt there is no water above, so this is the spot to camp.

The trail continues upward, passing under a cliff and opening into a wide, flat meadow—which, sad to say, has become a race track for the motorbikes the Forest Service allows here. At 6 miles, 6000 feet, the way attains Marmot Pass and panoramas westward.

The legendary Three Rivers Hike descended the trail 1½ miles to Boulder Shelter, followed Dungeness trail No. 833 to Home Lake and Constance Pass in Olympic National Park, climbed Del Monte Ridge, and plunged down the interminable short switchbacks of the Sunnybrook trail to the Dosewallips River trail, and thence to the road.

Fine as the views are from Marmot Pass, nearby are even better ones. For a quick sample, scramble up the 6300-foot knoll directly south of the pass. For the full display, turn north of the pass on trail No. 840, leading to Copper Creek, follow it 1½ miles to just short of Buckhorn Pass, and find a path climbing to the 6950-foot west summit of Buckhorn Mountain. Especially striking are the dramatic crags of 7300-foot Warrior Peak and 7743-foot Mt. Constance.

OLD	NEW
2812	28120
272	2720000

Headwaters of Silver Creek from Mt. Townsend

HOOD CANAL

88 Mount Townsend

Round trip 11 miles
Hiking time 6 hours
High point 6280 feet
Elevation gain 3500 feet
Best June through November
One day or backpack
USGS Tyler Peak

Climb to a northern outpost of the highlands. Look down to the Strait of Juan de Fuca, Puget Sound, Hood Canal, and across the water to Mt. Baker, Glacier Peak, and faraway Mt. Rainier. In the other direction, of course, see the Olympic Mountains. The steep southeast slopes of the trail route melt free of snow in early June, and usually only a few easy patches are encountered then. Mid-June is best, though, when the entire forest road is lined with rhododendron blossoms, spring flowers are blooming in the lowlands, and summer flowers on the south-facing rock gardens higher up.

Two popular trails lead to the summit of Mt. Townsend. The one from Townsend Creek, ascending the southeast side, is described here. The other, the Little Quilcene trail from Lake Water Camp, is slightly longer but perhaps cooler walking in mid-summer.

Drive US 101 south from the Quilcene Ranger Station .9 mile. Turn west on a paved, unsigned road that eventually is revealed as road No. 2812000. At all junctions stay with that number. At 13.6 miles turn left on road No. 276400. In ½ cliff-hanging mile is the road-end and trailhead, elevation about 2800 feet.

For the alternate trail, drive road No. 2812000 another 5 miles and turn left on road No. 2909000 for 2 miles, then left on road No. 2892000 for 3 miles to the Little Quilcene River trailhead, elevation 4000 (or is it 4000000?) feet.

The Townsend Creek trail ascends steadily in timber 1½ miles, then opens out and steepens somewhat to Windy Camp, 2½ miles, about 5000 feet. Pleasant camping around little Windy Lake.

The way continues upward in parkland with a scattering of small flower gardens. At just under 3 miles is an unmarked junction. The left fork climbs over a saddle, drops into Silver Creek, and climbs again to campsites at Silver Lakes, a sidetrip of 2½ miles each way; one small lake is on the trail and the other is hidden. The right fork heads up the mountain, topping the ridge at 4 miles, 6000 feet, then following the crest, passing 100 feet below the first summit at 4½ miles, and running to the most northerly part of the ridge and the second summit, connecting there with the Little Quilcene trail and a trail down to Silver Creek.

Which summit is the higher? They are so evenly matched—with only 50 feet difference—you must try both to know. Wander to the summit of your choice and soak up the view over the waters to the Cascades, and over the rolling meadow ridges of the Olympics. The rugged peaks to the south are Mt. Constance and its neighbors, and farther away, The Brothers.

OLD	NEW
2812	2812000
2764	2764000
2909	2909000
2892	2892000

89 Mount Angeles

One-way trip 10 miles
Hiking time 5 hours
High point 5900 feet
Elevation gain 1200 feet
Best mid-July through October
One day
USGS Mt. Angeles and Port Angeles
Park Service backcountry use permit
    required

Once upon a time this was a challenging hike from lowland forests to alpine meadows, then along a craggy peak to some of the most glorious views of Olympic National Park. Forests, meadows, and views remain, but the challenge accepted by those who start at the bottom is like a big balloon, punctured, when greeted on top by people in street shoes walking paved trails. Most hikers, therefore, prefer to forget the challenge—they begin at the top and work down to the tall timber. (Such a plan, of course, requires either two cars or a pickup below by a non-hiking friend.)

The trail, which does not go to the actual summit of Mt. Angeles, is rough in spots. For an alternate trip with almost the same views and better tread, take the Lake Angeles trail. Both routes have the same start and finish and are approximately the same length, but the lake trail has more people.

Drive 18 miles from Port Angeles to Hurricane Ridge and find the Lake Angeles-Klahhane Ridge trail at the east end of the Big Meadow parking lot, elevation 5225 feet.

The first few hundred feet of paved pathway lead east around a low green hill. Soon the trail becomes gravel and in ½ mile narrows to normal mountain tread winding 2 miles along Sunrise Ridge, sometimes on the crest and sometimes contouring small knolls. Just before crossing the south slope of Mt. Angeles, pass a meager boot-beaten path leading upward, the climbers' route to the summit. At 2½ miles is a junction with the Switchback trail, a steep ½-mile shortcut from the highway which saves the "bother" of hiking 2 of the best alpine miles of the whole trip. From the junction the main trail switchbacks up 900 feet to 5900-foot Heather Pass at 3½ miles and the junction of the Lake Angeles and Mt. Angeles trails.

The views here are superb, with Mt. Olympus in one direction and, in the other, Port

Mountain goat on Klahhane Ridge

Angeles, the Strait of Juan de Fuca, the San Juan Islands, Vancouver Island, and Mt. Baker. If mountain goats have not been seen before, look around carefully; there are many in the vicinity, as evidenced by their wool on trees, rocks, and thistles and by their numerous paths crossing shale slopes. (Warning: Goats may be harmful to your health. Remember they are wild animals with sharp horns. Stay 20 feet away. If you want closeup pictures, use a telephoto lens.) This side of Mt. Angeles is geologically unusual, having vertical erosion lines in tilted sedimentary strata.

From the junction the Lake Angeles trail follows along Klahhane Ridge about another 1½ miles and then descends meadows into woods, reaching Lake Angeles at 6½ miles, 4196 feet, and continuing down in timber to the trailhead behind the ranger's quarters at Heart of the Hills, 10 miles, 1817 feet.

From the junction the Mt. Angeles trail drops 300 feet into the head of Ennis Creek, traverses shale slides, and climbs over Second Divide at 4½ miles, about 5800 feet. The way through the shale is hard to follow; don't be misled by certain goat trails which look better than the people trail.

From Second Divide the path descends rapidly, traversing more shale and crossing a spur ridge to Heather Park at 6 miles, 5500 feet, featuring a meadow at the foot of an avalanche slope, some flowers, lots of heather, and great gobs of views. The remaining 4 miles are in trees, passing Halfway Rock at 8 miles, and finishing at the Heart of the Hills trailhead in 10 miles.

Moose Lake

STRAIT OF JUAN DE FUCA

90 Grand Valley

Round trip to Moose Lake 9 miles
Hiking time 6 hours
High point 6450 feet
Elevation gain 300 feet in, 1800 feet out
Best July through October
One day or backpack
USGS Mt. Angeles
Park Service backcountry use permit
   required

A Grand Valley it surely is, with two lakes and a half-dozen ponds in glacier-scooped bowls, but it would better be called "Kingdom of the Marmots." There are meadows to roam and rushing streams to drink and views to admire. However, the abundant wildlife is the outstanding feature: an occasional goat, numerous deer and grouse, and an unbelievable number of whistlers.

This is an upside-down trip—the trail starts high and descends to the valley; the hard hauling is on the return.

Drive US 101 to Port Angeles and turn south 17 miles on the Olympic National Park highway to Hurricane Ridge. Just before the lodge turn left on a narrow and scenic dirt road through parklands along the ridge crest. In 8½ miles, on the side of Obstruction Peak, is the road-end, elevation 6200 feet.

The drive is beautiful and so is the trail south along the meadow crest of Lillian Ridge a mile, with views over Elwha River forests to Mt. Olympus, then swinging around rocky slopes of a small peak to a notch in the ridge, 6450 feet. Now the way drops steeply down slate screes and lush flowers to open forest on the floor of Grand Valley, and a junction at 3½ miles, 5000 feet.

The left fork leads in ¼ mile to a shelter beside Grand Lake, 4750 feet, then descends Grand Creek to 4000 feet and climbs through Badger Valley to Obstruction Peak, reached in 5 miles from the junction. (The "badgers" actually are marmots; listen for their whistles.) This route makes an excellent loop-trip return to the road.

The right fork ascends ½ mile to Moose Lake, 5100 feet, and another ½ mile to little Gladys Lake. There are nice camps near Moose and Grand Lakes (remember the minimum camping distance from lakes or streams is 100 feet) but for privacy scout around secret nooks in the vicinity of Gladys.

For more alpine wanderings, continue on the trail to 6300-foot Grand Pass, 6½ miles from Obstruction Point, then scramble up Peak 6701 to the west, with views to the Bailey Range and Mt. Olympus and Mt. Anderson and more.

If the weather turns bad when it's time to go home, keep in mind that the last mile along Lillian Ridge can be a battle for survival, even in July and August. In such case it is wise to return via Badger Valley, several miles longer but mostly protected from the killing winds. Moreover, wood fires are permitted at two sites in Badger Valley.

Olympic marmot

STRAIT OF JUAN DE FUCA

91 Whiskey Bend
To Low Divide

Round trip to Low Divide 57 miles
Allow a week or more
High point 3602 feet
Elevation gain about 2500 feet plus many
ups and downs
Best June through October
USGS Mt. Angeles; Mt. Steel and Mt.
Christie
Park Service backcountry use permit
required

No whiskey, but a lot of waterfalls and forest scenery, can be found on the 28-mile Elwha River trail from Whiskey Bend to Low Divide. The valley is very heavily traveled in summer, especially below Elkhorn, but the natural beauty and historical interest more than compensate for crowds. Spend a day or weekend on the lower trail—or spend a week hiking the complete trail, loitering at lovely spots, taking sidetrips. Before setting out be sure to read Bob Wood's delightful book, **Across the Olympic Mountains: the Press Expedition, 1889-90.**

Drive US 101 west from Port Angeles 8 miles and turn left on the paved Elwha River road 2 miles to the National Park boundary. At 2.1 miles from the boundary, just past the Elwha Ranger Station, turn left on the Whiskey Bend road and drive 5 miles (sometimes rough and steep) to the road-end parking area, elevation 1100 feet.

The trail is wide and relatively level, with occasional glimpses of the river far below, to Cougar Mike's Cabin at 1½ miles. Here a ½-mile sidetrail descends to the old homestead of Humes Ranch, where elk may sometimes be seen, mainly from late fall to spring.

At 4½ miles, 1273 feet, is Lillian Camp beside the Lillian River. Pause for refreshment because the next stretch is the toughest of the trip, climbing 700 feet from the hot, dry Lillian Grade through an old burn, then dropping for the first time to the Elwha River at about 8 miles, 1242 feet. The trail goes up and down, never near the river very long, to Mary Falls, 8¾ miles, and a nice view of the falls. Now the way climbs again, passing a ¼-mile sidetrip to secluded Canyon Camp, and at 11½ miles, 1400 feet, reaches Elkhorn Guard Station and Shelter.

The trail crosses an alder bottom where elk or deer may be seen and passes an old summer-home cabin of pre-park days—Remanns' Cabin (13 miles, 1450 feet)—and climbs again and drops again into Press Valley. At the upper end of the valley, 16¾

Forest floor

miles, 1685 feet, are Hayes River Camp and Hayes River Patrol Cabin, built in 1969 by 40 volunteer boys enrolled in the Student Conservation Program. Here is a junction with the Hayden Pass trail (Hike 86).

At 21 miles, 1900 feet, is a shelter at Camp Wilder. Easily cross a footlog over Buckinghorse Creek and at 26 miles reach Chicago Camp, 2099 feet, a jumping-off point for Mt. Olympus climbers. The trail now leaves the valley bottom and switchbacks in forest to the meadows of Low Divide, 28¾ miles, 3602 feet, and there meets the North Fork Quinault River trail.

To complete the classic Press Expedition cross-Olympics journey, continue from the pass 18 miles down the valley to the North Fork Quinault River road-end, for a total of 45 miles.

Mt. Olympus from near Oyster Lake

STRAIT OF JUAN DE FUCA

92 Appleton Pass

Round trip to pass 10½ miles
Hiking time 7 hours
High point 5000 feet
Elevation gain 3000 feet
Best mid-July through October
  (or until road is closed)
One day or backpack
USGS Mt. Carrie
Park Service backcountry use permit
  required

One of the most popular trails in Olympic National Park climbs to green meadows sprinkled with flowers, to views of High Divide and Mt. Carrie, and to possible extensions of the route to near and far places.

Drive Highway 101 west from Port Angeles about 9 miles and turn left on Upper

Elwha River road, paved all the way, 12½ miles to the end at Boulder Creek Campground (site of Olympic Hot Springs), elevation 2000 feet.

From the upper end of the campground the trail sets out in nice big trees growing from a groundcover of moss. The calypso orchids stage an annual riot hereabouts, usually in early June or so. At a junction in ½ mile, keep straight. The first mile is a breeze with only minor ups and downs. Then the trail crosses West Fork Boulder Creek and the work begins, the way climbing past two waterfalls to South Fork Boulder Creek. An unusual feature of the trail is the superb quality of the bridges and puncheon, which were built by meticulous craftspeople, including close relatives and friends of one of the co-authors. The path presents no problems but steepness until about 4000 feet, where mud grows deep and lush vegetation crowds in. At 5 miles are snowpatches that may last all summer (ice axes advised for early-summer hikers). At 6 miles the trail tops 5000-foot Appleton Pass.

Views from here being limited, take an unsigned way trail on the east side of the pass and follow the ridge crest upward, through alpine forest past tiny Oyster Lake, into green meadows, and in 1½ miles to a 5500-foot viewpoint overlooking Cat Creek to glacier-draped Mt. Carrie.

The first 3 miles of the trail have several small camps. Camping is superb along the ridge, though there is only snow for water and stoves should be used.

From Appleton Pass the trail descends in 2¼ miles to the Soleduck River trail, reached at 6½ miles from Sol Duc Hot Springs.

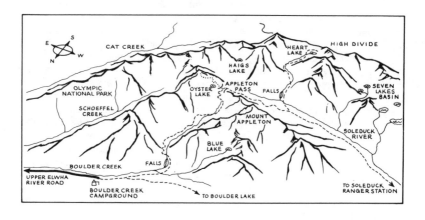

93 Pyramid Mountain

Round trip 7 miles
Hiking time 4 hours
High point 3100 feet
Elevation gain 2400 feet
Best late May to November
One day
USGS Lake Crescent

From Lake Crescent a delightful trail ascends magnificent forest to the 3100-foot site of a World War II airplane spotter's post. No enemy aircraft to watch for now except our own playboy-jockeyed military jets, screaming over the ridges and scaring the breakfasts out of hikers, but there are views of lake and mountains. A delightful trip, yes, but marred by a logging road to the very boundary of Olympic National Park. Ignore it, if you can.

Drive Highway 101 from Port Angeles to the west end of Lake Crescent and turn right on the road signed "Fairholm Campground." Drive 3.2 miles to a spacious parking lot, elevation 700 feet. Walk the road back a couple hundred yards to find the trail on the uphill side.

After a moderate start, gaining only 400 feet in the first mile, at 1½ miles the way steepens, crosses several small streams (perhaps dry by late summer), and goes through beautiful fir trees. The tread is mostly well-graded and wide but on crossings of steep shale narrows to meager inches.

At 2½ miles the trail switchbacks to a saddle in the ridge marking the boundary between Olympic National Park and Olympic National Forest. A logging road here is a jolting reminder of the different objectives of park and forest. It also is shocking evidence of a contempt for wilderness—the road could just as well have been built farther below the ridge crest, out of sight, not disturbing the mood. Even though the forest probably will be clearcut to the Park boundary, there was no need to put a permanent road that close—the logging could be done from temporary roads that afterward are put to bed. As it is, some hikers surely are going to feel so disheartened they'll drive the road and throw away the best part of the trip, making it a mere stroll.

From the saddle the trail stays on the National Forest side of the ridge, generally a few feet from the crest. At 3½ miles, 3100 feet, it ends at an abandoned cabin perched atop a cliff dropping off on three sides. Here and in many other places in the Olympics, during World War II, spotters lived the year around, watching for Japanese aircraft coming to attack Seattle and Bremerton. The view must have been better then; now greenery has encroached and one must peek around trees and shrubs to look down on the lake. On a sunny day the waters are dotted with boats. Directly across the valley is Storm King Mountain but trees make it hard to see.

Lake Crescent and Storm King Mountain from Pyramid Mountain

STRAIT OF JUAN DE FUCA

94 High Divide

Loop trip 20 miles
Allow 3 days
High point 5474 feet
Elevation gain 4000 feet
Best August through October
USGS Bogachiel Peak and Mt. Carrie
Park Service backcountry use permit
required

Soleduck forests, tarns and gardens of Seven Lakes Basin, meadows of the High Divide, and views across the green gulf of the Hoh River to glaciers of Mt. Olympus and far west to the Pacific Ocean. The trail is busy and the lakes crowded — sad to say, some are actually polluted — but the country is big and beautiful and offers a variety of wanderings short and long. By planning only to **look** at lakes and not to camp by them — alternative sites are numerous — hikers can enjoy solitude even now, when the fame of the area draws thousands of visitors annually. A loop trip is recommended as a sampler of the riches. (Actually, the bio-welfare of Seven Lakes Basin and the High Divide demands that the amount of camping in the fragile terrain be reduced, with more emphasis on day visits from camps in valley forests.)

Drive US 101 west from Lake Crescent (Fairholm) 2 miles to the Soleduck River road. Turn left 14.2 miles to the road-end and trailhead, elevation 2000 feet.

The trail ascends gently in splendid old forest 1 mile to the misty and mossy gorge of Soleduck Falls. Close by is the junction, 1950 feet, with the Deer Lake trail — see the concluding segment of the clockwise loop described here.

The Soleduck trail continues up the valley of gorgeous trees, passes the Appleton Pass trail (Hike 92) at 5 miles, 3000 feet, and soon thereafter crosses the river and climbs steeply to grasslands and silver forest of Soleduck Park and Heart Lake, 7 miles, 4800 feet.

Shortly above, at 8½ miles, the way attains the 5100-foot crest of the High Divide, and a junction. The left fork runs the ridge 3 miles to a dead-end on the side of Cat Peak, offering close looks at the Bailey and Olympus Ranges.

Turn west on the right fork into a steady ridge-top succession of views and flowers. At 10½ miles a sidetrail descends 1½ miles left to 4500-foot Hoh Lake, and from there

Avalanche lilies on High Divide, Mt. Olympus in distance

to the Hoh River (Hike 96). Here, too, a path climbs a bit to the 5474-foot summit of Bogachiel Peak and the climax panoramas. Plan to spend a lot of time gazing the full round of the compass.

The route swings along the side of the peak, at 11½ miles passing the sidetrail to Seven Lakes Basin, and traverses Bogachiel Ridge above the greenery (and often, a band of elk) in Bogachiel Basin. Snowfields linger late on this stretch and may be troublesome or dangerous for inexperienced hikers who try the trip too early in the summer.

The trail contours the ridge above the Bogachiel River almost 2 miles, then in subalpine trees drops to Deer Lake at 3500 feet and a junction with the Bogachiel River trail (Hike 95) at 15½ miles. Past the lake, the trail descends in lush forest to Soleduck Falls at 19 miles and in another mile to the road.

gachiel
ver

Round trip from Park boundary to
   Bogachiel Shelter 8 miles
Hiking time 5 hours
High point 560 feet
Elevation gain 260 feet
Best March through November
One day or backpack
USGS Olympic National Park or Spruce
   Mountain

One-way trip to Sol Duc Hot Springs via
   Deer Lake 30½ miles
Allow 2-3 days
High point 4304 feet
Elevation gain 4000 feet
Best July through October
Park Service backcountry use permit
   required

A beautiful hike through large old trees, rain-forest foliage, and luxuriant mosses. In autumn, the vine maple, alder, and bigleaf maple stage a glorious color show. Elk, deer, cougar, bear, and other animals may be seen by quiet and lucky hikers. A late-fall or winter visitor usually has the forest all to himself, the only footprints on the trail those of elk.

The valley offers a superb day trip for virtually any time of year, or a weekend for more extended enjoyment of wilderness greenery and streams, or a long, magnificent approach to alpine climaxes of the High Divide.

Drive US 101 to Bogachiel State Park. Turn east on the Bogachiel River road, passing several sideroads to homesteads; keep left at each intersection. After the last homestead, at 3.6 miles a spur road takes off from the main logging road and deadends in about 100 yards. From here, elevation 300 feet, the road is so rough it must be walked. The route is complicated—year to year, flood to flood, in different manners—along the old road 2 miles to the Park boundary, and 1½ mile more inside the park, amid artifacts of the logging done during World War II on the grounds of "national emergency" (some Forks gypo was out of work).

Amid second-growth forest look for giant stumps with springboard holes in both sides. Then virgin forest begins.

Bogachiel Shelter (emergency use only) and the old guard station, rebuilt by the

Bogachiel River (John Spring photo)

Student Conservation Program, are 4 miles from the Park boundary and make a good lunch stop and turnaround point for day hikers.

Near the shelter a branch trail climbs north over 1041-foot Indian Pass and drops to the Calawah River; at 6¼ miles another sidetrail climbs over the ridge south to the Hoh River road.

The valley path continues gently in lovely forest, never far from the river and sometimes beside it, to Flapjack Camp at 8¼ miles. At about 12 miles the river forks. While the trail follows the North Fork, the narrow but pristine main river valley can be explored on a sidetrip for 6 miles if you don't mind wading creeks and scrambling over high banks and fallen trees.

At 14¾ miles are Fifteen Mile Shelter and a bridge crossing the stream. At 15½ miles is Hyak Shelter, where the valley narrows to a slot, and at 18½ miles Twenty-One Mile Shelter, 2214 feet. At around 21 miles the trail abandons gentility, steeply ascends a dry hillside above the North Fork headwaters to 4300-foot Little Divide, then drops to Deer Lake at 24 miles, and climbs in parklands to the meadow crest of the High Divide. For alternative exits to Sol Duc Hot Springs, see Hike 94.

Round trip to Happy Four Shelter 11½ miles
Hiking time 6 hours
High point 800 feet
Elevation gain 225 feet
Best March through November
One day or backpack

Round trip to Glacier Meadows 37 miles
Allow 3 days
High point 4200 feet
Elevation gain 3700 feet
Best mid-July through October
USGS Olympic National Park or Mt. Tom
 and Mt. Olympus
Park Service backcountry use permit
 required

From around the world travelers are drawn to the Hoh River by the fame of the Olympic rain forest. Most of the 100,000 annual visitors are richly satisfied by the self-guiding nature walks at the road-end, but more ambitious hikers can continue for miles on the nearly-flat trail through huge trees draped with moss, and then climb to alpine meadows and the edge of the Blue Glacier.

Drive US 101 to the Hoh River road and turn east 19 miles to the Hoh Ranger Station and Campground, elevation 578 feet. The hike begins on the nature trail starting at the visitor center; before setting out, study the museum displays explaining the geology, climate, flora, and fauna.

The way lies amid superb, large specimens of Douglas fir, western hemlock, Sitka spruce, and western red cedar, groves of bigleaf maple swollen with moss, and shrubs and ferns. Gravel bars and cold rapids of the river are never far away, inviting sidetrips. Here and there are glimpses upward to snows of Mt. Tom and Mt. Carrie. In winter one may often see bands of Roosevelt elk; were it not for their constant grazing, the relatively open forest floor would be a dense jungle.

At 3 miles a way trail departs right, fording the river and ascending Tom Creek 1¼ miles to a dead-end far from crowds. Beside the Hoh River at 3¾ miles is the Park's largest known Sitka spruce, 51½ feet in circumference; the winter of 1975 it toppled, but is impressive even lying down.

Rain forest along Hoh River

Any distance can make a full day, what with long, lingering pauses. Happy Four Shelter, at 5¾ miles, elevation 800 feet, is a logical turnaround for a day hike, and also a good campsite for backpackers.

The trail remains level to the next camp at Olympus Guard Station, 9 miles, 948 feet. At 9¾ miles is a junction with the trail to High Divide (Hike 94). The valley trail then climbs a bit to the bridge over the spectacular canyon of the Hoh at 13¼ miles, 1400 feet, leaves the Hoh valley, and climbs more to the shelters at forest-surrounded Elk Lake, 15 miles, 2500 feet. (Crowded camping, stove required.)

Now the grade becomes steep, ascending through steadily smaller trees, with views across Glacier Creek of snows and cliffs, to the shelter at Glacier Meadows, 17¼ miles, 4200 feet. (Stove-camping only.) Wander a short way in flowers and parkland to a viewpoint near the foot of the Blue Glacier, where torrents pour down ice-polished slabs to the forest below. Or follow the trail ½ mile to the end on the bouldery crest of a lateral moraine. Admire crevasses and icefalls of the glacier, and the summit tower of 7965-foot Mt. Olympus.

PACIFIC OCEAN

97 Colonel Bob Mountain

Round trip, north side, 14½ miles
Allow 2 days
High point 4492 feet
Elevation gain 4270 feet
Best July to mid-October
USGS Quinault Lake, Grisdale, and Mt.
   Christie

Round trip, south side, 8.4 miles
Hiking time 7 hours
Elevation gain 3500 feet
One day or backpack

Climb to a western outpost of the Olympic Mountains, a former lookout site with views of Olympics nearby and, farther off, volcanoes of the Cascades—St. Helens, Adams, and Rainier. There's water to see, too—look down on sparkling Quinault Lake and out to the Pacific Ocean, particularly spectacular with the sun dunking into it of an evening.

There are two ways, both very steep, to Colonel Bob. The south approach gains 3500 feet; the north climbs 4270 feet and is 3 miles longer.

For the north side drive US 101 to near its crossing of the Quinault River and turn east on the South Shore road. In 2½ miles pass the Quinault Ranger Station and at 6 miles spot a sign, "Colonel Bob Trail No. 851." Turn in on a narrow road which promptly opens to a large parking lot, elevation 270 feet.

Near summit of Colonel Bob Mountain

The trail climbs through beautiful rain forest in long, sweeping switchbacks, ʋ sidehills, still going steadily up. At 3 miles is a crossing of Elwell's Creek and soon after are campsites of Mulkey Shelter, 2000 feet. Now the way switchbacks steeply to a 3000-foot pass and drops a bit, at 5½ miles reaching a junction, 2900 feet, with the trail from the south.

For the south-side approach to this junction, drive Highway 101 north 25½ miles from Hoquiam and turn east on road No. 2220-000, signed "Donkey Creek Road, Humptulips Guard Station." At 8.2 miles, where pavement ends, turn left on road No. 232-000, signed "Campbell Tree Grove Campground," and proceed 11 miles to a sign, "Pete's Creek Trail No. 858," near the crossing of Pete's Creek, elevation 1000 feet.

The trail starts on the uphill side of the road and is steadily steep and in places rocky. At 1 mile is a crossing of Pete's Creek, underground here most of the year. At 2 miles is a small camp, beyond which is a slide area and then, at 2½ miles, the junction.

About 1 mile beyond, at 6.4 miles from the north trailhead and 3.3 from the south, is Moonshine Flats, with all-year water, the most popular camp on the route. At 1¾ miles from the junction, the way emerging from forest into flowers, is the summit, the last few feet to the top blasted from rock.

Few traces of the old lookout cabin remain on the 4492-foot summit. But the views are glorious as ever. For sunset-watching, camps can be found ¼ mile back, 200 feet below the trail, on a wide, rocky bench covered with snow much of the summer. Bring a stove for cooking, melt snow for water.

OLD	NEW
220	2220-000
2302	2302-000

Enchanted Valley

Round trip 27 miles
Allow 2-3 days
High point 1957 feet
Elevation gain 1050 feet plus ups and
   downs
Best March through December
USGS Olympic National Park or Mt. Christie
   and Mt. Steele
Park Service backcountry use permit
   required

Walk beside the river in open alder and maple forest, and miles through cathedral-like fir forest where future generations of loggers will come to see what their grandfathers meant when they boasted of big trees. The climax is Enchanted Valley, a large alpine cirque ringed by 3000-foot cliffs. The trail has many ups and downs and during rainy spells is a muddy mess, but in such country, who can complain?

Drive US 101 to the south-side Lake Quinault road. Turn easterly, skirting the lake and winding up the valley. Pavement ends at 12 miles. In 13 miles pass the North Fork bridge and at 18 miles Graves Creek Campground. Continue on the final narrow road to the trailhead 18½ miles from US 101, elevation 907 feet.

The trail crosses Pony Bridge over the Quinault River at 3 miles; the lovely canyon under the bridge is worth a trip in itself. In another ½ mile climb around the canyon and drop back to the river. For the next 10 miles the way alternates, up and down, between flat bottoms (alders and maples) and terraces several hundred feet above the river (groves of tall fir and cedar). With any luck a hiker should see elk. At 7 miles pass a junction to O'Neil Creek Camp, ¼ mile off the main track.

All along are tantalizing glimpses of peaks above, but at about 10½ miles the change from lowlands to alpine is dramatic. Suddenly one leaves deep forest and bursts into the mountain world of rock and ice. To the left are cliffs of 6911-foot Chimney Peak. To the right is 6400-foot White Mountain. Both are dominated by the twin peaks of Mt. Anderson, divided by a small glacier: the sharp pyramid is 7366-foot West Peak, the highest point; the more massive peak in the middle is 7321 feet.

Coming down to earth, the valley has widened out. The lower part is floored with dense brush but farther up are flower fields. At 13½ miles cross the Quinault River, now a small creek. Walk a short bit through meadows to the three-story Enchanted Valley Chalet, built in 1930 as a commercial hotel and now maintained by the Park

Chimney Peak, left, and Mt. Anderson, right, above Enchanted Valley

Service as a public shelter. The structure often is full (only part of the flower floor now is open to camping) so be prepared to camp out. Be sure to carry a stove; cooking facilities are limited in the chalet and wood may be wet outside. Those unable to do the full 11 miles in a single day can stop overnight at any of a number of camps along the way.

Beyond the chalet the trail climbs 2500 feet in 5 miles to 4500-foot Anderson Pass and descends the West Fork Dosewallips River 10 miles to the road (Hike 85). Another trail leads to O'Neil Pass and Hart, Marmot, and Lake LaCrosse (Hike 99).

What's the best season for the trip? Well, some winters there is little snow in the lower valley, which thus can be walked in December or March when hardly any other country is open. Early spring is wonderful, when birds are singing and shrubs and maples are exploding with new leaves, and yellow violet and oxalis are blooming, and waterfalls and avalanches tumble and slide down cliffs. So is summer, when alders and maples canopy the valley bottoms in cool green. But fall is also glorious, with bigleaf maples yellowing and the trail lost in fallen leaves. Better try it in all seasons.

PACIFIC OCEAN

99 Lake LaCrosse-O'Neil Pass

One-way trip to Lake LaCrosse:
Via Quinault River and O'Neil Pass 26½ miles
Elevation gain 4000 feet
By any route, allow 5 days minimum
Best mid-July through September
USGS Mt. Steel
Park Service backcountry use permit required

In the heart of the Olympic wilderness, 16 miles from the nearest road, a group of beautiful alpine lakes sparkle amid a wonderland of heather and huckleberries. Quicker ways of reaching the lakes are mentioned in the last paragraph, but the one described here is the classic approach, via O'Neil Pass, on one of the most spectacular trails in the National Park, traversing ridges high above the Enchanted Valley of the Quinault, with many and magnificent views and flower fields.

To reach the O'Neil Pass trail, hike 17 miles and gain 2400 feet up the Enchanted Valley (Hike 98) to the beginning at about 3400 feet (incorrectly shown as 3100 feet on the USGS map).

The O'Neil Pass trail starts from the Enchanted Valley trail beside a small torrent and heads westward and up, in a few yards going by a small camp. The way alternates between forest and wide-view meadows. At 1 mile are campsites and a crossing of White Creek; a hillside beyond gives the best look at Mt. Anderson.

At 1½ miles is a mountain hemlock with a sign saying it is 6 feet, 3 inches in diameter and 136 feet tall—a midget compared to the lowland species of hemlock but huge at this elevation. At 2 miles is an Alaska cedar identified as 7 feet, 6 inches in diameter and 114 feet tall.

The trail climbs to 4500 feet and then contours for miles, mainly in grass and blossoms. Directly across the valley is Chimney Peak, an impressive 6911 feet high. Views are breathtaking down the Quinault River to Lake Quinault and, if lucky, the ocean. The trail drops a bit, rounds a shoulder of the ridge, and ascends to O'Neil Pass, 7½ miles (25 miles from the road), 4900 feet, and close-ups of Mt. Duckabush.

Lake LaCrosse

Still in meadows, the way descends to Marmot Lake, 8½ miles, 4400 feet. The O'Neil Pass trail ends here in a junction with the Duckabush River trail.

Scattered through higher gardens are Hart Lake, Lake LaCrosse, and Buck Lake. To get there, find the trail behind Marmot Lake Shelter and switchback upward ¾ mile to a junction. The left fork contours ½ mile to Hart Lake, enclosed on three sides by vertical cliffs; good camps. The right fork continues ¾ mile uphill to Lake LaCrosse, 4800 feet, perhaps the most splendid alpine lake in the Olympics, with views across the water to massive 6233-foot Mt. Duckabush and more graceful 6300-foot Mt. Steel. Another mile farther is Buck Lake, too small for fish and thus more private; there is no trail, but an experienced hiker can find the way from Lake LaCrosse west over a 5500-foot saddle and down to the 5000-foot shores. Camping is great at all the lakes.

The camping is stove-only, no wood fires, at Marmot, Hart, and LaCrosse lakes and O'Neil Pass. Marmot Lake is the most crowded.

The lakes can be approached in various other ways. For one, hike the Dosewallips trail (Hike 85) and drop over Anderson Pass 1½ miles, losing 1100 feet, to the start of the O'Neil Pass trail. Or, hike directly to the lakes by way of the Duckabush River trail 20 miles to Marmot Lake, gaining 4500 feet including some major ups and downs. For another, hike the North Fork Skokomish River trail (Hike 81) 19½ miles to Marmot Lake, gaining 5200 feet counting ups and downs. The lakes can also be included in imaginative one-way and loop trips.

100 Point of the Arches

Round trip to Point of the Arches 7 miles
Hiking time 4 hours
High point 150 feet
Good all year
One day or backpack
USGS Cape Flattery and Ozette Lake
Park Service backcountry use permit
  required

Here, perhaps, is the most scenic single segment of the Washington ocean coast, with needle-like sea stacks, caves, and arches to explore, tidal pools, and miles of sand beaches. Once threatened with roadbuilding and subdivision, in 1976 Shi-Shi Beach and the Point were added to the wilderness-ocean section of Olympic National Park; however, land exchanges must be completed before the Park Service can begin management.

Drive from Port Angeles on narrow, tortuous State Highway 112 to the Makah village of Neah Bay. At the west end of town turn left and follow signs to "Air Force Base and Ocean Beaches," crossing and recrossing a private logging road—stay on the public road. In 3 miles turn left over the Waatch River on a concrete bridge, again avoid the private road in favor of the public road, in about 6 miles cross the Sooes

Point of the Arches

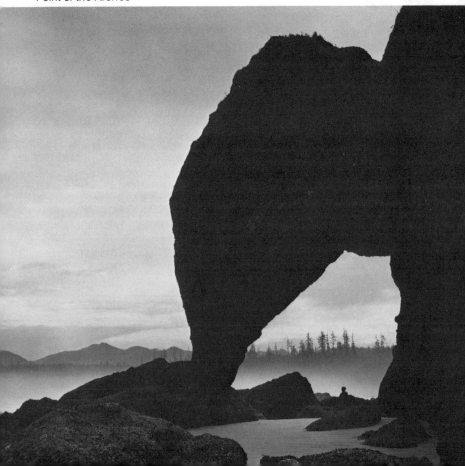

River, and pass a cluster of Makah homes on Mukkaw Bay at 6½ miles. Beyond the settlement the road climbs into woods above the beach and in 1 mile deteriorates rapidly. Park either near the houses or where the road gets sloppy. Overnight hikers do best to ask at one of the houses for parking space for a fee; car-looting is a problem here.

The parking area and road are on the Makah Indian Reservation. The ocean beach and all adjacent land belong to the Makahs so private property rules apply.

The virtually-undrivable road over Portage Head is pleasant walking under a canopy of trees. During wet weather be prepared for much mud. In about 1 mile push through the roadside brush for dramatic looks down to the surf. At 1½ miles, where the road comes to the edge of the bluff for the first unobstructed views of the ocean, are two "trails," side by side. The first drops like a shot to the north end of Shi-Shi Beach and is slippery and even scary. The other, several yards away, is steep enough but descends amid trees that provide handholds and a feeling of security. (If the tide is high, follow the road, which dwindles to a jeep track and in a mile nearly touches the beach.)

A short distance from the foot of the trail is the south end of Portage Head, with spectacular sea stacks, tidal pools, and a shipwreck. Hike about 2 miles south on the beach, leaving the reservation, passing a number of good camps (the most reliable source of water in summer is Petroleum Creek), to the fabled Point of the Arches. The long string of stacks and islands can be reached and explored at very low tide; the going is rough over sharp and slippery rocks and involves some wading.

The Point is rounded by crossing the headland. Travel to the south can be difficult, since there are several heads with no trails over the tops, requiring a very low tide to get around the bases or considerable bushwacking to go over the tops. Before going over, look for the thinnest salal and on top of the heads stay in the forest where there is little brush. About 6 miles from Point of the Arches is the Ozette River; a bit north of the river a road (closed to public vehicles) leads inland 4½ miles to Ozette Lake.

In dry spells in calm weather at low tide the Ozette River may be only knee-deep, permitting sturdy hikers to wade and continue to Cape Alava (Hike 101).

PACIFIC OCEAN

101 Rialto Beach
To Cape Alava

One-way trip 22 miles
Allow 3 days
High point 100 feet
Good all year
USGS Olympic National Park or La Push
  and Ozette Lake
Park Service backcountry use permit
  required

Olympic National Park first became famous for rain forests and glaciers set within a magnificently large area of mountain wilderness. Now, though, it is known far and wide for still another glory—the last long stretch of wilderness ocean beach remaining in the conterminous United States. North and south from the Quillayute River extend miles and miles of coastline that are now almost exactly as they were before Columbus—except that in 1492 (and until fairly recent times) Indians had permanent homes and temporary camps at many places along the coast now deserted.

Winter and early spring often offer the best hiking weather of the year, but storms can be hazardous. Facing a cold rain with miles of beach to hike is miserable and can lead to hypothermia.

The north section, from Rialto Beach to Cape Alava, makes a longer but easier walk than the south section described in Hike 102. There are no really difficult creek crossings, only one headland that cannot be rounded at low tide, and most of the way

Sea stack near Hole in the Wall

Near Norwegian Memorial

is simple sand and shingles, interrupted occasionally by short stretches of rough rock.

Be sure to obtain a tide chart beforehand and use it to plan each day's schedule. Much of the route can be traveled at high tide, but at the cost of scrambling over driftwood and slippery rocks, plodding wearily through steep, loose gravel, and climbing up and down points. Moreover, some headlands cannot be climbed over and the beach at low tide provides the only passage. Be prepared to hike early in the morning or late in the evening, with layovers during the day, if the tides so dictate.

Drive US 101 to 2 miles north of Forks. Turn west on the La Push road 8 miles, then turn right on the Mora Campground-Rialto Beach road 5 miles to the parking lot at the beach.

In ½ mile is Ellen Creek, the first possible campsite. Here and elsewhere the "ocean tea," the creek's water colored by bark tannin dissolved in headwaters swamps, is perfectly drinkable, but due to the possibility of invisible giardia, the cause of "beaver fever," should be boiled. At 1½ miles, just beyond the sea stack with the Hole in the Wall, are meager camps and the first headland, which has several small points, one requiring low tide to get around. At 2½ miles are camps near the Chilean Memorial, which commemorates one of the countless ships wrecked on this rugged coast, and at 3 miles begins the long, rough rounding of Cape Johnson, which has no trail over the top and can be passed at low tide only, as is true of another rough point immediately following. A point at 5 miles must be climbed over on a short trail and one at 6 miles rounded at low tide. At 6½ miles is Cedar Creek (campsites) and immediately beyond is a point that can be rounded at low tide or crossed on a steep, short path.

At the Norwegian Memorial (another shipwreck and more camps), 7½ miles, a rough, abandoned trail leads inland 2¼ miles to Allen's Bay on Ozette Lake. (There is no trail along the lake, so unless a boat pickup by the resort has been arranged, this is not a shortcut to civilization.) Passing campsites every so often and at 10 miles a low-tide-only point, at 13½ miles the way comes to Yellow Banks, the point at the north end of which must be rounded at low tide.

At 15 miles a way trail heads inland 2 miles to Ericsons Bay on Ozette Lake. At Sand Point, 15½ miles, is an emergency shelter, innumerable campsites in the woods, and a trail leading 3 miles to the Ozette Lake road.

Don't stop here. Continue on the wilderness beach 3 miles to Cape Alava, 18½ miles, where an archeological dig has uncovered a Makah village that was overwhelmed by a mudslide 500 years ago. The Makahs are planning an interpretive center here. To finish your trip, follow the trail 3½ miles back to the lake, 22 miles.

102 Third Beach
To Hoh River

One-way trip 16 miles
Allow 3 days
High point 250 feet
Good all year
USGS Olympic National Park or La Push
   and Forks
Park Service backcountry use permit
   required

Wild forest and wild ocean, woods animals and sea birds, tidal pools and wave-carved stacks, the constant thunder of surf, and always the vast mysterious horizon of the Pacific. This south section of the Olympic National Park wilderness ocean strip is shorter but more complicated than the northern one described in Hike 101, requiring detours inland to cross headlands and creeks and demanding even closer attention to the tide chart.

Warning: Goodman, Falls, and Mosquito Creeks are high all winter, and after a period of heavy rain or melting snow are virtually unfordable.

Drive US 101 to 2 miles north of Forks. Turn west on the La Push road 12 miles to the parking lot at the Third Beach trail, elevation 240 feet.

Warning: Cars at the Third Beach parking area have been frequently broken into. Do not leave any belongings visible inside the car.

Hike the forest trail, descending abruptly to the beach and campsites at ¾ mile. Head south along the sand and in ½ mile look for a prominent marker on a tree above the beach, the start of the trail over Taylor Point—which cannot be rounded at the base. The trail climbs into lovely woods, dropping to the beach at 3 miles and a small head which can be rounded at any time except high tide; a path climbs over.

At 3½ miles is a point which can be rounded at low tide or climbed over by a short trail to reach Scott Creek, with campsites in the woods; another very small point immediately south can be rounded in medium tide or climbed over. At 4½ miles is Strawberry Point, low and forested and simple, and at 5½ miles, Toleak Point, ditto. Shortly beyond is Jackson Creek (camps).

At 6½ miles a trail ascends a steep bluff and proceeds inland through beautiful forest to crossings of Falls and Goodman Creeks (cliffs rule out a shore passage), returning to the surf at 7¾ miles. The beach is then easy to Mosquito Creek, 10 miles; ford the stream at low tide. (Camps here.) Climb small points at 10½ and 10.9 miles, and at 11.1 miles round another at low tide (the way over the top is strenuous). Two more points in the next mile can be crossed on rough paths but are better passed at low tide.

At 12 miles a trail climbs the large promontory of Hoh Head, which cannot be rounded in any tide, and regains the beach at 12¾ miles. Going by a campsite or two, at 13½ miles the way comes to the last point, a heap of big rocks which must be

Toleak Point

rounded at low tide. From here a narrow, low-tide-only strip of beach leads to the mouth of the Hoh River, 14¾ miles. A trail follows the river inland to the Oil City road-end, 15½ miles.

Hikers forced off the beach by high tide can follow the trail along the hillside from Mosquito Creek to the Hoh River; keep careful watch on small children in the party lest they sink without a trace in a mudhole.

The Oil City road reaches US 101 in 12 miles, at a point about ½ mile north of the Hoh River bridge.

STILL MORE HIKES IN THE ALPINE LAKES, SOUTH CASCADES, AND OLYMPICS

The 102 hikes represent all provinces of the Cascades from Stevens Pass to the Columbia River, and of the Olympics. Heaviest emphasis has been placed on areas close to major population centers. There are countless other great hikes in the two ranges, and below is an additional list of 149.

To take the following hikes, consult the books referred to, if any, or obtain the applicable maps and make your own way. The lack of detailed "recipes" or, in some cases, even a trail, may be compensated for by a greater degree of solitude.

Skykomish

West Fork Miller River: An abandoned road, now a pleasant forest trail beside the stream. (See **Footsore 2**.)

Deception Creek: Beautiful forest and creek from Highway 2 to Pacific Crest Trail at Deception Pass. Combines with Surprise Lake trail (Hike 6) for excellent loop.

Hope Lake: 2 miles up North Fork Tunnel Creek to the Pacific Crest Trail and the lake.

Lake Josephine: Reached from Stevens Pass on the Pacific Crest Trail.

Nason Creek

Lanham Lake trail No. 1589: 1¾ miles to lake under cliffs of Jim Hill Mountain. (Closed to bikes and horses.)

Glacier Creek trail No. 1573: An access via Chiwaukum Creek to meadows on east side of Chiwaukum Mountains. A dead-end trail after 1½ miles—needs maintenance.

Lake Ethel trail No. 1585: Steep 4½ miles. Passes through a grove of lodgepole pine with contorted trunks.

Painter Creek trail No. 1575: Pleasant forest and meadows—long hike.

Hatchery Creek trail No. 1577: Access to Icicle Ridge trail.

McCue Ridge trail No. 1574: From trail No. 1584A to trail No. 1591.

White Pine Creek: From White Pine Creek road to Icicle Creek Trail No. 1551.

Icicle Creek

Icicle Ridge trail No. 1570: 25-mile ridge walk with lots of ups and downs and lots of views. 4-5 days hike.

Fourth of July Creek trail No. 1579: 5 miles to an old lookout site and Icicle Ridge trail.

Trout Lake trail No. 1555: 5 miles to shallow Trout Lake. Trail goes on to Windy Pass and Eight Mile Creek.

Icicle Creek trail No. 1551: 12-mile access to Crest Trail past Lake Josephine.

Jack Creek trail No. 1558: 11½ miles to meadows and Stuart Pass.

Solomon Creek trail No. 1593: Meadows. Long trail via Jack Creek or shorter from Cle Elum River.

Snowall-Cradle Lake trail No. 1560: Long loop trip to meadows from Meadow Creek-French Creek trail.

French Creek trail No. 1595: 12 miles to Paddy-Go-Easy Pass. Good trail in timber but boggy in meadows.

French Ridge trail No. 1564: Open meadows on a steep loop trail between Icicle Creek trail and French Creek trail.

Lake Leland trail No. 1566: Long hike in woods to lake on edge of meadow country.

Square Lake trail No. 1567: Interesting trail to meadows and views.

Chain Lakes trail No. 1569: Very steep trail from 10 miles up Icicle Creek trail to a chain of meadow lakes. View of spires on Bulls Tooth from hill north of lakes. Trail continues over a pass to Doelle Lakes and onward to Frosty Pass country. Map shows Doughgod Creek trail but this is abandoned and impassable.

Klonaqua Lakes trail No. 1563: Steep trail (and long access) to two alpine lakes.

Mission Ridge Area (all the below are open to motorbikes)

Devils Gulch trail No. 1220: Good trail 12 miles up Mission Creek to Beehive road and return on ridge via trail No. 1201. Good in May.

Red Hill trail No. 1223: Hike to top of 3800-foot hill in May.

Squilchuck trail No. 1200: 2-mile hike through alpine forest. Access to Clara and Marion Lakes.

Ingalls Creek

Hansel Creek Ridge and return to Ingalls Creek; abandoned trail.

North Bend Area

Mt. Teneriffe: 7 miles up a jeep road from valley and then ¾-mile trail to summit. (See **Footsore 2**.)

Granite Creek: Abandoned road and fishermen's path to Granite Lakes and Lake Thompson and connection with Defiance trail No. 1007. (See **Footsore 2**.)

Lake Thompson: From Granite Creek road and trail.

Pratt River: Possible for 7 miles but must first ford the Middle Fork Snoqualmie River.

Rainy Lake trail (not a trail) from Camp Brown: Route very difficult to find. 6 or 7 hours to lake.

Quartz Creek: Very difficult route to Rainy Lake or a ¾-mile fishermen's trail to Blethan Lake.

Nordrum Lake: Rough trail around logs and up creek beds from Taylor River to Nordrum Lake. Gateway to alpine country.

Middle Fork Snoqualmie valley trail: Unmaintained trail across river from road. Forest Service plans to rebuild this trail when money is available.

Rock Creek trail: Unusual approach from valley trail to Snow Lake (Hike 25). Trail not used much because of difficult river crossing.

Trail No. 1018 from Silver Peak to Hanson Creek: Presently closed through watershed and unmaintained for 15 years or more.

Cle Elum Area

Roaring Ridge: Find abandoned road near Lost Lake. Follow it to road-end, then take a short trail to old lookout site.

Snowshoe Butte: Cross-country travel from road No. 204B or from Pacific Crest Trail between Tacoma Pass and Stampede Pass.

Lookout Mountain: Inquire at Cle Elum Ranger Station.

Cole Butte: Begins on the High Line Canal near Easton to Goat Peak and along jeep road to saddle between Log Creek and Big Creek.

Silver Creek: 16 miles to hanging valley, a beautiful meadow of berries and subalpine timber. Can also be reached from Cooper Pass.

Red Mountain trail No. 1330: 7 miles long, connecting with the Kachess Ridge trail a mile short of the Thorp Mountain lookout.

Davis Peak trail No. 1324: Steep 5½ miles to an old lookout site and broad views. Possible roaming out along Goat Ridge.

Paris Creek trail No. 1393: A short 8 miles to open basin where trail is difficult to follow. One could spend a week here without retracing path, since the trail joins the Teanaway, Jolly Mountain, and Boulder-De Roux trails.

Boulder-De Roux trail No. 1392: 4-mile jeep trail connecting to the Paris Creek trail and others.

Gallagher trail No. 1335: 4-mile jeep trail to mining claim and south to Boulder Creek, Paris Creek, Jolly Mountain, and Sasse Ridge.

Fortune Creek spur trail No. 2342: Jeep trail from Van Epps Pass.

Trail Creek trail No. 1322: From Waptus River to Fish Lake. Must ford the river.

Michael Lake trail No. 1336: Sidetrip from Trail Creek trail. Best reached from the Fish Lake end.

White River

Huckleberry Mountain: A once-popular trail now nearly obliterated by logging.

Noble Knob trail No. 1184: From Corral Pass, 8½ miles in alpine trees and meadows with grand views of Mt. Rainier to road No. 72.

Dalles Ridge trail No. 1173: Starts from trail No. 1184, 3½ miles of scenic trail with views of Mt. Rainier. Ties to road No. 72.

Ranger Creek trail No. 1197: Being constructed by volunteers of the Boy Scouts of

America. 8 miles to Dalles Ridge trail No. 1173. Good view overlooking White River in 2¼ miles. (See **Footsore 1**.)

Crystal Mountain trail No. 1163: 8½ miles from Silver Creek trail No. 1192 past Hen Skin Lake over top of Crystal Mountain (also reached by chairlift) down the ridge to Crystal Mountain highway.

White River trail No. 1199: 5-mile lowland trail in big timber paralleling US 410. (See **Footsore 1**.)

Deep Creek trail No. 1196: A steep 5 miles to Noble Knob trail No. 1184. Last ½ mile in open alpine country.

Lost Lake trail No. 1185: Starts 3¼ miles up the Greenwater trail. Passes Quinn Lake, Lost Lake, and goes through alpine country to join the Noble Knob trail. Trail is 5½ miles long.

Maggie Creek trail No. 1186: Starts 5½ miles up the Greenwater trail. In 5¼ miles, all in timber, reaches Pacific Crest Trail.

Arch Rock trail No. 1187: Steep 3½-mile access to Pacific Crest Trail starting 7½ miles up the Greenwater trail. Last ½ mile in apline country.

Carbon trail No. 1179: 9½-mile trail from Flip-O-Way road No. 74 to a junction with Summit Lake trail No. 1177. Scenic around Bearhead Mountain.

Cedar Lake: Steep, 1-mile fishermen's trail to lake, then ½ mile more to Celery Meadow.

American River

Bismark Peak trail No. 983: Reached from Bumping Lake or Indian Creek trails.

Fife's Peaks trail No. 954: Steep, dry trail to views of rugged cliffs. Map shows a nonexistent trail around the peak.

Richmond Mine trail No. 973: Long route from Bumping River to Rattlesnake Creek.

Mt. Aix trail No. 982: From Rattlesnake Creek road to Mt. Aix.

Rattlesnake trail No. 981: Long route to the headwaters of Hindoo Creek; due to numerous fords is best in low water of late summer.

Randle Area

Langills Peak trail: Long scenic ridge walk. Water at Grasshopper Lake and Bear Creek.

Vanson Peak trail No. 217: Best reached from Ryan Lake over Goat Mountain. North end of trail is in private land (U.S. Plywood-Champion Papers).

Vanson Lake trail: A 1-mile sidetrip from trail No. 217.

Blue Lake: A large lake surrounded by virgin forest reached by a 3-mile trail from road No. 123. Trail is heavily used by motorcycles.

Tongue Mountain trail No. 294: Early season hike from road No. 111 or 123.

Trail No. 119: 3½-mile ridgetop trail from Blue Lake to Mouse Lake.

Packwood Area

Lake Christine trail No. 249A (901A on old maps): Near southwest corner of Mount Rainier National Park.

Puyallup trail No. 248 (900 on old maps): On west side of Mount Rainier National Park.

Carlton Ridge trail No. 42: Old-growth Douglas fir, views of narrow valley, and access to Crest Trail at Fish Lake.

Cowlitz and Jug Lake trails, Nos. 44 and 43: Access to Crest Trail and shallow Jug and Fryingpan Lakes. Many marshy meadows.

Sand Lake trail No. 60: A way to Crest Trail.

Cartright Creek trail No. 57: Access to Crest Trail.

Bluff Lake trail No. 65: Long route to Coyote Ridge and Goat Rocks Wilderness.

Clear Fork trail No. 61: River access to Goat Rocks Wilderness.

Trail No. 83: On Snyder Mountain, joining trail No. 86 in 1 mile.

Angry Mountain trail No. 90: Ridge hike to Lily Basin.

Jordan Creek trail No. 94: Long access route to Goat Ridge.

South Point trail No. 123: A lookout and a long ridge hike on a dry access route to Klickitat trail (Hike 57).

Coleman Weed Patch trail No. 121: Access route to the Crest Trail. A timbered plateau with small lakes.

Teeley Creek trail No. 251: Can start on road No. 84 for longer hike to Granite Lake.

Pompey Peak: 5 miles to excellent view of St. Helens and Cowlitz valley. Shelter cabin halfway up.

Tieton Area

Sand Ridge: Long, dry, flat, and wooded ridge hike from near Rimrock Reservoir to Blankenship Meadows.

Spiral Butte (Big Peak): A sidetrail from Sand Ridge up a little volcano. Goes through a recent burn. Excellent view of Mt. Rainier and Mt. Aix area.

Tenday Creek trail No. 1134: Starts from Conrad Meadows. A long creek and ridge route to Cirque Lake. Just above lake is a fine view of Goat Rocks.

Jump-off Lookout: Trail to lookout. Jeep road on other side of ridge.

North Fork Tieton trail: Forest trail to Crest Trail at Tieton Pass, not far from McCall Basin to the south, Shoe Lake to the north.

Trout Lake Area

Snipes Mountain trail No. 11: From road No. 80, trail climbs along a lava flow 5 miles to alpine meadows and a junction with Adams Highline Trail.

Cold Springs trail No. 72: 15-mile loop hike is possible by starting on trail No. 11, going to the Adams Highline Trail, following it westward to timberline, then down the timberline road to trail No. 72, to trail No. 40, and walking road No. 80 ¾ mile back to car.

Bird Lake trail No. 100: Beautiful flower walk—see **Trips and Trails, 2**.

St. Helens Area

Some trails survive but as of 1981 most are in the Red (closed) Zone. Check with Gifford Pinchot National Forest; as the years go along routes may be opened.

Lewis River

Quartz Creek trail No. 5: Miles of forest and creek. The largest virgin forest in the area. Trail crosses clearcuts.

Snagtooth Creek trail No. 4: Climb from Quartz Creek to Boundary Trail.

Wright Meadow trail No. 80: Through forest between roads 2327 and 93.

Trail No. 17: Recently reopened 2.5 miles from road No. 9341 to Craggy Peak trail No. 3.

Wind River Area

Soda Peaks trail No. 133: To a small gem-like lake near Government Mineral Springs.

Falls Creek trail No. 152: 2-mile trail from road No. 30 to a falls in a secluded little valley.

Little Huckleberry Mountain trail No. 197: Starts from road No. 6801. Camping near the top and views from the rounded 4202-foot mountain. Crossed by Crest Trail.

Silver Star Mountain: Impassable jeep road to a lookout in the Yacolt Burn.

Hamilton Mountain, in Beacon Rock State Park: 4-mile hike to a tremendous overlook of the Columbia River. (See **Trips and Trails, 2**.)

Table Mountain: 3-mile hike to views of the Oregon and Washington volcanoes.

Dog Mountain: 2½-mile hike from the Columbia River to the top of the mountain.

Thomas Lake trail: 3 miles to Crest Trail and the heart of Indian Heaven.

Huffman Peak trail No. 129: 8 miles from road No. 5701 starting in forest, climbing to a ridge top with panoramic views, and ending at road on top of Siouxon Peak, an old lookout site.

Siouxon trail No. 130: 9 miles from road No. 5701, following Siouxon Creek through forest and past a small waterfall in the Siouxon Roadless Area.

East Side Olympic Peninsula

Mt. Washington trail No. 800: Starts from Big Creek road No. 24190000. An easy grade 1½ miles to ridge top. Does not go to summit of mountain.

Mt. Rose trail No. 814: Steep, strenuous climb 3 miles to within ¼ mile of the 4301-foot summit. For experienced hikers only.

Dry Creek trail No. 872: Starts from road No. 23510000 near the Park boundary. The first 1½ miles are along the shores of Lake Cushman. Ideal for family hiking.

Wagon Wheel Lake way trail: Located near Staircase. Trail is a steep (12 to 15 percent) 3-mile climb to a small tarn. Good views of Mt. Lincoln and upper Slate Creek Basin.

Six Ridge trail: From North Fork Skokomish River trail. Long, steep, dry way trail to subalpine meadows, elk country.

Putvin trail No. 813: Starts at head of Hamma Hamma valley near Boulder Creek. A long-abandoned trapper's trail to alpine country. Extremely steep but offers access to Mt. Stone, Mt. Skokomish, and acres of flowers and wildlife.

Constance Pass: Scenic route between the Dosewallips and Dungeness valleys.

Graywolf trail: 20-mile hike to 6150-foot Graywolf Pass and descent to Dosewallips. Can be shortened by starting at Deer Park.

Cameron Creek trail: Reached from the Graywolf trail. A very long hike to 6400-foot Cameron Pass and on over Lost Pass to Dose Meadows.

North Side Olympic Peninsula

Grand Ridge trail: 8-mile ridge walk from Deer Park to Obstruction Point. Splendid alpine hike. Carry water.

Little River trail: Lovely and little-traveled 8-mile route to Hurricane Ridge.

Lake Creek: Begins at Heart of the Hills Campground, Loop E. 2-mile woods walk, no lake.

Cox Valley way trail: Starts 1 mile along Obstruction Point road. Trailhead not marked. Goes into Cox valley.

P.J. Lake: A way trail starting at base of Eagle Mountain on the Obstruction Point road. ½ mile down to lake. Way trail not marked.

Storm King way trail: 1½-mile steep trail to viewpoint of Lake Crescent on side of Mt. Storm King.

Barnes Creek trail: Indistinct way trail through forest to Aurora Ridge trail. Fades out as it reaches 5000-foot Lookout Dome.

Aurora Creek way trail: 3½-mile shortcut to Aurora Ridge trail. Very steep.

Aurora Ridge trail: 16-mile ridge walk, mostly in trees, then down to Olympic Hot Springs. Some good views of Mt. Olympus.

Long Ridge trail: From the Elwha trail to Dodger Point, a long, dry ridge with views. Ends in scenic meadows. Route to Bailey Range. Good trail.

Boulder Lake trail: 3½ miles from Olympic Hot Springs to Lake Crescent.

Happy Lake Ridge trail: Long hike with views and a lake, starting from Olympic Hot Springs road. Can be a loop with the Boulder Lake trail. 3½ miles between trailheads.

Martins Park way trail: 2-mile sidetrip from the Elwha trail at Low Divide to glorious meadows and views.

North Fork Soleduck trail: Woods walk 9 miles to dead-end.

West Side Olympic Peninsula

Geodetic Hill trail: Very indistinct route, abandoned in 1945, from the Bogachiel to forested Spruce Mountain.

Hoh-Bogachiel trail: Follows the Park boundary from the Hoh over and down into the Bogachiel at Flapjack Shelter.

Indian Pass trail: Forested route from the Bogachiel River to Calawah River and on to Rugged Ridge and Forest Service road.

South Fork Hoh trail: Short trail to canyon. Very easy. Fades out in unspoiled rain forest. Trailhead difficult to find.

Mt. Tom Creek trail: A difficult ford of the Hoh River leads to seldom-visited forest.

Queets River trail: A difficult ford of the Queets River leads to 15-plus miles of primitive rain forest.

Kloochman Rock trail: From Queets trail past largest Douglas fir tree to lookout site. Officially abandoned.

Tshletshy Creek trail: From the Queets to Quinault; not maintained and very difficult to follow.

Higley Peak trail: 3-mile climb from Lake Quinault or a short walk from logging road. View of lake. (See **Trips and Trails, 2**.)

Elip Creek trail: Intersects the Skyline Trail from North Fork Quinault. 4½ miles.

Skyline Trail: Long, strenuous, scenic way trail to Low Divide. A late-summer trip, since snow obscures route at head of Promise Creek. Minimal way trail between Seattle Creek and Kimta Creek.

Three Lakes trail: Starts at North Fork Quinault Ranger Station. A 7-mile trail connects at divide above Three Lakes with Tshletshy Creek trail 18 miles from Three Lakes to Queets River.

Graves Creek trail: 9-mile hike from the Quinault to Six Ridge Pass and Sundown Lake.

Second Beach (Near La Push): (See **Trips and Trails, 2**.)

INDEX 102 HIKES